data processing

APPLICATIONS TO POLITICAL RESEARCH

KENNETH JANDA

NORTHWESTERN UNIVERSITY PRESS • Evanston 1965

DATA PROCESSING

To Charles S. Hyneman

EDITOR'S FOREWORD

In each of several capacities—as a friend, as a former colleague, and as editor of *Handbooks for Research in Political Behavior*— I welcome the occasion to enter a Foreword to Kenneth Janda's manual on the processing of political data.

I first met Mr. Janda in 1957, a few weeks after he undertook graduate study in political science at Indiana University and a few weeks after I had completed mine at Northwestern University. At the request of Professor Charles Hyneman, he was kind enough to drive me from Bloomington to Mitchell, Indiana, to board a train. From the moment our conversation began, it was clear to me that Professor Hyneman's new student had learned to execute research differently from one of Hyneman's most recent students. Janda's first year of graduate training introduced him to machinery that most of my classmates rarely used and less often fully comprehended. Janda began instructing me in the kinds of data processing available to political scientists. He has continued that instruction off and on ever since. In the meantime, I have come to look back on 1957 as a watershed in the development and application of technical skills in political research. Few political scientists whose doctoral sheepskins bear an earlier date were systematically trained in the use of data processing equipment; those whose degrees antedate 1957, for the most part, have had to teach themselves to use the equipment as part of a continuing effort to pull themselves up by the bootstraps.

When Dr. Janda joined the Northwestern Department of Political Science in 1961, he introduced to his undergraduates, as well as to his graduate students and his faculty colleagues, the conveniences of data processing machinery—keypunches, verifiers, reproducers, counter-sorters, and computers. That Janda inspired students, and effectively communicated these conveniences to them, is evidenced by the several who as undergraduates and later as graduate scholars assisted and contributed to research much earlier than beginning scholars usually do. Both at Northwestern and at The Ohio State University I have had a number of Janda-trained students. Their early introduction to research techniques has hastened their contributions to scholarship and made them valued colleagues much earlier than is customary.

The great merit of introducing undergraduates to the advantages of data processing is not, however, to quicken the professionalization of political scientists. Rather, the merit of providing this instruction to undergraduates is that it contributes to fulfilling the goals of the liberal arts tradition, the curriculum of general education. Stated quite broadly, liberal education, as it applies to the social sciences, embraces values, science, and policy.

Topics with respect to values include identifying the ends or objectives of social and political institutions; evaluating the objectives that should be uppermost on the public and private agendas; discovering standards for distributing existing resources, usually scarce compared to demand; judging in what order new resources should be created.

Topics of science include the historical analysis of trends with respect to preferences among values; the explanations of why some goals have been preferred to others; the description of ways in which they have successfully or unsuccessfully been pursued by institutions.

Topics of policy are those that involve finding and inventing courses of public and private action that, insofar as available evidence will reveal, are most likely to realize certain objectives.

Each of these three primary concerns of a liberal education—values, science, and policy—involve empirical questions. A liberal education is a house of many mansions and is not exclusively empirical. Nevertheless, the identification of values, the discovery of trends and conditions underlying their realization, and the invention of policies most likely to affect values include many empirical inquiries.

The undergraduate who can occasionally bring data to bear on questions of value, science, and policy will have a wider appreciation of the intellectual tasks of the liberally educated man than one who can not. If students are to devote part, but not all, of a course to data analysis, they can be assisted by convenient steps of processing and analysis. Election data, census tracts, legislative records, judicial opinions, international documents, interviews, letters of public figures—these and many other sources are subject to quantitative manipulation, providing one knows the rather simple rules for organizing, arranging, and sorting them. Dr. Janda's volume provides precisely this kind of instruction for students of politics.

To involve the student directly in research adds a special feature to the liberal education. Knowledge is not, after all, a finite number of objects to be communicated. Knowledge expands; new items are added regularly, so that the agenda of education continuously lengthens. Knowledge also molts; some things that once were included in curricula are now shed. If knowledge changes, is it not appropriate to share with students an appreciation of the process of acquiring knowledge, as well as the content?

One of the purposes of this Series is to provide undergraduates with manuals that will instruct them in how political knowledge is acquired. I have been asked often, however, why special volumes should be necessary for political scientists. Are not the same techniques described in advanced texts for sociologists, economists, and psychologists? Why not send our students to those materials? And why not enroll our students in methodology courses in other social science departments?

I believe, as do most of the authors in this Series, that special circumstances with respect to political science justify a special set of volumes. (I omit the argument that differences in the nature of data often cause economists to use variations of common techniques that differ from those of psychologists or sociologists.) I am persuaded that students enter political science for a variety of reasons, not all of which are associated with an aptitude for empirical techniques. Some enroll because they are attracted by the humanistic concerns of political philosophy; some take up the subject out of aesthetic or scientific motives to understand an aspect of human activity; others join the field to acquire practical information in carrying a precinct, in conducting a public opinion poll, or in working in an administrative bureau. Political science, probably more than any other social science, is a liberal education within a liberal education.[1] It is a subject devoted to values as much as science, to science as surely as policy, and to policy no less than values.

If empirical and quantitative skills are to be communicated to an audience with such diverse, yet related, purposes, it will help to use political examples to illustrate techniques. Method in the context of substance is most likely to appeal to this audience. If this is regarded as sugar-coating the pill of empiricism, so be it.

JAMES A. ROBINSON

Columbus, Ohio
February 22, 1965

NOTE

[1] Harold D. Lasswell imaginatively presents a similar and fuller statement of this perspective in *The Future of Political Science* (New York: Atherton Press, 1963), pp. 208-42.

ACKNOWLEDGMENTS

The idea for writing this book came from James A. Robinson, who also contributed valuable advice and criticism on the manuscript. Ralph Bisco suggested many improvements in the organization and content of Chapter V. James Aagaard commented on Chapters III and IV, and Joe Mayer reviewed Chapter III.

Joy Neuman of Northwestern University Press was extraordinarily patient and helpful—as was Will Norman, who did the artwork for the book.

Miss Louise Cowen, Supervisor; Dr. James E. Van Ness, Director; and the entire staff of the Northwestern University Computing Center cooperated in every way possible.

Finally, I thank Professor Charles S. Hyneman, who originally stimulated my interest in political science and trained me in political research. To him I dedicate this book.

K. J.

Evanston
January, 1965

CONTENTS

DATA PROCESSING

CHAPTER I **INTRODUCTION**

This book introduces political scientists to some applications and advantages of punchcard data processing technology. It will show ways in which various types of political information can be recorded on punchcards and processed by mechanical equipment and electronic computers. Since this material is intended for political scientists who in the main are unfamiliar with research applications of punchcard data processing techniques, there will be no discussion of the use of computers in executing complex statistical analyses of political data. This book is for the beginner, and hopefully its "how-to-do-it" character will encourage more political scientists to expand their research, and ultimately their theory, through the use of modern technology.

THE MEANING OF "DATA PROCESSING"

The term "data processing" as used here requires some elaboration. The term is widely used in writings on mechanical aids in research, and many authors use it to describe the several steps involved from the time the data are gathered through the analysis of the findings.[1] The United Nations publication, *Handbook on Data Processing Methods*, compares the term "processing" to its counterpart in manufacturing, where "the processing of any material consists of taking it in one form and changing it to some other required form."[2]

Punchcard data processing in political research means recording information on punchcards, manipulating or rearranging this information mechanically, compiling new information about the data, and statistically analyzing the results to produce more new information. The essential stages in the process are *recording, manipulating, compiling,* and *analyzing.* The function performed at the first stage—*recording* information in punchcard form—is self-explanatory and needs no further description in this section. However, the distinguishing characteristics of the other stages may not be so obvious and require some elaboration.

Manipulation of punchcard data differs from *compilation* and *statistical analysis* in that no "new" information is produced when data are manipulated. A good example of a manipulative operation would be using punchcards and data processing equipment to alphabetize the names of all legislators who served in a given legislature during a period of twenty-five years. Another example of a manipulative operation would be grouping the world's nations according to some classification of legislative-executive structure. A manipulative operation merely *arranges* the data in a certain manner, adding no new information to that already gathered.

On the other hand, the last two stages in the process *do* produce new information about the data and must be differentiated from each other. The distinction between compilation and statistical analysis is drawn from the U. N. *Handbook on Data Processing Methods,* in which "compilation" refers to counting, summating, computing percentages and averages for the data, and "statistical analysis" refers to testing for significance, determining correlations, and other more sophisticated statistical procedures.[3]

As the opening paragraph of this chapter indicates, this work will not deal at length with statistical analysis. Given the present state of methodology in political science, the greater need is for a handbook concentrating on the early stages of data processing, particularly the recording of relevant data on punchcards.

Many political scientists may be unaware of the punchcard's suitability as a means of recording relevant information. Even as automation-oriented a group as urban planners (who deal in such patently quantitative variables as assessed valuations of homes, percentage of owner-occupied dwellings, and taxation rates) are not always aware of the benefits of this process. Addressing such a group in 1961, Robert McCarger said, "It is not immediately obvious how many different kinds of information, *which we may not ordinarily think of as data,* can be represented in, or mapped into a number system by a human being and then subjected to machine processes."[4] To quote McCarger further, "Hence the newcomer may underestimate the range of forms subtended by the word 'data' and the range of machine functions subtended by the words 'data processing.'"

By illustrating the varied uses of punchcards in recording political science data, this book aims to stimulate students of politics to consider their research in terms of punchcard data processing. Obviously not *all* political science research can be facilitated by punchcard methods. But these fundamentals of punchcard data processing coupled with concrete examples may help the researcher judge the suitability of the methodology for his needs.

THE USE AND DISUSE OF THIS HANDBOOK

Researchers need instruction in how and when punchcards and data processing equipment can be used. Instructional material that explains the applications of these tools to political science problems is not readily available now. Although political science journals do report many studies that use modern data processing techniques, these journals contain few articles on the general method of data processing. The situation is somewhat different in the other behavioral sciences, especially psychology. However, discussions of data processing in psychological research have focused on the use of computers in performing complex statistical analyses.[5] These esoteric writings are of little value to the political scientist who wants guidance at earlier stages of data processing.

Many standard statistical routines in psychology can be applied appropriately and profitably to political data—once political scientists learn to record their data in a form amenable to computer analysis. However, collecting and recording political data is a problem for students of politics, not for psychologists. Learning how and when to use data processing equipment is a burden to be assumed by those who want to make use of the method. William Cooley's discussion of the "cultural lag" in realizing the potential of modern data processing techniques in *educational* research is equally relevant to political research. Cooley speaks of the difficulty in familiarizing educational research workers with the techniques of modern data processing:

It certainly is not going to be done through general courses in educational research, especially if recent texts introducing research are typical of the content of such courses.

My plea is not that all graduate students in education be trained to be computer programmers! However, we must develop a core of students thoroughly familiar with modern data processing techniques. These people are needed to develop the specific applications of these techniques to educational research (no one else will do it for us), and to guide their colleagues in computer applications as the need arises.[6]

No one else will do it for educators, and no one else will do it for political scientists.

This book is designed to stimulate students of politics to develop specific research applications of data processing techniques. Many books on methodology contain an initial declaration that no prior knowledge of the subject on the part of the reader is assumed, but this promise is often lost sight of in subsequent pages. This book makes that declaration and it will attempt to adhere to it throughout. The examples herein emphasize information familiar to political scientists, and the discussion of these examples is concrete and specific. In further keeping with its how-to-do-it character, this book presents a general computer program for cross-tabulating qualitative or categorized data and also discusses the use of a standard program for computing correlations from quantitative data.

This specific and concrete how-to-do-it approach aims to dispel what Oliver Benson has referred to as the "unnecessary air of mystery" that, for many political scientists, seems to overhang the university's computing center.[7] Hopefully, such an approach will also lead to an early obsolescence of this book. Any how-to-do-it manual becomes obsolete when better ways are discovered for doing what is to be done. When better methods are developed, progress takes place, and progress produces obsolescence. Progress in data processing can come through two major routes, and from the standpoint of the growth of knowledge, one is far more satisfying than the other.

One major source of progress in data processing lies in advances in machine technology. These technological advances may be separated into developments in machine "hardware" and "software." The hardware aspect of computing equipment refers to the actual physical capabilities of the machines. Harold Borko predicts several likely advances in hardware designs: greater operating speeds, greater storage capacity, ability to read printed characters as well as punched holes, and changes in machine logic.[8] The software aspect of computing equipment refers to the means by which humans "program" machines to process their data. Borko predicts that advances in software may eventually enable researchers to use simple English in writing computer programs.[9]

Important as these developments may prove to be, they depend on the efforts of the equipment manufacturers—not on the efforts of political scientists. From the standpoint of political science, obsolescence of the techniques reported in this book would be more satisfying if it came from more sophisticated and imaginative application of data processing techniques in political research. The methods in this book already may be obsolete in comparison to those employed by other researchers. In that event, perhaps this book will stimulate discussion of data processing methodology—a neglected topic in contemporary political science literature.[10]

Regardless of the origin of better data processing methods in political research, this book will surely be rendered obsolete— and the sooner the better.

ADVANTAGES IN USING PUNCHCARDS

Many benefits have been claimed for the punchcard as a data-gathering medium. These include *speed, convenience, neatness, accuracy, permanency, flexibility,* and *reproducibility.*[11] When might a researcher wish to record his information on punchcards? Many considerations figure in such a decision, but at least three factors deserve special attention: (1) the number of cases or observations under examination, (2) the uses intended to be made of the data and, (3) the possibilities of using the data for purposes other than those included in the original design. Each of these considerations will be discussed in turn:

1. *How many cases in the study?* The punchcard becomes an especially useful data-recording medium when the number of

cases or observations is large (e.g., more than one hundred, to choose an arbitrary figure). In fact, the punchcard was invented by Dr. Herman Hollerith of the U.S. Census Bureau to cope with problems of compiling information on large numbers of cases. In 1885 the Census Bureau was still compiling data collected in the Census of 1880. "It was obvious," writes Herbert Hyman, "that if the country's rate of growth continued, the time would not be far off before a new census would have to be undertaken before the previous one had been published."[12] Hollerith experimented with mechanical methods of tabulation, developing a punched-hole technique that was first used in the 1890 census.

Speed is a major advantage in using punchcards to record large numbers of cases, but it is not the only important one. The accompanying advantages of *convenience, neatness,* and *accuracy* should not be underestimated in conducting large-scale studies. The keypunch machine, which prepares the punchcard records, can be programmed for automatic operation, swiftly positioning the cards to receive the information to be recorded. As the operator presses the machine keys, information is neatly printed across the top of the card as holes are being punched into it. The contents of the cards can easily be printed on sheets of paper or totaled as many times as desired, and the cards themselves can be conveniently filed for later use. The cards are durable enough to resist wear, and worn or damaged cards can be duplicated automatically. Compare these features with problems raised by managing hundreds or thousands of sheets of hand-written records, frayed or smeared from repeated handling.

Shortly after punchcard equipment was made available at colleges and universities, students of politics undertook research involving huge numbers of cases. As early as 1931, Charles Samenow began recording information on punchcards in a study that eventually would involve more than 35,000 court cases.[13] Not long afterwards, Charles Hyneman published his classic comparative studies of 7,500 legislators serving in thirteen states during all legislative sessions from 1922 to 1935.[14]

With the advent of the sample survey as standard methodology in political research,[15] political scientists were frequently faced with problems in studying large numbers of cases. Herbert Hyman observes that because survey research studies are massive in size (often involving 1,500 or more respondents), "It is almost universal in current survey research that automatic or machine methods of processing data are used. It is therefore a further demand upon the survey analyst that he have considerable familiarity with machine methods."[16] Because of speed, convenience, and neatness, punchcards are recommended for recording political information when the number of observations or cases is large.

2. *What use is intended to be made of the data?* If the researcher plans to undertake some form of statistical analysis that would be laborious, unfeasible, or practically impossible without the use of computers, then the answer is easy and obvious: record the information in punchcard form. When the researcher plans nothing more than some manipulations and compilations of his data and the number of observations is not large, then an answer becomes more difficult. In *calendar time* it is not always "faster" to employ punchcard techniques to research a topic. Ironically, this is especially true when the use of a computer is contemplated.

If it is *Monday*, and an answer to a given question must be obtained by *Wednesday*, (and the data are not already recorded on punchcards), often the surest way of meeting the calendar deadline is to burn the midnight oil and do the job manually. In certain instances, there are definite reasons for preferring manual to mechanical methods of data processing. An obvious set of reasons is associated with the uncertainties attending mechanization: Machines sometimes break down; they are often being used by other people just when we need them; and they indiscriminately accept our own erroneous instructions, failing to execute the operation or producing useless results. This acceptance of erroneous instructions is especially frustrating when a computer is being used to meet a deadline.

Although the uncertainty of punchcard data processing must be calculated in the amount of calendar time needed to answer a given question, that is probably not the most important factor in determining the punchcard's appropriateness as a medium for recording data in smaller studies. More important is the use to which the data will be put after being recorded on cards. To some extent, the problem is akin to the "direct-production" or "indirect-production" distinction in economics. If a shipwrecked sailor on an island wants a drink of water, the quickest and easiest way to get it is to go to the pond and get it. But he could avoid a trip to the pond every time he is thirsty by constructing a piping or irrigation system. So it is with punchcards: the initial investment in the preparation of the data *may* be greater when recording in punchcard form, but the eventual payoff is assured in terms of *permanence* and *flexibility*.

A well-planned punchcard format will permit processing the data to answer many questions, some of which may not yet have occurred to the researcher. In her pre-World War II studies of the legislative histories of more than 1,100 bills in the Ohio legislature, Mona Fletcher points out the problems involved in answering questions concerning the flow of legislation through committees:

> The compiling of answers to such queries as these has been a laborious task, usually done by laying off a chart and tallying the desired information. This procedure, in addition to its tediousness, does not provide a permanent record, nor does it give an opportunity to make other comparisons than those contemplated at the beginning of the study.[17]

She found that the punchcard made it possible "to provide accurate and permanent records, available at any future time for additional analyses." Punchcards are a reusable and flexible data-recording medium. If the researcher contemplates manipulating, compiling, and analyzing his data in a variety of ways, then it may well pay him to record the data on cards, even if the number of cases or observations involved is small.

3. *What other uses might be made of the data?* Few of us are altruistic enough to incur expense solely to help fellow researchers. Yet, in the emerging era of cooperative research, punchcards do perform this often-unintended function. The punchcard format encourages development of such bold new plans for the pooling and sharing of data as the data repository program of the Inter-University Consortium for Political Research.[18] The Consortium, a partnership association between the University of Michigan's Survey Research Center and forty other

educational institutions, established an "Inventory of Data Resources" and now provides a clearinghouse for scores of studies conducted by individual researchers across the nation. Ralph Bisco of the Consortium staff holds that this clearinghouse makes it feasible to view any data collection ultimately as the property of the entire academic community.

> Unlike much natural science data, most social science data is not limited to the testing of a limited set of hypotheses devised within the constraints of a particular discipline. The verbal responses of interviewees to one specific question might be used to test theories about knowledge, perceptual processes, or attitudes; historians, political scientists, psychologists, sociologists, and anthropologists can use the same basic data for quite different purposes. As new concepts are developed, prior collections can be re-examined for evidence of change in the operation of individual or social processes.[19]

The Consortium promotes the sharing of data for political research by formulating policies and standards for recording data and by aiding in the reproduction and distribution of punchcard data and other machinable records. In addition to the advantages already mentioned—especially that of flexibility—it is the *reproducibility* of punchcard data that makes this pooling and sharing possible. Charles Backstrom and Gerald Hursh have stated:

> Machine data cards quickly have become a universal shorthand for communicating volumes of data. Scholars remote from each other can exchange information by having a duplicate deck of cards made and sending along a copy of the coding manual and questionnaires as the Rosetta stone to interpret the cards.[20]

Therefore, the use of punchcards is also recommended if the data might be of value to other researchers, to students, or for future study—even though the number of cases studied may not be large and the analysis may not be complex.

This discussion of the punchcard as an information-carrying medium has been very general. The discussion in the next chapter is more technical and specific, explaining how political data can be recorded on punchcards.

NOTES

[1] "Data processing" is used in this broad manner, for example, in Edward F. R. Hearle and Raymond J. Mason, *A Data Processing System for State and Local Governments* (Englewood Cliffs, N. J.: Prentice Hall, 1963), p. 3; Francis B. Martin, "Punch-Card Equipment," in Richard D. Duke (ed.), *Automatic Data Processing* (East Lansing: Institute for Community Development and Services, Michigan State University, 1961), p. 17; and Joyce Cole Vialet, *Fundamentals of Electronic Data Processing* (Wellesley Hills, Mass.: Minneapolis-Honeywell Regulator Company, 1963), p. 3.

[2] U. N. Statistical Office (New York: Columbia University Press, 1959), p. 2.

[3] *Ibid*, p. 9.

[4] Robert S. McCarger, "Data Processing and Planning," in Richard D. Duke (ed.), *Automatic Data Processing* (East Lansing: Institute for Community Development and Services, Michigan State University, 1961), p. 72.

[5] See E. Lowell Kelly and James C. Lingoes, "Data Processing in Psychological Research," in Harold Borko (ed.), *Computer Applications in the Behavioral Sciences* (Englewood Cliffs, N. J.: Prentice-Hall, 1962), pp. 173-203.

[6] William W. Cooley, "Research Methodology and Modern Data Processing," *Harvard Educational Review*, 31 (Summer, 1961), 62.

[7] Oliver Benson, "The Use of Mathematics in the Study of Political Science," in James C. Charlesworth (ed.), *Mathematics and the Social Sciences* (Philadelphia: The American Academy of Political and Social Science, 1963), p. 51.

[8] Harold Borko (ed.), *Computer Applications in the Behavioral Sciences* (Englewood Cliffs, N. J.: Prentice-Hall, 1962), pp. 597-601.

[9] *Ibid.*, pp. 601-3.

[10] Curiously, the literature of the 1930's reveals more on data processing methodology than the contemporary literature. For example, see Mona Fletcher, "The Use of Mechanical Equipment in Legislative Research," *The Annals of the American Academy of Political and Social Science*, 195 (January, 1938), 1-8; and "Bicameralism as Illustrated by the Ninetieth General Assembly of Ohio: A Technique for Studying the Legislative Process, *American Political Science Review*, 32 (February, 1938), 80-85. See also, Charles S. Hyneman, "Tenure and Turnover of Legislative Personnel," *American Academy of Political and Social Science Annals*, 195 (January, 1938), 21-31. A variety of punchcard applications to social science research in general is reviewed in G. W. Baehne (ed.), *Practical Applications of the Punched Card Method in Colleges and Universities* (New York: Columbia, 1935).

[11] The amenability of punchcards to statistical analysis by computers

is more often implicitly understood than explicitly included in an enumeration of their advantages.

[12]Herbert Hyman, *Survey Design and Analysis* (Glencoe, Ill.: The Free Press, 1955), p. 19.

[13]Charles U. Samenow, "Judicial Statistics in General," in Baehne, *op. cit.*, pp. 319-26.

[14]Charles S. Hyneman, *loc. cit.* and "Who Makes Our Laws?" in John C. Wahlke and Heinz Eulau (eds.), *Legislative Behavior* (Glencoe, Ill.: The Free Press, 1959), pp. 254-65. Reprinted from *Political Science Quarterly*, 55 (1940), 556-81.

[15]See Charles H. Backstrom and Gerald D. Hursh, *Survey Research* (Evanston: Northwestern University Press, 1963).

[16]Hyman, *op. cit.*, p. 19 [emphasis in original].

[17]Fletcher, *op. cit.*, p. 1.

[18]The Consortium is described in Warren E. Miller, "The Inter-University Consortium for Political Research," *American Behavioral Scientist*, 7 (November, 1963), 11-12 and in Warren E. Miller and Philip E. Converse, "The Inter-University Consortium for Political Research," *International Social Science Journal*, 16 (1964), 70-76.

[19]Ralph Bisco, "Policies and Standards for Coding Data," Inter-University Consortium for Political Research, Memorandum (1964), pp. 1-2.

[20]Backstrom and Hursh, *op. cit.*, p. 166.

CHAPTER II **RECORDING POLITICAL DATA**

ON PUNCHCARDS

When a governmental official acts in an unexpected manner, computer-oriented political scientists may be taunted by the question, "How are you going to put *that* on punchcards?" This question, taken literally, suggests the existence of an important communications gap among political scientists. Some students of politics may be genuinely curious about "how" political data are put on punchcards. Knowledge of this process is basic for understanding the use of data processing equipment in political research, and this chapter describes ways in which various political data are recorded on punchcards.

The familiar "IBM card" will be discussed as an information-carrying medium. Next, standard procedures for recording different types of political information on punchcards will be briefly outlined—avoiding details that might confuse the beginner. Appendices A-1 through A-6 contain detailed descriptions of punchcard formats and codes actually used in recording the information that prompted the examples in this chapter. Punchcard processing of political data will be treated later in Chapters VI and VII.

THE PUNCHCARD

Although several types of punchcards are in use today, the most popular type is the 80 column card pictured in Figure II-1.[1] Each of the 80 vertical columns contains 12 punching positions that appear as horizontal rows across the card. Numbers from 0 to 9 are printed across the bottom ten rows. Above the 0 row are two unmarked positions—the 12 and 11 rows. Information can be entered into a card by punching holes in the proper rows and columns. These holes then are "read" by data processing equipment and are interpreted as numbers, letters, or special characters according to the coding system devised by Herman Hollerith around 1900 and now referred to as "Hollerith code."

Any number from zero to nine can be represented by a single punch in the 0-9 positions in any given column. A single punch in the 12 row (for any column) is ordinarily interpreted as a plus sign; a punch in the 11 row ordinarily indicates a minus sign. Letters of the alphabet are produced by combining in a single column a "digit" punch (1-9) with a "zone" punch (12, 11, or 0). Special characters can be produced by certain combinations of two or more punches per column. The characters punched in the columns can be printed simultaneously at the top of the card at the time it is punched. Figure II-1 shows the common punchboard characters printed above the hole combinations that produce them.

To understand how these holes in thin cardboard can contain political data, one must become familiar with the term "field." The 80 columns on a card can be allocated so that certain columns are reserved for one type of information and other columns for other types. A *field* is a group of adjacent columns reserved for a given type of information. A field may vary in width from one to eighty columns, depending on the number of columns needed to record the information. The arrangement or layout of fields for recording data is called the card *format*. The format for recording a particular type of information is determined before the data are punched into the card, and all cards in a given study generally follow the same format.

The manner in which these fields are used to record information depends on the nature of the data. *Quantitative* data, such as election returns or governmental expenditures, can be recorded on a card simply by punching the numerical value directly into the proper field. These punches can be given a literal interpretation: the digits "300" punched into a three-column field *mean* the number "three hundred."

Given the fact that a punchcard can carry alphabetical as well as numerical information, it may seem that *qualitative* data, which is of great interest to political scientists, could also be put on cards simply by punching directly into fields of adequate

FIGURE II-1

A PUNCHCARD AND PUNCHING POSITIONS*

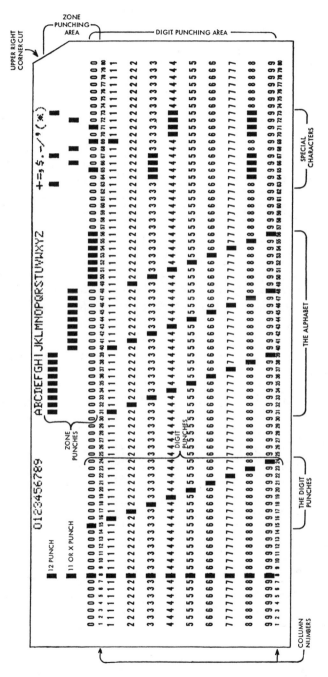

* Courtesy of International Business Machines Corporation.

length. In truth, this can be done, but a number of technical problems exist in processing alphabetical information. These problems are not present in processing numerical data.

Using computing equipment to manipulate and analyze words and sentences is sometimes called *information processing* or *information retrieval* instead of "data processing." More will be said on this subject in Chapter VIII, but for now it is sufficient to say that qualitative data are not usually recorded directly on cards and instead are "coded" into numerical categories, which then are punched into appropriate fields. The punches in these fields defy literal interpretation, and their meaning must be deciphered with a code book that identifies punches that represent specified information.

Some concrete examples of political data in punchcard form will soon be presented to illustrate this discussion. But first, it is helpful to stress a basic similarity between the punchcards used by a researcher and the common 3x5 or 4x6 index cards. Punchcards and ordinary index cards both carry information. The main difference between the two lies in their representation of information. Information is carried on punchcards in the form of holes, while it is written or typed on index cards. The information on either type of card depends on the research problem and the researcher's decisions.

The researcher who uses index cards to study generals in battles must decide whether the data should be organized by generals or by battles. Whether he uses a different card for each general or a different card for each battle depends on the organization of information in his sources and the questions he wants to answer. He then has to decide what information to record, on what part of the card to record it, and how to label or mark the cards so he can pull out the information he needs when he wants it.

These considerations also are involved when punchcards are used instead of index cards. The researcher still must decide how to organize his data, what to record, where to record it, and how to label his units of observation. Many decisions are similar because the *function* of both types of cards is similar when carrying research information. The punchcard's essential advantage as an information-carrying medium is that punchcards can be read, manipulated, and analyzed by machines; index cards cannot. The payoffs from machine processing of punchcard data were enumerated in Chapter I. Examples of computer analyses in political research will be given in later chapters. The following section illustrates how various types of political data can be put on punchcards. Election returns, responses to public opinion surveys, biographical information about political actors, characteristics of political institutions, roll call votes in legislative bodies, legislators' committee assignments, legislative histories of bills, instances of human conflict, and interactions in United Nations committee meetings have been selected as illustrations.

ELECTION RETURNS

The votes cast in precincts, wards, counties, and states for Democratic and Republican candidates are a basic source of data for students of American government and political behavior. Official election returns constitute one type of *aggregate* data— observations reported on groups of people living in a given area rather than on particular individuals. Familiar examples of aggregate data can be found in census-type information, such as the percentage of non-white population in a city block or the number of persons in a county engaged in farming. The same considerations and procedures involved in recording election returns on punchcards can be applied to various types of aggregate data. In general, aggregate data are easily put on punchcards and are especially suited to the powerful arithmetical capabilities of modern computers (see Chapter VII).

Voting returns for major state and national offices contested in recent elections are available in official state publications. In general, the county is the most common unit for reporting these returns. Figure II-2 shows a page from the official Illinois publication of the 1962 vote by counties for the office of U.S. Senator. The counties are listed alphabetically along with the votes cast within each county for the Republican and Democratic candidates. Most states publish their official election reports in similar format.

FIGURE II-2

RECORDING ELECTION RETURNS ON PUNCHCARDS

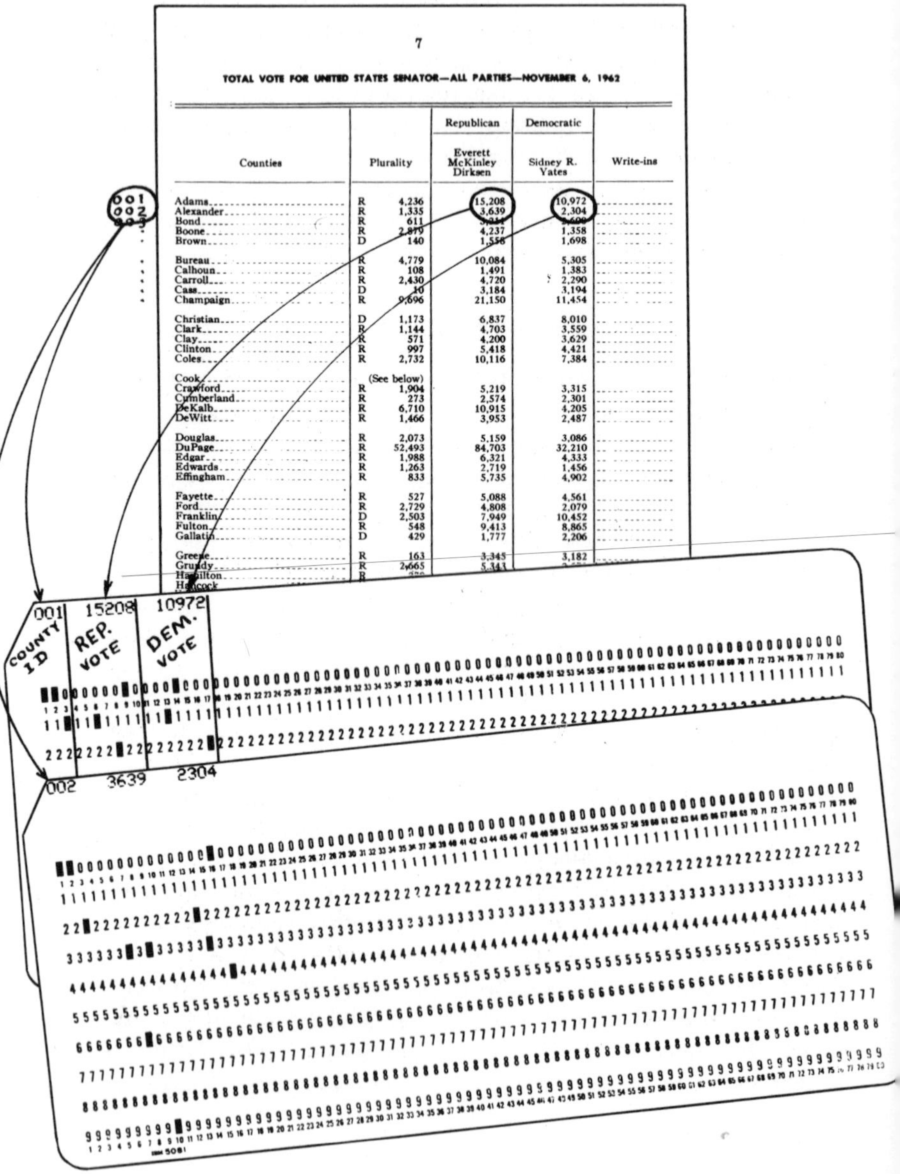

The standard method of putting election returns on cards is to use different cards for votes cast in given areas for given offices. Figure II-2 shows separate cards used in recording votes from Illinois' Adams and Alexander counties. Because Illinois has 102 counties, 102 cards are needed to record the votes from all counties for each statewide election. If it is considered desirable to break down the Cook County (Chicago and suburbs) vote by wards and townships, additional cards may be used to record votes in these subdivisions.

Transcribing information from official reports to punchcards involves both "direct" and "coded" punching. In Figure II-2, three separate fields are arbitrarily laid out on the card for recording (1) the county identification code, (2) the Republican vote, and (3) the Democratic vote. The first field (columns 1-3) contains a simple three-digit code that assigns numbers to the counties according to their alphabetical order. The Republican vote is punched directly into the second field (columns 4-10) and the Democratic vote into the third field (columns 11-17). Note that the commas in official vote reports are not recorded on the card, and the figures are entered in the card fields with the units position at the extreme right-hand side, leaving blank spaces at the left. This is called a "right-justified" field. It is standard practice to right-justify numerical data entered in fields that are wider than the number of digits in the data. In general, card fields are made wide enough to accommodate the largest anticipated value, and the vote fields in Figure II-2 were made seven digits wide to handle votes in the millions as might be cast in Cook County.

The simple card format discussed here captures only the most essential facts: the county identification codes and the party vote. The parties' pluralities in each county are not usually recorded because the computer can calculate pluralities from the vote totals far more easily and accurately than they can be recorded on cards from the published report. It often is desirable, however, to punch other information in the cards while the raw data are being recorded. If the cards are to become part of a large library of punchcard holdings, it is useful to include codes for the offices being contested and for the election years. Estimates of the eligible electorate in each county should also be recorded if the computer is to calculate the percentage turnout at the polls. Additional information of this sort has been recorded in the election studies on file at Northwestern University. Details of the card format and codes for these studies are contained in Appendix A-1.

PUBLIC OPINION SURVEYS

Punchcards perhaps are used most often in behavioral research for recording individual responses to questions asked in survey interviews and public opinion polls. These questions normally elicit qualitative responses that must be translated into numerical coding categories before being punched onto cards. The standard practice is to use a different card for each person interviewed. The respondents are identified by code numbers—usually punched on the lefthand side of the cards—and their responses are punched in separate fields laid out on the remaining columns. Figure II-3 illustrates how an interviewer's notations of a respondent's answers to two typical survey questions might be transcribed on punchcards. In actual practice, of course, responses to many questions would be recorded, and holes would be punched throughout the card.

Some survey questions elicit easily anticipated answers that can be coded in a few obvious categories. Others produce rich and varied responses that need to be studied carefully before coding categories can be constructed. Both types of questions are contained in the sample interview schedule in Figure II-3.

The question, "Did you vote for a candidate for Congress?" usually produces answers that the interviewer can record simply by circling the appropriate code number. Answers to the question, "What is the most important reason you voted for him?" are best handled by having the interviewer record them verbatim and by constructing codes after a sample of responses is studied. The appropriate code number for the response is then written alongside the question on the interview schedule, and the schedules are given to keypunch operators with instructions to punch all circled numbers.

FIGURE II-3

RECORDING INTERVIEW RESPONSES ON PUNCHCARDS

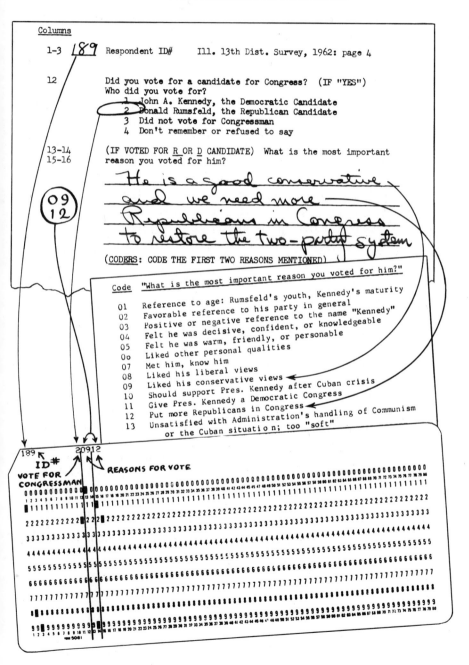

The general subject of questionnaire design and coding considerations in survey research deserves its own book-length treatment. Backstrom and Hursh treat this and other topics thoroughly in *Survey Research*, an earlier book in this series of Handbooks for Research in Political Behavior. Although Chapter V contains some suggestions for developing coding categories that have relevance for survey data, this book does not devote much additional attention to this subject. Complete examples of interview schedules and punchcard codes have been published in the appendices of many survey studies.[2]

POLITICAL INSTITUTIONS

The practice of "coding" information into numbered categories has long been used for response to survey questions, but it only recently has been applied to information on political institutions. Students of government often deal with such institutional variables as a nation's legislative-executive structure, the nature of its party system, and the role of interest groups in the political process. Many political scientists may not think of this information as "data"—a term that has quantitative connotations. Nevertheless, institutional variables can easily be recorded on cards and profitably analyzed with data processing equipment.

Political institutions can be categorized and counted in the same manner as can responses to interview questions. Admittedly the job may be far more difficult, but in principle the tasks are the same. Information on political institutions is not "hard" data, and careful judgment must be exercised in constructing categories and in classifying these variables on the basis of incomplete and often conflicting evidence. Once the data have been recorded on punchcards, however, the researcher can avail himself of the advantages of data processing equipment in analyzing political institutions. These advantages are especially helpful in comparing political institutions in many different governmental units.

A Cross-Polity Survey, the landmark work of Arthur S. Banks and Robert B. Textor, indicates what can be done with this approach to comparative politics at the international level.[3] Banks coded 115 of the world's independent "polities" according to 57 different political and environmental characteristics. He then used Textor's special computer program to cross-classify each characteristic against every other and to print out the resulting table when a relationship was statistically significant. This effort produced a massive 1,300 page book composed mainly of computer output. While it yields no theory about comparative politics, this book does provide comprehensive pictures of the relationships between many pairs of variables for virtually all nations. The resulting information can be used for theory-building.

The use of punchcards for information on political institutions will be illustrated with two variables chosen from *A Cross-Polity Survey*. Banks sought to classify each nation according to its legislative-executive structure and the status of its legislature in making governmental policy. The following sets of categories were constructed for these variables.[4]

Code   *Legislative-Executive Structure*

1 *Presidential:* characterized by the presence of an elected official (whether directly or indirectly designated) who serves for a stated term as both Head of State and Chief Executive, or as Head of State and *effective* executive, in conjunction with a "weak" premier not dependent upon a parliamentary majority.

2 *Presidential-Parliamentary:* has a "strong" president serving as Head of State and as effective executive, in conjunction with a "weak" premier who is dependent upon parliamentary support.

3 *Parliamentary-Republican:* differs from the presidential-parliamentary in that the power positions of president and premier, respectively, are reversed.

4 *Parliamentary-Royalist:* differs from the parliamentary-republican in that the Head of State is a "weak" monarch, rather than an elected president.

5 *Monarchical-Parliamentary:* has a "strong" monarch serving as Head of State and as effective executive, in conjunction with a "weak" premier dependent, at least to some degree, upon parliamentary support.

6 *Monarchical:* has a "strong" monarch serving as Head of State and as Chief Executive, or as Head of State and effective executive, in conjunction with a "weak" premier not dependent upon parliamentary support.

7   *Communist:* the legislature has complete *formal* control over the appointment and tenure of both the Head of State and the Premier. Effective control, however, is exercised by the party hierarchy.

8   *Ambiguous, irrelevant,* or *unascertained*

Code   *Current Status of the Legislature*

1   *Fully effective* (performs normal legislative function as reasonably "co-equal" branch of national government)

2   *Partially effective* (tendency toward domination by executive, or otherwise partially limited in effective exercise of legislative function)

3   *Largely ineffective* (virtually complete domination by executive or by one-party or dominant party organization)

4   *Wholly ineffective* (restricted to consultative or "rubberstamp" legislative function)

5   *Ambiguous, irrelevant,* or *unascertained*

Although Banks presented his sets of categories for most variables, he did not disclose the evidence underlying the coding decisions for individual nations. Therefore, Figure II-4 shows how one *might* use published material to classify a nation according to its legislative-executive structure and the status of its legislature in making governmental policy. In an actual study, again, the card would be punched full of coded information.

In the Banks and Textor scheme, nations constituted observational units, and the data were recorded on a one-card-per-nation basis. Figure II-4 shows a punchcard carrying information about the governmental structure and role of the Japanese legislature. Japan's identification number is punched in the first field. Columns 6 and 9 respectively contain Banks's codes for legislative-executive structure and status of the legislature in policy making. Note that the arrows do not go directly from the data to the card but go first to a ruled sheet of paper. This is called a "coding sheet" and is used when the coding process is too complex to allow cards to be punched directly from source documents. Trained personnel enter code numbers on coding sheets with the use of detailed code books. The code sheets they prepare are

FIGURE II-4

RECORDING INFORMATION ABOUT POLITICAL INSTITUTIONS*

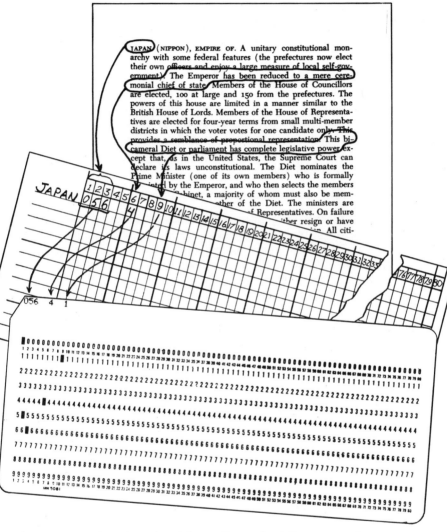

JAPAN (NIPPON), EMPIRE OF. A unitary constitutional monarchy with some federal features (the prefectures now elect their own officers and enjoy a large measure of local self-government). The Emperor has been reduced to a mere ceremonial chief of state. Members of the House of Councillors are elected, 100 at large and 150 from the prefectures. The powers of this house are limited in a manner similar to the British House of Lords. Members of the House of Representatives are elected for four-year terms from small multi-member districts in which the voter votes for one candidate only. This provides a semblance of proportional representation. This bi-cameral Diet or parliament has complete legislative power except that, as in the United States, the Supreme Court can declare its laws unconstitutional. The Diet nominates the Prime Minister (one of its own members) who is formally appointed by the Emperor, and who then selects the members of the cabinet, a majority of whom must also be members of either House of the Diet. The ministers are responsible to the House of Representatives. On failure of a vote of confidence they either resign or have the Diet dissolved for a new election. All citi-

*By permission from Samuel A. Johnson, *Essentials of Comparative Government* (Great Neck, New York: Barron's Educational Series, Inc., 1964), page 201.

given to keypunch operators who punch the numbers into cards on a one-card-per-line basis. The heavy black lines that follow every fifth column serve as reference markers for coders and keypunch operators.

Much remains to be learned about categorizing and coding information on political institutions, for this use of punchcards in political research is still relatively new. This method could be extended to include collections of data on other observational units such as governmental agencies and political parties, but most uses of punchcards for institutional variables have made the nation the unit of observation. Appendix A-2 illustrates codes used for data on fifteen political variables collected on eighty-two nations as part of the Dimensionality of Nations Project at Northwestern and Yale universities.

BIOGRAPHICAL MATERIAL

Governments and private agencies periodically collect and publish biographical information on prominent public personalities and various groups of political actors. The biographical sketches in these "who's who" publications have been used in intensive studies of individual careers and in comparative studies of the careers of whole classes of political actors, such as the Hoover Institute elite studies in the 1950's.[5] When biographical information is sought for purposes of intensive research on individual careers, punchcards offer few or no advantages over ordinary note cards. But when background characteristics are to be gathered and analyzed for scores (or hundreds) of political actors, punchcards should be considered.

Figure II-5 illustrates the punchcard procedure for recording biographical information on members of the Soviet Academy of Sciences.[6] Information about each entrant is packed into a paragraph following his name. The relevant data in these paragraphs are put on punchcards by translating the information into code numbers which are then entered on coding sheets. Each line on the sheet represents a different individual, and the cards are punched on a one-card-per-individual basis. The following codes provide information on membership in the Communist Party and the Soviet Academy of Sciences:

Code   *Communist Party membership*
0 Not a member
1 Former member from (year: *col. 14-15*) to (year: *col. 16-17*)
2 Current member since (year: *col. 14-15*)

Code   *Soviet Academy of Sciences membership*
0 Not a member
1 Indeterminate association with the Academy
2 Current regular member
3 Current honorary member   } since (year: *col. 21-22*)
4 Current corresponding member
5 Former regular member   { from (year: *col. 21-22*)
6 Former honorary member   to (year: *col. 23-24*)
7 Former corresponding member

These categories are incorporated in a code book that serves as a reference for translating published information into numbers on code sheets. Even when working with well-prepared manuals, coders must exercise their own judgment in deciding how to handle ambiguities and unanticipated problems in the data. It is useful for them to enter these decisions in "diaries" that can be reviewed by the researcher who can modify the coding instructions if necessary.

The coding categories devised for biographical data depend on the research objectives and information available in the sources. Appendix A-3 describes the punchcard format and codes for background data collected on all members of the Indiana General Assembly from 1925 to 1961. Similar biographical data on members of state legislative bodies have been used in research to determine "who makes our laws."[7]

ROLL CALL VOTING

Published records of votes cast by members of governmental bodies constitute a major source of data for political scientists.[8] Analyses of roll call votes have been conducted on city councils, state legislatures, both houses of Congress, foreign legislatures, the United Nations, and the Supreme Court. The voting patterns

FIGURE II-5

RECORDING BIOGRAPHICAL INFORMATION*

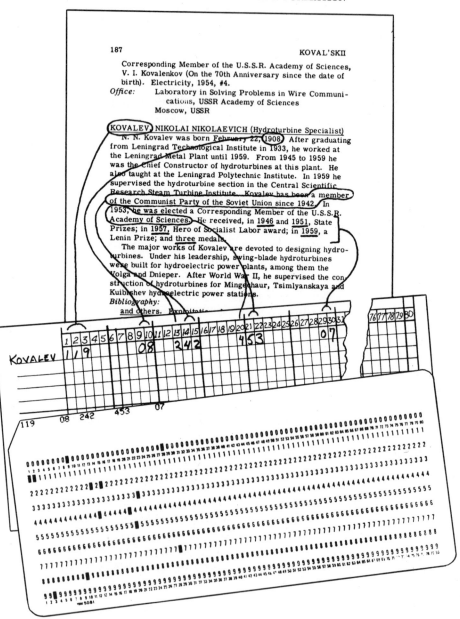

of all members on many different issues are usually studied in these analyses. Often the researcher must analyze the voting positions of more than one hundred members on more than one hundred roll calls. This amount of information could hardly be managed by traditional methods, but once the data are put on punchcards, complex analyses of this enormous information matrix becomes almost routine.[9]

Roll call votes usually are recorded on punchcards by using one card for each member, reserving a separate column on the card for each roll call, and punching a code number for each legislator's vote on a given roll call in the proper column of his card. A simple code is *1* for *yes, 2* for *no,* and *3* for *not voting.* Figure II-6 shows how this code may be applied to the official report of roll call votes on Senate Bills No. 146 and No. 367 as published in the *Senate Journal* of the 1963 Illinois General Assembly.

A record must be kept to indicate which roll calls are recorded in which columns. Supposing that the card format in Figure II-6 limits the recording of roll calls to columns 11-80, the voting positions of one member on as many as 70 different roll calls can be contained on one punchcard. Because some legislatures may have several hundred roll calls in one session, it often is necessary to use more than one voting card per individual. In this case, every card assigned to a given legislator is punched with the same identifying number, but another column is punched to indicate whether it is his first card, second card, and so on.

The format in which legislative votes usually are reported makes it necessary to record the data on coding sheets before the cards can be punched. This process is a tedious error-inviting task. One person can do the job, but a team of two—one reading off the votes and the other entering code numbers—usually operates more economically as they produce fewer errors that must later be corrected. Although a great deal of effort is required to transcribe large numbers of roll calls onto punchcards via coding sheets, the flexibility and reusability features of punchcard data make the effort worthwhile.

The one-card-per-member format for recording roll call votes provides considerable flexibility in analysis. The researcher can

FIGURE II-6

RECORDING ROLL CALL VOTES

On motion of Senator Canfield, Senate Bill No. 146, a bill for "An Act to amend Section 1-10 of the 'Public Assistance Code of Illinois', approved August 4, 1949, as amended."

Having been transcribed and typed and all amendments adopted thereto having been printed, was taken up and read at large a third time.

And the question being, "Shall this bill pass?" it was decided in the affirmative by the following vote: Yeas, 31; nays, 16.

The following voted in the affirmative:

Bidwill	Fawell	Green	Larson	Peters
Broyles	Friedrich	Harris	Laughlin	Peterson
Canfield	Gilbert	Hart	Little	Schlagenhauf
Carpentier	Gottschalk	Hatch	Martin	Sours
Collins	Graham, J. A.	Hoffelder	McGloon	Sprague
Davis	Graham, Paul	Kerr	Osinga	Swanson
Drach				Yeas—31.

The following voted in the negative:

Coulson	Downing	Kocarek	McCarthy	Simon
Cronin	Finley	Kusibab	Neistein	Smith
Dixon	Kinnally	Lyons	O'Brien	Ziegler
Dougherty				Nays—16.

This bill, having received the votes of a constitutional majority of the members elected was declared passed.

Ordered that the title be as aforesaid, and that the Secretary inform the House of Representatives thereof and ask their concurrence therein.

On motion of Senator Simon, Senate Bill No. 367 a bill for "An Act to amend Section 4d of the 'Personnel Code', approved July 18, 1955, as amended."

Having been transcribed and typed and all amendments adopted thereto having been printed, was taken up and read at large a third time.

And the question being, "Shall this bill pass?" it was decided in the negative by the following vote: Yeas, 9; nays, 34.

The following voted in the affirmative:

Cherry	Dixon	Eberspacher	Neistein	Smith
Coulson	Dougherty	McGloon	Simon	Yeas—9.

The following voted in the negative:

Bidwill	Fawell	Harris	Little	Sours
Broyles	Finley	Hart	Martin	Sprague
Carpentier	Friedrich	Hatch	McCarthy	Swanson
Collins	Gilbert	Hoffelder	Osinga	Sweeney
Davis	Graham, J. A.	Kerr	Peters	
Downing	Graham, Paul	Larson		
Drach				

	1	2	3	4	5	6	7	8	9	10	11	12	13	14	15	16	17	18	19	20	21	22	23	24	25	26	27	28	29	30	31	32	33	34
ARRINGTON	0	1								3	3																							
BIDWELL	0	2									1	2																						
BROYLES	0	3									1	2																						
CANFIELD	0	4									1	3																						

VOTE ON BILL NO. 146   VOTE ON BILL NO. 367

combine individual members' cards to analyze their votes according to common characteristics such as party, occupation, and character of the districts represented.[10] In principle only the members' code numbers need be known to form these groupings, since the identification codes permit individual cards to be selected and grouped as desired. However, it is more convenient to code these common variables for each individual and to include them on the card in addition to the identification code. Data processing equipment can then arrange the members into analysis groups. Appendix A-4 contains a roll call vote study that includes such additional variables on each legislator's data cards.

COMMITTEE ASSIGNMENTS

Legislators' committee assignments have been chosen to illustrate how punchcards can be used for less common types of political data. Political scientists take great interest in legislators' memberships on committees. Especially in Congress, a legislator's influence is determined by his membership on committees, and his career in the chamber is reflected in his movement through the committee structure. In spite of the publication of several recent analyses of initial assignments and membership changes on congressional committees, the need continues for additional research assessing the effect of committee membership on roll call voting and comparing congressional committees with those in state and foreign legislatures. Such research can be facilitated with data processing techniques if the data are recorded on punchcards.

Various governmental and private publications issue reports on committee assignments of congressmen and state legislators. A page from the *Congressional Directory* of the 88th Congress, 1st session, is reproduced in Figure II-7. The senators' names are listed alphabetically and followed by the committees on which they served. Chairmanships are also specified. This information can be recorded conveniently on coding sheets by using a separate line for each senator and arbitrarily reserving a separate column for each committee. If the senator is a member of a given committee, the appropriate column can be marked 1. If he is the chairman of that committee, the column can be marked 2. The column can be left blank or punched zero if the senator did not serve on the committee.[11] Other codes are possible: the field for each committee might be expanded to two columns and the number of years served on the committee could be entered in place of the simple code above. Whatever the code, the data would be punched into cards on a one-card-per-member basis, and some record should be kept to tell which committees' assignments were recorded in which columns.

As stated in the previous section on recording roll call votes, it is often desirable to supplement a man's identification number with other information punched in the data card. For example, analyses of the background of members on various committees would be facilitated if codes for the standard party, occupation, and district variables were punched in the cards along with identification numbers and committee assignments. Appendix A-5 describes data collected on committee assignments in the Indiana legislature, in which members serve on many committees with constantly shifting assignments. Complete information on the card format and coding categories used for the data are given.

HISTORIES OF BILLS

Students of legislatures want to know what happens after bills are introduced into the chamber. Knowledge about whose bills go to which committees and what eventually happens to them is especially important for comparative studies of legislative processes. Because hundreds of bills are introduced in some legislative sessions, punchcards and data processing techniques are virtually essential if one is to acquire such knowledge. Even with this technology, an enormous amount of work is involved in comprehensive comparisons of the histories of legislation.[12]

The main problem in recording legislative histories on punchcards lies in getting access to information. Information relevant to the history of any given bill is likely to be scattered throughout a legislature's house and senate journal. Detailed and accurate indexes to the journals are a great help at the recording stage, but the task is still a tedious one. Figure II-8 shows how one facet of a bill's history is reported in an official journal of a legislature

Figure II-7

RECORDING COMMITTEE ASSIGNMENTS

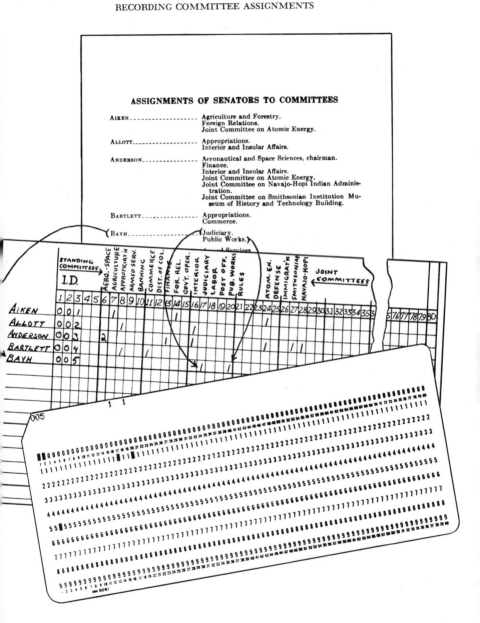

ASSIGNMENTS OF SENATORS TO COMMITTEES

AIKEN — Agriculture and Forestry.
Foreign Relations.
Joint Committee on Atomic Energy.

ALLOTT — Appropriations.
Interior and Insular Affairs.

ANDERSON — Aeronautical and Space Sciences, chairman.
Finance.
Interior and Insular Affairs.
Joint Committee on Atomic Energy.
Joint Committee on Navajo-Hopi Indian Administration.
Joint Committee on Smithsonian Institution Museum of History and Technology Building.

BARTLETT — Appropriations.
Commerce.

BAYH — Judiciary.
Public Works.

and transcribed in punchcard language on a one-card-per-bill basis.

The page reproduced in Figure II-8 is from the Indiana *House Journal* for 1961. The information shows that the House adopted the majority committee report that House Bill No. 149 pass without amendment. House reactions to committee reports can be reported with such categories as the following:

Code Chamber action on the Majority Report of the Committee

1 The bill was not reported out of committee so no action was taken

2 Adopted the report: that the bill pass without amendment

3 Adopted the report: that the bill pass after amendment

4 Adopted the report: that the bill should not pass

5 Adopted the report: that the bill be recommitted to another committee

6 No committee report: the bill was taken from committee by action of the chamber

7 The chamber adopted the minority report of the committee (see Chamber Action on Minority Report)

The exact coding categories formulated for recording the legislature's actions on a bill depend on the rules governing operation of the legislative process in the chamber. Appendix A-6 contains a detailed description of codes used in recording legislative histories of bills introduced in several sessions of the Indiana General Assembly. Because the categories were constructed several years ago when it was considered important to squeeze all information into single-column fields on one card only, the codes require revision.[13] They are reproduced in Appendix A-6 for purposes of illustration only.

DOMESTIC AND FOREIGN CONFLICT

Conflict over "who gets what, when, and how" lies at the very heart of the study of politics. Surprisingly, however, the comparative study of political conflict within and between nations has not drawn much attention from political scientists.[14] This neglect

FIGURE II-8

RECORDING THE HISTORIES OF LEGISLATION

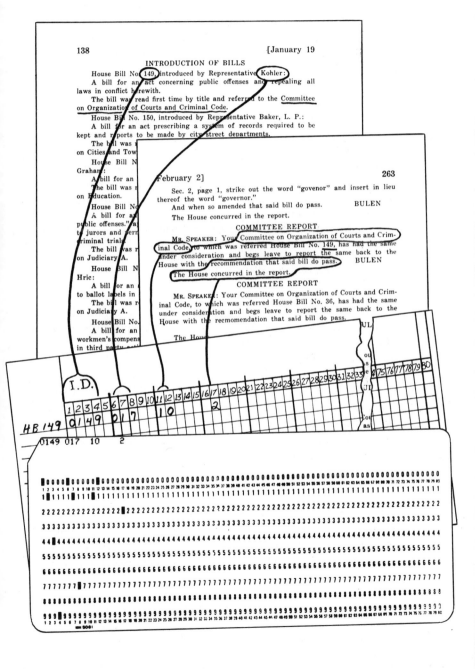

is due largely to the enormous data collection and analysis problems involved in making systematic and comprehensive comparisons of domestic and foreign conflict behavior. World-wide comparative studies of political conflict have become feasible only recently through the advent of punchcards and modern data processing techniques.

One approach to the comparative study of conflict behavior within and between nations is represented in the work of Rudolph Rummel and Raymond Tanter.[15] Rummel collected and analyzed data on twenty-two measures of domestic and foreign conflict for seventy-seven nations during 1955, 1956, and 1957. Tanter replicated Rummel's study and extended the data collection and analysis across eighty-three nations for 1958, 1959, and 1960. Intercorrelations among variables, factor analysis, and multiple regression were the principal methods of data analysis in both studies. Both research designs recorded conflict behavior on punchcards and used computers to process the data.

Rummel and Tanter studied nine measures of domestic conflict and thirteen measures of foreign conflict. For measures of domestic conflict, they selected the presence or absence of *guerrilla warfare* within a country and the number of *assassinations*, general *strikes*, major *governmental crises, purges, riots, revolutions*, anti-government *demonstrations*, and *killings* in all forms of domestic violence. For measures of foreign conflict, they selected the presence or absence of *military action* and the number of anti-foreign *demonstrations*, negative *sanctions, protests, severed relations, recalled* or *expelled ambassadors, recalled* or *expelled lesser diplomatic officials, threats, wars, troop movements, mobilizations, accusations*, and *killings* in all forms of violent interchange between countries. The basic data for each of these measures were obtained through systematic examination of such sources as *The New York Times Index, Brittanica Book of the Year*, and *Facts on File* for 1955-1957 and 1958-1960. The process of recording these conflict data on cards is illustrated in Figure II-9 which shows how a news item in *The New York Times*, July 6, 1959, is recorded in the assassination data for Haiti during 1958-1960 (the second time period).

FIGURE II-9
RECORDING FOREIGN AND DOMESTIC CONFLICT BEHAVIOR

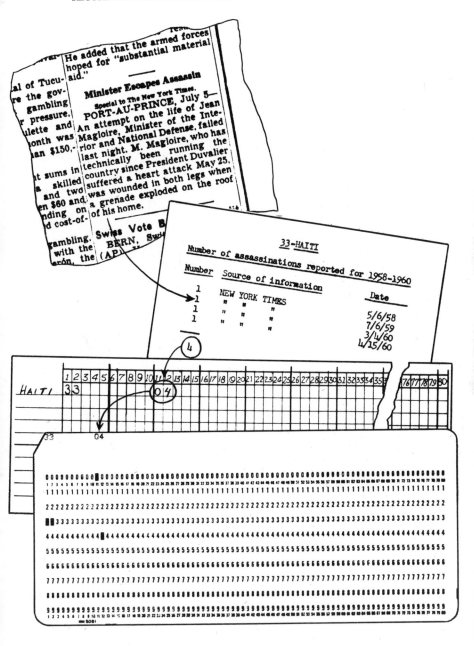

In the Rummel and Tanter studies, an assassination was defined as

> The politically motivated murder or attempted murder of a high governmental official or politician. Among high governmental officials are included the governors of states or provinces, the mayors of large cities, members of the cabinet, and members of the national legislature. Among high politicians are included members of the inner core of the ruling party or group and leaders of the opposition.[16]

The incident reported in the newspaper item in Figure II-9 was entered on an index card that lists assassination data on Haiti; the total number of assassinations reported during 1958-1960 were recorded on the coding sheet and punched into Haiti's data card. Similar operations were involved in recording data on the remaining twenty-one conflict measures for the other nations studied.

INTERACTION ANALYSIS

The political process involves interactions among people. Sometimes these interactions occur in places where they can be easily observed. Members of city councils and legislative committees, for example, talk to one another and to private citizens in public meetings. They ask questions, provide answers, get angry, show pleasure, and so on. While only a small portion of the political process may be reflected in public meetings, this part may be studied directly through intensive analysis of interactions. However, analysis of observed interactions among governmental officials has not been a subject of much research.[17] This neglect has certainly not been due to lack of data, for the careful observer can quickly fill a note pad with the interactions recorded during one evening's attendance at a lively city council meeting. The problem lies not in obtaining the data but in handling the data once obtained. Here again, punchcards and data processing equipment offer a solution.

Chadwick Alger's work on communication patterns in the United Nations[18] provides an examples of punchcard methods

FIGURE II-10

RECORDING INTERPERSONAL INTERACTIONS IN THE UNITED STATES*

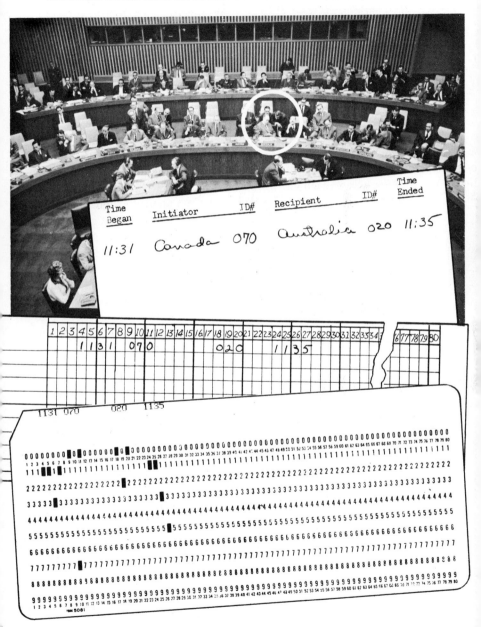

*Photograph courtesy of the United Nations.

applied to interaction analysis. Alger and an assistant pains-
takingly and systematically recorded their observations of private
discussions on the floor during meetings of the Fifth Committee (Administrative and Budgetary Committee) during the
17th Regular Session in 1962 and the 4th Special Session in 1963.
The researchers noted who talked with whom, when, and for
how long. When possible, they recorded the initiator of the interaction as well as the recipient. They also noted diplomatic posts
held by the discussants and the agenda item under discussion at
the time. As a result of these observations, data were collected on
3,488 interactions in seventy meetings of the Fifth Committee in
1962 and on 1,796 interactions in twenty-two meetings in 1963.
These data were punched into cards as shown in Figure II-10,
using a separate card for each observed interaction.

Once the data were on cards, Alger was able to analyze thousands of interactions with the help of data processing equipment.
He isolated patterns among member nations and determined
which nations tended to be initiators and which were recipients.
He also identified the *individuals*—not only the nations—highest
in interactions and the types of diplomatic posts they occupied.
This information can now be related to other knowledge to provide a more complete picture of the political process in the
United Nations.

CONCLUSIONS

These examples have been presented to show ways in which
punchcards might be used to record widely different types of
political information. These certainly are not the only possible
uses of punchcards for political data, and with some imagination,
entirely new applications of punchcards can be devised to cope
with practical problems of political research. In order to think
effectively about new applications of punchcard methodology,
however, it is necessary to know something about the simple
mechanics of data processing. This is the subject of the next two
chapters.

NOTES

1 Remington Rand (UNIVAC) cards have the same dimensions as IBM cards, 7⅜ x 3¼ inches. Early Remington Rand machines read only 45 columns of information from each card; the same size card was later organized into 90 columns. In both versions, the punched holes were round instead of rectangular as in IBM cards. Modern Remington Rand equipment, however, is compatible with the IBM standard. Different types of punchcards are compared in Burton Dean Friedman, *Punched Card Primer* (Chicago: Public Administration Service, 1955).

2 The interview schedule and codes for one of the major voting studies is given in Bernard R. Berelson, Paul F. Lazarsfeld, and William N. McPhee, *Voting* (Chicago: University of Chicago Press, 1954). Lester Milbrath's *The Washington Lobbyists* (Chicago: Rand McNally, 1963) provides the questions and codes used in his interviews with 114 lobbyists.

3 Banks and Textor, *A Cross-Polity Survey* (Cambridge: M.I.T. Press, 1963).

4 Although the categories used here are essentially the same as those in the Banks and Textor book, it should be pointed out that the *codes* associated with the categories are *not* similar to theirs. Banks and Textor used letters of the alphabet as coding symbols in order to accommodate more categories in a single column than provided by the digits 0 to 9. This procedure is not recommended for the variety of reasons discussed in Chapter V. Banks and Textor had to develop their own special computer program to process their alphabetically coded variables.

5 Harold D. Lasswell *et. al.*, *The Comparative Study of Elites* (Stanford: Stanford University Press, 1952).

6 For a recent article describing the relevance of such a biographical analysis to political research, see Arthur M. Hanhardt, Jr. and William A. Welsh, "The Intellectuals-Politics Nexus: Studies Using a Biographical Technique," *American Behavioral Scientist*, 7 (March, 1964), 3-7.

7 See Charles S. Hyneman, "Who Makes Our Laws?" in John C. Wahlke and Heinz Eulau (eds.), *Legislative Behavior* (Glencoe: The Free Press, 1959), pp. 254-265. Reprinted from *Political Science Quarterly* 55 (1940), 556-81.

8 There has, however, been considerable argument generated about the utility and validity of roll call analysis. Most of the important points in the debate have been packaged nicely in the Bobbs-Merrill Reprint number PS-92, which binds together three items: (1) David R. Derge's "Metropolitan and Outstate Alignments in Illinois and Missouri Legislative Delegations," *American Political Science Review*, 52 (December, 1958), 1051-65; (2) Richard T. Frost, "On

Derge's Metropolitan and Outstate Legislative Delegations," *American Political Science Review*, 53 (September, 1959), 792-95; and (3) Derge, "On the Use of Roll Call Analysis: A Reply to R. T. Frost," *American Political Science Review*, 53 (December, 1959), 1097-99. For additional views see Wilder Crane, Jr., "A Caveat on Roll-Call Studies of Party Voting," *Midwest Journal of Political Science*, 4 (August, 1960), 237-49; and Fred I. Greenstein and Elton F. Jackson, "A Second Look at the Validity of Roll-Call Analysis," *Midwest Journal of Political Science*, 7 (May, 1963), 156-66.

[9] A thorough treatment of roll call analysis will be the subject of another Handbook for Research in Political Behavior, now under preparation by Lee Anderson, Carl McMurray, Meredith Watts, and Allen Wilcox.

[10]Although the one-card-per-member format probably offers the greatest flexibility in analysis, a one-card-per-vote format may be better suited to a special analytical technique, like Q-technique factor analysis.

[11]See Chapter V for some comments on the use of blanks as codes.

[12]Punchcards were used in studying the histories of legislation as early as 1938. See Mona Fletcher, "Bicameralism as Illustrated by the Ninetieth General Assembly of Ohio: A Technique for Studying the Legislative Process," *American Political Science Review*, 32 (February, 1938), 80-85; Fletcher, "The Use of Mechanical Equipment in Legislative Research," *The Annals of the American Academy of Political and Social Science*, 195 (January, 1938), 1-8; and Lloyd M. Short, "The Legislative Process in Minnesota," *The Annals of the American Academy of Political and Social Science*, 195 (January, 1938), 123-28.

[13]See Chapter V regarding the inadvisability of sacrificing variables or code categories in order to squeeze all information into single-column codes on a single-card-per-case basis.

[14]For a review of "comparative conflict research," see Rudolph J. Rummel, "The Dimensions of Conflict Behavior Within and Between Nations," *General Systems Yearbook*, 8 (1963), 1-50. Rummel could find only twenty-four published studies on domestic conflict between 1945 and 1961. Although he found many more studies on foreign conflict, most of these dealt only with the most violent form —war.

[15][Rummel's work is cited in footnote 14.] Tanter's study is "Dimensions of Conflict Behavior Within and Between Nations, 1958-1960," unpublished Ph.D. thesis, Indiana University, August, 1964. For an approach to conflict analysis that focuses on voting behavior in the United Nations, see Hayward R. Alker, Jr., "Dimensions of Conflict in the General Assembly," *American Political Science Review*, 58 (September, 1964), 642-57.

[16]Rummel, *op. cit.*, p. 25.

[17]A study of interactions among legislators was made as early as 1938. See Garland C. Routt, "Interpersonal Relationships and the Legislative Process," *Annals of the American Academy of Political and Social Science*, 195 (January, 1938), 129-36. I know of no other published studies since, however, that have analyzed *observed* interactions among legislators; although the following studies have been made of interaction patterns based on interview data: Samuel C. Patterson, "Patterns of Interpersonal Relations in a State Legislative Group: The Wisconsin Assembly," *Public Opinion Quarterly*, 23 (Spring, 1959), 101-9; and Wayne L. Francis, "Influence and Interaction in a State Legislative Body," *American Political Science Review*, 56 (December, 1962), 953-60.

[18]At the time of this writing, Alger has not yet published his findings. But see Chadwick Alger, "Interactions in a United Nations Committee," scheduled for publication in J. David Singer (ed.), *International Yearbook of Political Behavior Research*, Vol. 7 (New York: The Free Press, 1965).

CHAPTER III UNIT RECORD MACHINES

Data processing equipment can be divided into two basic types—computers and "unit record" machines. "Unit record" derives from the common use of punchcards to carry information on a one-item-per-card basis, which makes them *unit records.* Computers are *electronic* devices that function primarily through tube, transistor, or solid-state circuitry; unit record equipment operates through *electromechanical* principles—involving motors, gears, wheels, brushes, and magnets. Computers will be discussed in Chapter IV; this chapter will concentrate on unit record equipment.

Unit record machines perform such specific physical functions as sorting punchcards into groups or printing the cards' contents on paper. With the increased importance of computers in data processing, these specific-function machines have also become known as "auxiliary" equipment as they often are used only to prepare data for computer analysis.

In the years before computers ("B.C."),[1] all stages of data processing—from recording through analysis—were executed on what today is called "auxiliary" equipment. The development of computers has changed the usage of unit record equipment, but it has not made these machines obsolete. A great deal of preliminary processing is usually required before data are ready for computer analysis. Because of problems in conceptualizing, acquiring, and recording political data, knowledge of the functions and operating principles of different types of unit record equipment is especially important for researchers.

A thorough review of all the various types, makes, and models of unit record equipment would be out of place in this handbook.[2] Instead, this discussion will pertain to equipment most likely to be available at colleges and universities. From a practical standpoint, this means describing products of the International Business Machines Corporation.[3] The discussion aims to be sufficiently specific to be instructive for those who have access to IBM equipment, while still being general enough to be informative for those who use other manufacturers' products.

With one exception, the machines discussed in this chapter perform specific functions in the preparation and manipulation of punchcard data. Most important of these functions are punching; verifying; counting and sorting; reproducing and gangpunching; tabulating and printing; interpreting; and selecting, merging, and collating. These functions are performed, respectively, by the *keypunch, verifier, counter-sorter, reproducer, tabulator, interpreter,* and *collator.* The exception is the *electronic statistical machine,* which combines several manipulative functions with a capacity for data analysis and operates through electronic as well as electromechanical principles. Each of these machines will be discussed in turn.

THE KEYPUNCH[4]

Information normally is recorded on a punchcard by means of a keypunch machine.[5] The most common keypunch machines in use today are the IBM 24 Card Punch and the IBM 26 Printing Card Punch. The machines are virtually identical except for the IBM 26's ability to print information above the columns in which it is punched. The IBM 26 is pictured in Figure III-1.

Information is punched in a card by operating a typewriter-style keyboard, which punches letters, digits, or special characters into card columns. Cards pass through the machine as illustrated in Figure III-2. The operator presses the "feed" button on the keyboard which moves a card down from the hopper. When the "register" button is depressed, the first column of the card is positioned under the punching station. The cards are punched from left to right, one column at a time (column 1 to column 80). After each column is punched, the card is automatically positioned for the next column. After all 80 columns are punched, the card automatically is registered under the reading station, through which it passes—column by column—in phase with the card following it at the punching station. When the card at the

FIGURE III-1
THE IBM 26 PRINTING CARD PUNCH*

* Courtesy of International Business Machines Corporation.

punching station is released, the card at the reading station moves into the card stacker.

FIGURE III-2

THE PATH TAKEN BY CARDS THROUGH THE IBM 26°

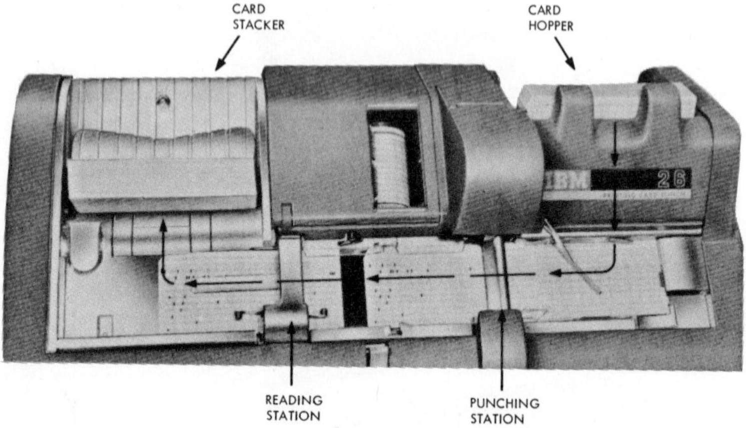

* Courtesy of International Business Machines Corporation.

Because passage through the reading station is in phase with passage through the punching station, holes sensed at the reading station can be duplicated into the trailing card passing under the punching station. The ability to duplicate information from card to card reduces the amount of manual punching needed. Data common to a group of cards—such as a date—may be punched into the first card of a group and duplicated into the remaining ones. Depressing the "duplicate" key can accomplish this, or it can be done automatically by the keypunch operating under preplanned control.

Other functions that can be put under automatic control are printing, skipping columns, and ejecting and feeding cards. These automatic operations are especially valuable when cards for a given research project are punched in batches. According to the requirements of the card format, a pattern often can be established so that the keypunch can skip columns, duplicate fields, or release the card when punching is finished but before column 80 is reached. Figure III-3 illustrates how these automatic controls operate in punching names, identification numbers, background characteristics, and sessions of service into cards forming a master file of 650 members of the Illinois House of Representatives who served from 1933 to 1961.[6]

Instructing the keypunch to skip, duplicate, or release upon reaching certain column locations is known as *programming*. (Programming the keypunch, however, is considerably different from programming computers—see Chapter IV for computer programming.) The operator programs the keypunch by punching a *control card*, wrapping the card around a cylinder or drum, and inserting the drum on a spindle in the machine. The holes in the card control the operation of the machine, causing it to perform specified functions automatically.

THE VERIFIER[7]

After cards have been punched, they should be checked for accuracy of keypunching. Cards can be verified visually by comparing the characters printed at the top of the card to information on coding sheets or in source documents. It is somewhat easier on the eyes to have the tabulator print the contents of the cards on paper (see below) and proofread from the tabulator printout.

However, "repunching" the cards on the verifier is the most accurate method of verification. The most common verifying machine—the IBM 56 Verifier—appears almost identical to the IBM 26 keypunch, and the verifying operation is quite similar to keypunching. *Punched* cards are fed from the hopper into position under a verifying station instead of a punching station. Working from the same coding sheets or source documents, the operator begins "repunching" the information on the cards. If the operator hits the same key that was depressed on the keypunch, a thin metal plunger passes through the hole or holes previously punched in the card. This permits the card to advance to the next column. If an error was made in the original punching, the plunger has no opening through which to pass and the card cannot advance. In this case, a red light flashes and the keyboard locks, preventing additional repunching.

FIGURE III-3

KEYPUNCHING UNDER PROGRAM CONTROL, SHOWN ON A CARD FROM A
MASTER FILE OF ILLINOIS STATE REPRESENTATIVES, 1933-1961

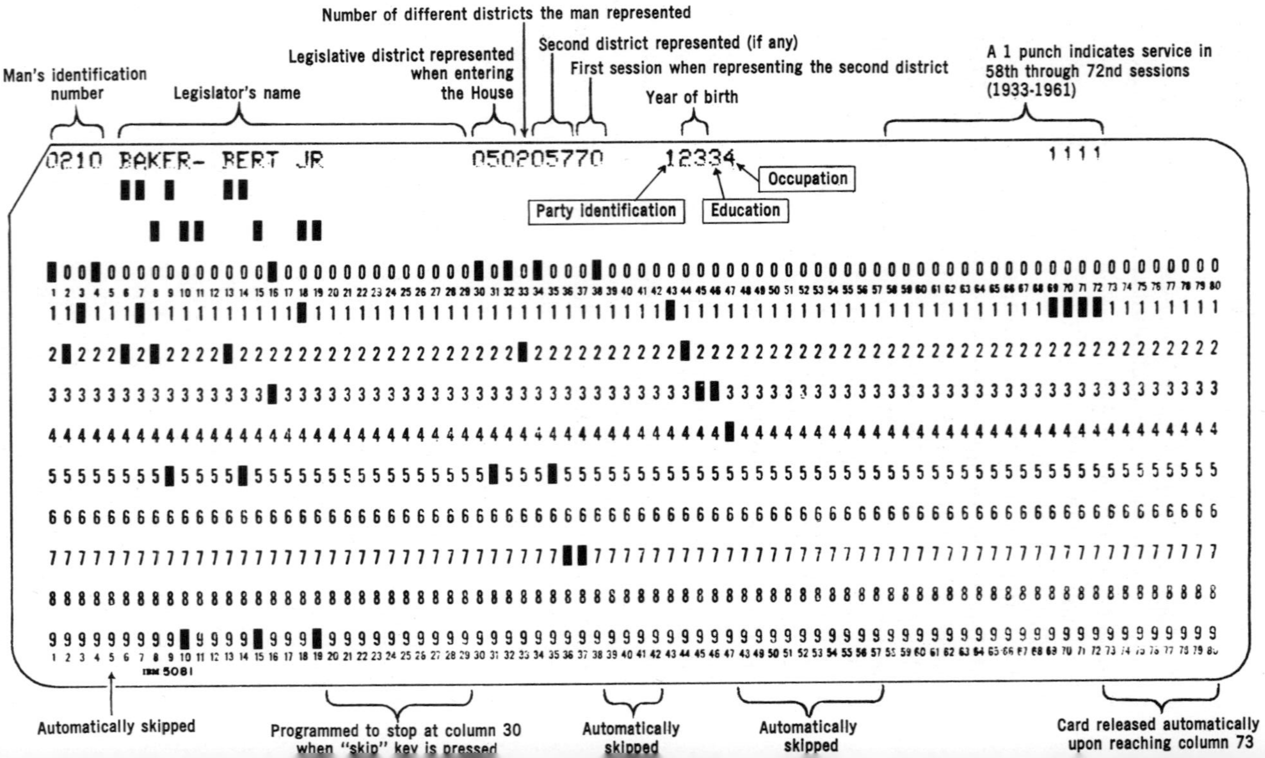

The operator can check his source information and column location. Depressing an "error" key permits the operator to try repunching that column. If the operator depressed the wrong key in *verifying* the information and subsequently depresses the correct one, the light goes out and the card proceeds to the next column. But if in fact the operator is depressing the correct key according to the original information and the card contains an incorrect punch, the red light will flash again.

This provides a second opportunity to recheck the source information and repunch the column. A third mismatch between the thrust of the plunger and the hole in the column will cause the machine to put a notch over the incorrect column as shown at the top of Figure III-4. This marks the error for easy correction later. If the verification process proceeds without a single error being detected on the card, a notch is made instead in the right-hand edge of the card as shown at the bottom of Figure III-4.

The keypunch and verifier are used at the recording stage of data processing. The other unit record machines to be discussed deal primarily with subsequent stages of manipulating and compiling data.

THE COUNTER-SORTER[8]

A researcher often needs to sort his data into groups or order his data according to case number. Frequently he also wants a tally of the total number of cases or the number in each grouping. A *sorter* will rapidly and accurately arrange punchcards in groups or in numerical sequence. A sorter with a *counter* attached will provide the necessary tallies. The counting attachment is extremely valuable in processing political data but is not always available on computing center sorters. This discussion will refer to sorters that *do* have counters attached.

Perhaps the most common sorting machines are the IBM 82—which sorts cards at a rate of 650 cards per minute—and the newer IBM 83—which sorts 1,000 cards per minute.[9] These machines are pictured in Figure III-5. The counting attachment, which fits on top of the sorter, is shown in Figure III-6. Both machines operate by "reading" punched holes and producing

FIGURE III-4

ERROR AND VERIFICATION NOTCHES MADE IN VERIFYING, SHOWN ON A
CARD FROM A MASTER FILE OF ILLINOIS STATE REPRESENTATIVES, 1933-1961

corresponding electrical impulses. This principle is basic to the operation of all remaining unit record machines.

The manner in which the cards are read to produce electrical impulses from punched holes is illustrated in Figure III-7. The contact between a wire brush and a brass roller is interrupted after a card is fed into the machine from the hopper. If the brush is positioned over a column punched with a hole, the brush makes contact with a source of electricity (the metal contact roller), creating an electrical impulse for machine use. The impulse is of short duration, lasting only as long as contact is maintained between the brush and the roller. If there is no hole in a column, no circuit is completed, and no impulse is created.

The impulses produced by different holes in a column occur at specific "times" in a machine *cycle*—one revolution of a central shaft in the machine. Because each punched hole is converted into a timed electrical impulse, the machine can distinguish among the various punching positions in the card. A hole in the 3 position gives an impulse at a different time in the machine cycle than does a hole in the 4 position. What the machine *does* with these impulses depends upon the type of machine it is.

The counter-sorter has a movable reading brush that can be positioned above any of the 80 columns on the card (see Figure III-8). Suppose someone wished to sort out from the master file of Illinois State Representatives all members serving in the 72nd Session (1961) of the General Assembly. As indicated in Figure III-3, service in that session is represented by a 1 punched in column 72. To sort out the members in the 72nd session, the brush would be positioned to read column 72, and the master file of legislators would be placed in the hopper. The position in which the cards are placed in the hopper is important on all machines. For the counter-sorter, the cards should be placed *face down*, with the 9-edge toward the brush and roller.

When the start key is pressed, the cards begin entering the machine one at a time from the bottom of the stack in the hopper. The cards are advanced under the sorting brush and over the metal roller (Figure III-9). If there is a 1 punched in column 72 on any card, an electrical circuit is closed impulsing the magnetic coils under the chute blades and pulling down an armature. This

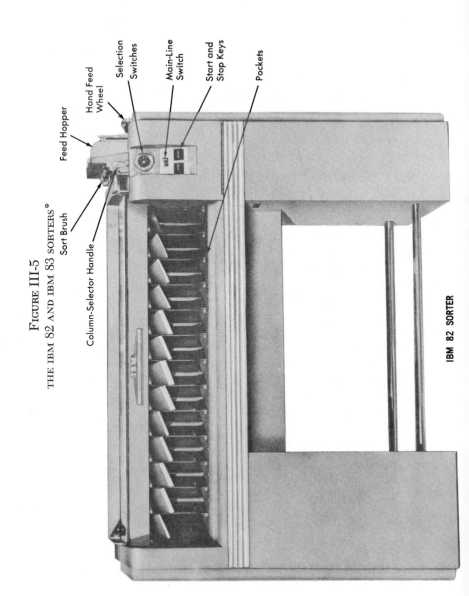

FIGURE III-5
THE IBM 82 AND IBM 83 SORTERS*

Feed Hopper

Hand Feed Wheel

Selection Switches

Main-Line Switch

Start and Stop Keys

Pockets

Sort Brush

Column-Selector Handle

IBM 82 SORTER

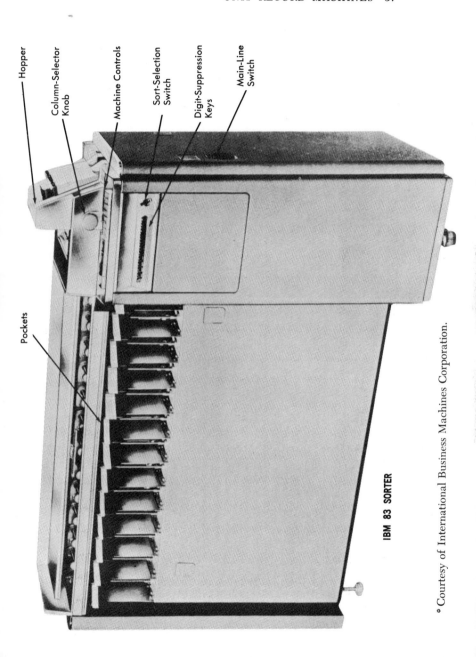

Hopper

Column-Selector Knob

Machine Controls

Sort-Selection Switch

Digit-Suppression Keys

Main-Line Switch

Pockets

IBM 83 SORTER

* Courtesy of International Business Machines Corporation.

drops all blades ahead of the leading edge of the card and causes the card to be directed into the passage between the chute blades. Carrier rolls then convey the card over the proper chute blade into pocket 1. Figure III-9 shows the process for a card being sorted in pocket 4.

FIGURE III-6

COUNTING UNIT ATTACHMENT FOR IBM SORTERS[*]

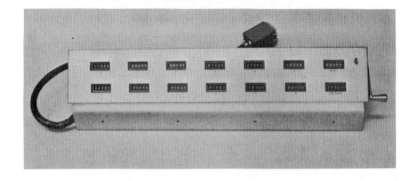

* Courtesy of International Business Machines Corporation.

The cards for legislators who did not serve in the 72nd Session will contain no punch in column 72. Therefore, the brush will not make contact with the roller, and the chute blades will not be pulled down. The cards will then proceed into the reject pocket. Cards that have two punches in one column (as in alphabetic characters) will sort according to which punch is read first. This will be the punch nearest the 9-edge of the card.

After sorting the master file of legislators on column 72, we find those who served in the 72nd Session in pocket 1 and all others in the reject pocket. The counting attachment on top of the machine would have tallied 177 cards in pocket 1, corresponding to the number of men serving in that session. The counters would show 473 cards in the reject pocket. The total number of cards read by the machine (650) is also recorded.

FIGURE III-7

READING HOLES IN PUNCHCARDS*

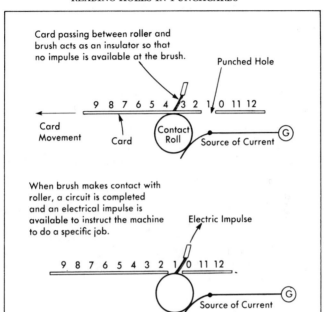

*Courtesy of International Business Machines Corporation.

The sorting process could be continued to determine the party breakdown within the 72nd Session. The cards from pocket 1 would be transferred to the hopper, the sorting brush would be moved to read party identification in column 43, and the counters would be restored to zero by two turns of a crank. Pressing the start key would sort the legislators into pockets 1 and 2 (Democrats and Republicans) and would count the number of cards falling in each pocket. (If desired, the machine could be instructed *only* to count the number of 1 and 2 punches and *not* sort the cards. In this instance, all cards would go into the reject pocket.)

The counter-sorter can be used to construct cross-classifications or cross-tabulations of variables through this process of sorting

Figure III-8
MOVABLE SORTING BRUSH ON THE IBM 82 SORTER*

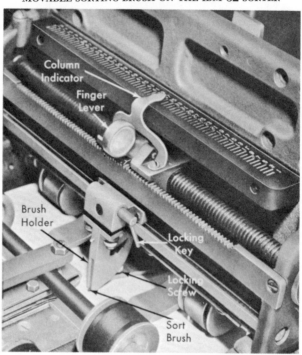

* Courtesy of International Business Machines Corporation.

cards first into groups and then sorting the groups individually. The computer, however, is a far more powerful tool for this method of analysis (see Chapter VI).

The counter-sorter has an important function other than sorting cards into groups; it also can arrange cards in numerical order according to an identification code. Sequencing is accomplished by sorting the cards on each column in the identification field, starting with the *units position first,* then the tens, the hundreds, and so on across the width of the field. After each sort, the cards should be removed from the 0 pocket first, followed by those from the 1 pocket, etc. They should then be placed in the hopper with the 0's on the bottom, 1's on top of them, etc.

FIGURE III-9

SCHEMATIC OF CARD FEED ON THE IBM 82 SORTER *

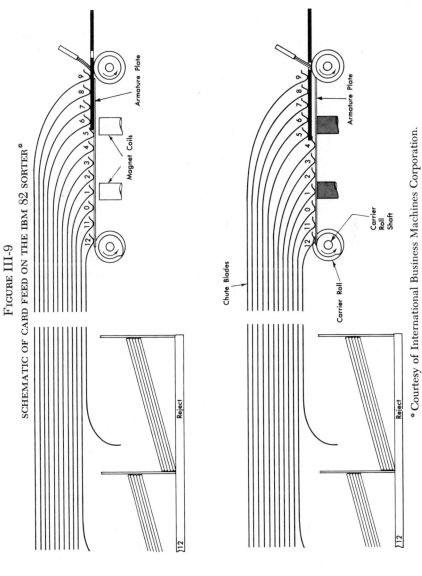

* Courtesy of International Business Machines Corporation.

Figure III-10 shows the path—from hopper to pockets—of fifteen cards punched with the numbers 11 to 23. They are in miscellaneous order when placed in the hopper. On the first sort, with the sort brush on the *units* column of the two column field, cards punched *1* in the units column (11, 21) fall into pocket 1; cards punched *2* (12, 22) fall into pocket 2; cards punched *3* (13, 23) fall into pocket 3. The cards then are removed from the pockets and placed in the hopper face down in ascending sequence so that the cards punched *1* are first, followed by cards punched *2* and *3*.

On the second sort, the sort brush is moved to the *tens* column. Cards punched *1* in the tens column (11, 12, 13) fall into pocket 1, and cards punched *2* (21, 22) fall into pocket 2. When removed from the pockets in order, the file will be in numerical sequence from 11 to 23.

The same procedure is followed for larger fields of numerical codes. The presence of *two* punches per column complicates the process somewhat if legislators' names are to be alphabetized on the counter-sorter, but this can be done.[10]

THE REPRODUCER[11]

One of the main advantages of punchcard data is its reproducibility. As already noted, cards can be duplicated on the keypunch. Information on a card at the reading station can be transferred—column by column—into another card at the punching station. But this process is far too slow and cumbersome for reproducing large numbers of cards. The appropriate machine for this is the reproducer, which transfers information into a card *row-by-row* and can punch the same digit simultaneously in all 80 columns. The difference in the process is schematized in Figure III-11.

The most common reproducers available on college campuses are the IBM 519 Document-Originating Machine and the older IBM 514 Reproducing Punch. Both machines reproduce cards at the same speed—100 cards per minute. Both machines also look much the same—the main difference being in the format of the control panel (discussed below). The machine pictured in Figure III-12 is the IBM 514 Reproducing Punch.

FIGURE III-10

SCHEMATIC OF NUMERICAL SEQUENCING ON THE SORTER*

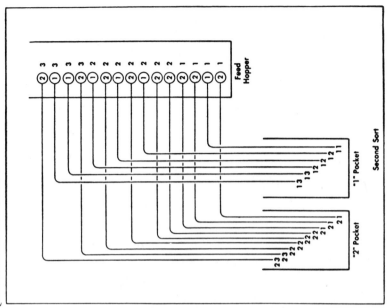

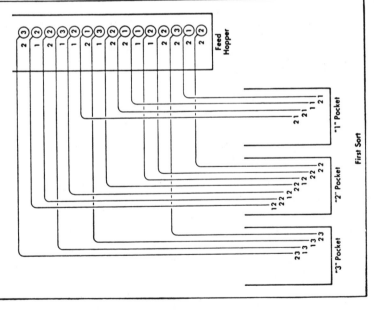

*Courtesy of International Business Machines Corporation.

Figure III-11

SCHEMATIC OF COLUMN-BY-COLUMN AND ROW-BY-ROW PUNCHING*

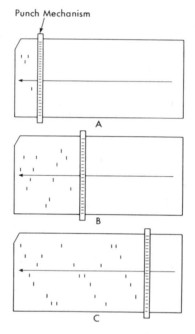

COLUMN-BY-COLUMN PUNCHING

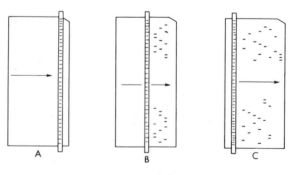

ROW-BY-ROW PUNCHING

* Courtesy of International Business Machines Corporation.

FIGURE III-12
THE IBM 514 REPRODUCING PUNCH *

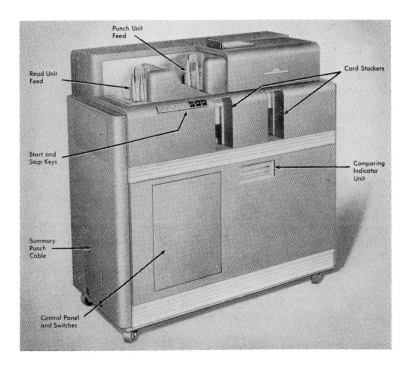

* Courtesy of International Business Machines Corporation.

Suppose someone wanted a duplicate set of cards for the master file of Illinois State Representatives. A duplicate set could be prepared in minutes on the reproducer through 80-80 reproduction—transferring all 80 columns of information from the original cards into the same 80 columns on blank cards. The reproducer's operation in this process can best be understood by referring to the diagram in Figure III-13.

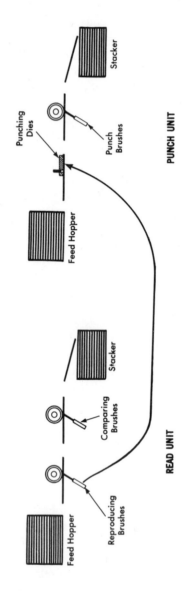

Stacker

Punching
Dies

Punch
Brushes

PUNCH UNIT

Feed Hopper

Stacker

Comparing
Brushes

Feed Hopper

Reproducing
Brushes

READ UNIT

* Courtesy of International Business Machines Corporation.

The original cards are placed in the feed hopper on the left-hand or *read* side (face down and 12-edge toward the brushes), and blank cards are placed in the feed hopper on the right-hand or *punch* side (also face down and 12-edge toward the brushes). As the cards feed in one by one from the read unit, they pass over a set of 80 "reproducing" or "reading" brushes that transmit impulses to the punching dies in the punch unit. Blank cards pass under the punching dies in phase with those passing over the reading brushes.

After the old card is read and a new one punched, both cards pass over additional sets of brushes. On the read side these are known as "comparing" brushes. Their function is to re-read the original card and send impulses to 80 electromagnets that constitute *one side* of a set of comparing units. On the punch side, the punch brushes read the newly punched card and send impulses to 80 electromagnets that constitute the *other side* of the comparing units (see Figure III-14).

FIGURE III-14

SCHEMATIC OF COMPARING OPERATION ON THE REPRODUCER[*]

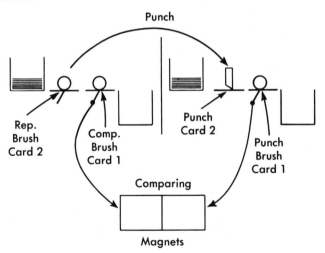

Punch

Rep.
Brush
Card 2

Comp.
Brush
Card 1

Punch
Card 2

Punch
Brush
Card 1

Comparing

Magnets

[*] Courtesy of International Business Machines Corporation.

If a column on the original card has been reproduced properly, both sides of each comparing unit will be impulsed simultaneously—as in Figure III-15. If an error has been made in reproducing the column, one of the two magnets in a comparing unit will be impulsed before the other, attracting an armature that closes a circuit—as in Figure III-16—and causes the machine to stop. The comparing unit indicator then lights up, illuminating a marker that discloses which columns have been incorrectly reproduced.

In addition to 80-80 reproduction, the reproducer is capable of offset reproducing—transferring information from certain columns on one card to different columns on another. This operation is performed by wiring a removable control panel or "board." In fact, even 80-80 reproduction is accomplished through control panel or board wiring, but straight 80-80 reproduction is so common that every computing center has a board already wired for that purpose—it need only be inserted into the machine. Extra control panels usually are available for offset reproducing and other specialized operations. A control panel for the IBM 514 is pictured in Figure III-17.

The small holes in the panel are called "hubs." All hubs are connected by internal wiring to various parts of the machine: the reading, comparing, and punch brushes; the punch magnets (underneath the punch dies); and the magnets in the comparing units. The light wires in Figure III-17 connect the reproducing (reading) brushes for columns 22-25 to the punch magnets for columns 8-11. This will cause the information in columns 22-25 of the original card to be punched into columns 8-11 on another card. The dark wires in the same figure show the wiring necessary to compare the new punches with the original information. The wires go from punch brushes 8-11 (reading the new card) to one side of the comparing units and from comparing brushes 22-25 (reading the original card) to the other side.

Through proper control panel wiring, data on party, education, and occupation can be transferred from the master file of legislators into a set of cards containing the legislators' votes. While transferring this information, the machine can compare identification numbers of both cards involved in each transfer to insure

FIGURE III-15

SCHEMATIC OF COMPARING UNIT, BOTH MAGNETS IMPULSED AT THE SAME TIME*

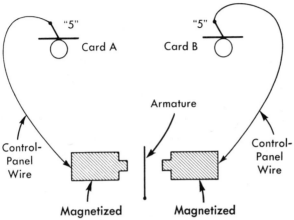

FIGURE III-16

SCHEMATIC OF COMPARING UNIT, LEFT MAGNET IMPULSED BEFORE RIGHT MAGNET*

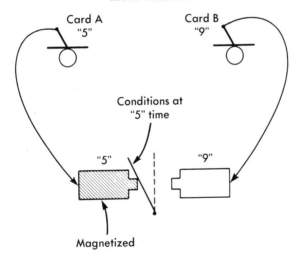

* Courtesy of International Business Machines Corporation.

that information being taken from one man's master card is in fact being transferred to the *same* man's roll call card.

In addition to straight and offset reproducing, the reproducer can punch the *same* information into a group of cards through an operation known as "gangpunching." Such an operation may be helpful, for example, when one wants to punch a "study identification code" into all cards produced in a given study.[12] Only the punching unit of the reproducer is used in gangpunching. The cards to be gangpunched—punched with the same information— are preceded in the punch hopper by a card that is prepunched with the desired information. As the prepunched card passes over the punch brushes, impulses are sent by control wiring to the punch station. The trailing card then carries the desired information when *it* passes over the punch brushes. The impulses are again sent to the punch station for the next card, and so on.

THE TABULATOR[13]

Information punched in cards can be summarized and printed on paper with the tabulator. Because of its ability to add, subtract, accumulate totals, and prepare reports, the tabulator has been used extensively in the business world as an "accounting machine." However, in most university computing centers, the tabulator is seldom used for anything other than printing contents of cards—an operation that is called "detail printing" or "listing." The most common tabulators available at educational institutions are either the IBM 403 or the newer IBM 407, pictured in Figure III-18.

The IBM 403 Accounting Machine can print 88 characters or less on a line at speeds up to 100 lines per minute. The printing unit consists of two sections of typebars. The left section contains 43 typebars, each capable of printing any alphabetic or numeric characters. The right section has 45 typebars that print numerical information only. The IBM 407 Accounting Machine, on the other hand, can print 120 characters on a line at speeds up to 150 lines per minute. The printing unit of the 407, moreover, uses printwheels that permit printing any alphabetic or numeric characters in any location on the line. Because the IBM 403 Accounting Machine is being replaced by the faster and more flex-

FIGURE III-17
CONTROL PANEL WIRING FOR THE IBM 514

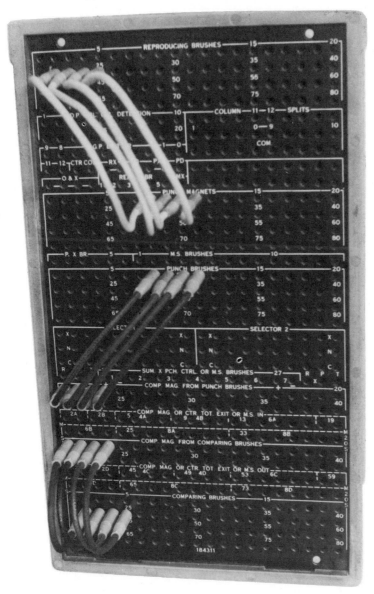

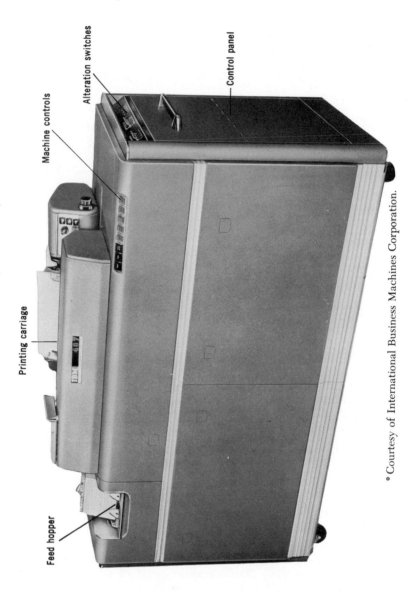

FIGURE III-18
THE IBM 407 ACCOUNTING MACHINE (TABULATOR) *

Alteration switches

Machine controls

Control panel

Printing carriage

Feed hopper

* Courtesy of International Business Machines Corporation.

ible 407, our discussion of the tabulator will be based on the IBM 407. However, aside from references to the printing mechanism almost everything said about the 407 will also apply to the 403.

Like the reproducer, the tabulator operates through control panel wiring, although wiring a tabulator board is much more complicated. Wiring is especially tricky if the tabulator is to function more as an accounting machine than as a card-to-paper printer. Fortunately for researchers who have access to computers, it is not necessary to develop a knowledge of control panel wiring for the tabulator. Time can be spent far more profitably by learning to use the computer, which can perform the same functions more efficiently.

For the purposes of this handbook, it is sufficient to point out that the tabulator has capabilities ordinarily not used in university computing installations. A computing center may own only one control panel for its tabulator. Usually, this panel is "permanently" wired to perform various types of listing operations. Flexibility in listing is obtained by changing "alteration" switches on the side of the machine. For example, one alteration switch may provide the option of single or double spacing in listing. Another may provide or eliminate a count of the total number of cards listed. These switches operate in conjunction with the prewired control panel. The user does not need to know anything about control panel wiring to obtain a simple listing of his data cards. An example of tabulator printout of data cards is given in Figure III-19, which is a partial listing of the alphabetized file of Illinois State Representatives, 1933-1961.

The contents of cards can be printed simply by placing them in the hopper (face down, 9-edge in), inserting a standard listing control panel in the machine, and pressing the "start" button. Cards are fed from the bottom of the deck past the first of two reading stations (see Figure III-20). Each reading station has 960 stationary reading brushes and, instead of a contact roller, 960 metal "segments" below the reading brushes. All possible punches in all columns can be read simultaneously (960 equals 12 positions in each column multiplied by 80 columns). Each reading station also contains 80 commutators—or revolving arms —that rotate from the 9 position to the 12 position.

FIGURE III-19

TABULATOR LISTING OF PART OF THE ALPHABETIZED MASTER FILE OF
650 ILLINOIS STATE REPRESENTATIVES, 1933-1961

0010 ACKER- JOHN	012		1
0020 ADAMOWSKI- BENJAMIN S	025		1111
0030 ADDUCI- JAMES J	002	29474	111111111 1
0040 ALEXANDER- JAS P	048		1
0050 ALLEN- GEORGE B	020		11
0060 ALLEN- HENRY C	035		111
0070 ALLISON- ROBERT H	030	29451	1111111111
0080 ALPINER- BEN W	059		11111
0090 ALSUP- JOHN W	047	11292	11
0100 ANDERSON- FRED W	036	1 51	1
0110 ANDERSON- THOMPSON	024		1
0120 ARMSTRONG- CHARLES F	022	11951	111
0130 ARMSTRONG- STANLEY C	006		1111
0140 ARNOLD- LAWRENCE F	046		11
0150 ARRINGTON- W RUSSELL	006	20651	11111
0160 ASHCRAFT- ALAN E	006		11
0170 ATKINS- JAS L	028	20037	11
0180 AUSTIN- ROBERT	039	21256	11
0190 AUTH- A L	027		111 1111
0200 BAIRSTOW- JACK	008203170	10251	11111
0210 BAKER- BERT JR	050205770	12334	1111
0220 BALTZ- MEADE	037	21274	1
0230 BARBOUR- JAMES J	006		1
0240 BARNES- LIZZIE	048		1
0250 BARRY- TOBIAS SR	037204070	19579	1111 1
0260 BAUER- GEORGE J	042		11111
0270 BAUMGARTEN- JOHN	010		1
0280 BECKMAN- LOUIS E	020204170	21456	1111
0290 BECKMEYER- G R	044	22094	1
0300 BEDERMAN- EDWIN B	025		1
0310 BENEFIEL- NORMAN L	056	12498	1
0320 BENSON- O E	039		111
0330 BERMAN- LOUIS G	005	1 94	1111111111
0340 BEST- ALAN	031	20606	1111
0350 BILLHARTZ- WARREN O	042205570	22753	111
0360 BINGHAM- JOHN A	012		111111
0370 BLACK- WILLIAM Z	024		1
0380 BLOMSTRAND- HAROLD R	025		1
0390 BOLGER- THOMAS A	008		1111111111
0400 BOLTON- JOHN M	002		11
0410 BONK- CHARLES STANLEY	015	12076	1
0420 BOOKWALTER- WALTER J	022		1
0430 BORDERS- GROVER C	049		1
0440 BOTTINO- LOUIS F	037	20753	11
0450 BOWEN- E N	050		1
0460 BOWLER- MAX L	049		1
0470 BOYLE- JAMES P	049		1111
0480 BOYLE- JOHN F	004		111111

Each card pauses momentarily at the read stations. For each hole in the card, contact is made between the reading brush and the metal segment for that specific column and row. This contact is sensed by one of the 80 commutators and an electrical impulse is available at the appropriate hub in the control panel.

Printing normally is accomplished by impulses generated at the second reading station, while impulses originating at the first reading station are used in accounting functions. Impulses from the second reading station hubs in the control panel are transmitted by wires to hubs connected to the machine's printwheels.

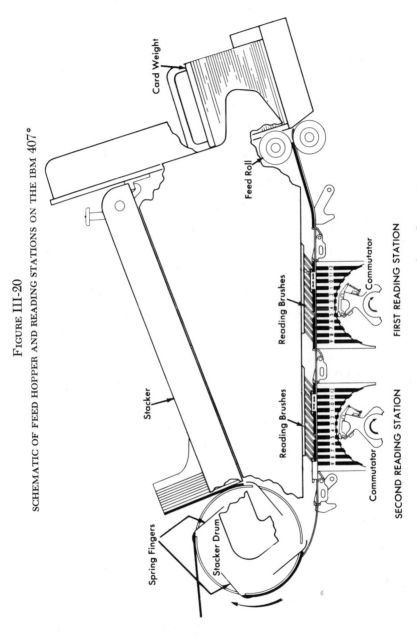

FIGURE III-20

SCHEMATIC OF FEED HOPPER AND READING STATIONS ON THE IBM 407*

* Courtesy of International Business Machines Corporation.

If a printwheel is impulsed, it rotates to the proper position and is pressed against the paper moving through the machine, imprinting a digit, letter, or special character. The paper is fed through in continuous forms that are perforated for easy separation. More than one copy can be made during one machine run by using special forms with carbon paper between sheets. It also is possible to print on forms made of spirit masters, mimeograph stencils, or multilith masters.

<h2 style="text-align:center">THE INTERPRETER[14]</h2>

As already noted, the keypunch can print the contents of a card above the columns as they are being punched. When a new set of cards is reproduced from the originals, this printing is not reproduced, and one must decipher the holes to determine what information the card contains. As its name implies, the interpreter is a machine for translating punched holes into printed characters. The most common interpreting machines are the IBM 548, which operates at a speed of 60 cards per minute, and the IBM 557, which interprets 100 cards per minute. Their internal functions differ somewhat, but they are operated in much the same manner. The IBM 557 is pictured in Figure III-21.

A punchcard that has been reproduced and then interpreted is shown in Figure III-22. The card in that figure contains the same information as the one in Figure III-3. In comparing the figures, one should note that the interpreter printing is larger and better defined than the keypunch printing. However, the larger size of the characters in Figure III-22 prevents them from being printed directly over the columns in which they are punched.

Only 60 characters printed by the interpreter occupy the length of a punchcard. In fact, the interpreter has only 60 printing positions available. In order to print all 80 columns of information, cards have to be run through the interpreter twice. Part of the information is printed at the top of the card on the first pass through the machine, and the rest is printed in the space between 11 and 12 punch positions on the second pass. This procedure has been followed in interpreting the card in Figure III-22, which shows the information in the first 40 columns of the card printed above the information in the last 40 columns.

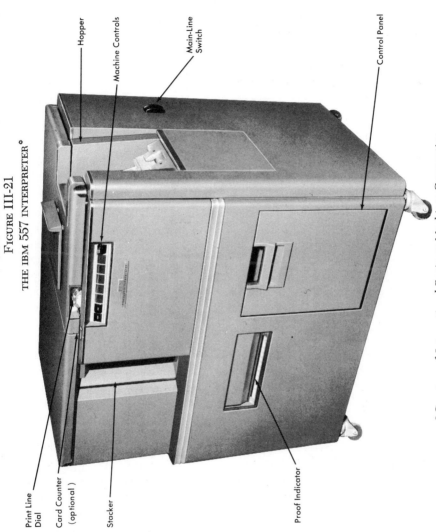

FIGURE III-21
THE IBM 557 INTERPRETER *

Print Line
Dial

Card Counter
(optional)

Stacker

Hopper

Machine Controls

Main-Line
Switch

Control Panel

Proof Indicator

* Courtesy of International Business Machines Corporation.

FIGURE III-22

AN INTERPRETED CARD FROM THE MASTER FILE OF ILLINOIS STATE REPRESENTATIVES, 1933-1961

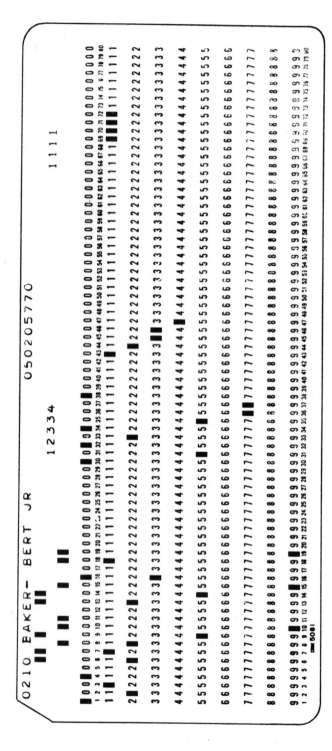

A dial on the machine controls the line on which information is to be printed. On the IBM 557, the dial can be set to print at any of 25 locations on the card. Again, control panel wiring determines which columns will be printed during a pass through the machine. Although an interpreter control panel is not difficult to wire, it is unlikely that the researcher will need to know how to wire one. Most computing centers maintain several prewired control panels for interpreting columns 1-40, 41-80, 1-60, 61-80, and so on. Interpreting cards becomes merely a matter of selecting the desired panel and inserting it into the machine. Depressing the start key causes cards in the hopper (face down, 12-edge in) to feed in and be interpreted.

THE COLLATOR[15]

Collators are designed to match (compare) fields of data in two groups of cards, to merge two groups into one, to select particular cards out of a group, and to sequence-check cards for correct ascending or descending orders. A combination of these functions may be performed at the same time. The most common types of collators are the IBM 85, 87, 88, and 188. The IBM 85 and 87 both read at the rate of 240 cards per minute; they differ in that the 85 deals only with numeric information while the 87 handles both alphabetic and numeric punches. The newer IBM 88 and 188 operate at a rate of 650 cards per minute, and both accept alphabetic and numeric information. The main difference between the two is that the 188 has expanded memory capacity. The IBM 88 is pictured in Figure III-23.

Although the collator performs some very useful manipulative functions with punchcard data, it is not a commonly-used machine at university computing centers, mainly because the manipulative functions performed by the collator are less relevant to the data processing needs of physical scientists than of social scientists. This point will be elaborated on in the next chapter, but data processing problems confronting physical scientists seem to involve little manipulation and much analysis. Social scientists often manipulate more than they analyze. Because computing centers are organized and run largely for physical

FIGURE III-23

THE IBM 88 ALPHABETICAL COLLATOR*

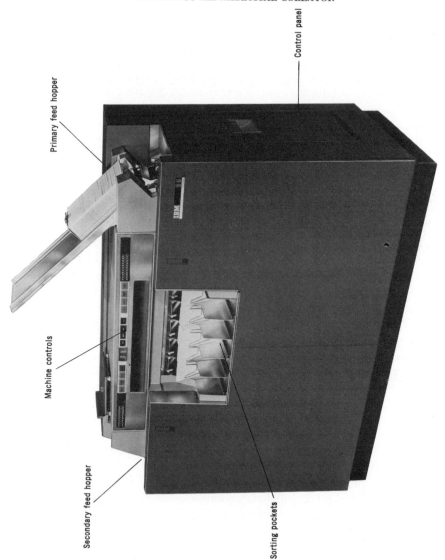

Control panel

Primary feed hopper

Machine controls

Secondary feed hopper

Sorting pockets

*Courtesy of International Business Machines Corporation.

scientists (who are the biggest users of computer time) a collator ordinarily is not considered a top priority machine. Another reason for the collator's lack of popularity is the relative complexity of its control panel wiring. Wiring a collator control panel is not as complex as wiring a tabulator board, but once a tabulator board has been wired, the same one can serve a variety of users. Because the punchcard fields involved in matching, merging, selecting, and sequencing vary from job to job, at least part of the control panel for the collator must be wired anew for each job. Computing centers normally are not interested in providing this service, and few researchers are inclined to learn how to wire collator panels.

A schematic diagram of the IBM 88 collator is given in Figure III-24. Cards can enter the collator from two feed hoppers. For such operations as comparing and merging, cards are placed in both hoppers. But for such other operations as selecting and sequence-checking, only the primary feed hopper is used. All operations are performed by wiring the hubs from the various read stations to the appropriate comparing units or "sequence" units. Conditions of equality or inequality sensed by these units cause cards to fall in one of four pockets, depending on the job to be done and on the nature of the control panel wiring.

THE ELECTRONIC STATISTICAL MACHINE[16]

Many functions of the previous machines are combined in the IBM 101 Electronic Statistical Machine, which can perform the following operations at the rate of 450 cards per minute:

1. Sort cards in numerical or alphabetical sequence.
2. Arrange cards into any desired pattern.
3. Check cards for consistency of coded information.
4. Check accuracy of sorting.
5. Search files of cards for specific facts or combinations of facts.
6. Count cards for as many as 60 different classifications in one run.
7. Add two 5-digit amounts in punchcards to accumulate two 8-digit totals, or add one 9-digit amount to accumulate one 12-position total.

8. Print results in final form on one or two report forms.
9. Print group identifications.
10. Print a check symbol on each line of report to indicate that totals printed on line cross-check.
11. Summary-punch totals in cards when summary-punches are connected to machine.

The 101 is available in two models: Model 1 is a full-capacity machine with two printing units and sixty unit counters; Model 2 is a smaller capacity machine with one printing unit and fifteen unit counters. Model 1 is pictured in Figure III-25.

The design of the 101 incorporates several characteristics of other unit record machines. For example, it is quite similar to the sorter in appearance. But while the sorter has only one movable brush to control sorting, the 101 has 80 sorting brushes. And, like the reproducer, tabulator, and collator, the 101 has an additional set of 80 brushes at a second reading station for comparing, counting, accumulating, and so on. The reading stations on the 101 are diagrammed in Figure III-26.

The 101 also operates through control panel wiring. Wiring a 101 control panel is a relatively complex procedure—as it is for the tabulator and collator. Although panels for the 101 can be prewired to accomplish basic types of operations, the user still must know something about control panel wiring to use the machine at all. In this respect, the machine shares a disadvantage of the collator. And like the collator, the 101 is not a common machine in university computing centers, whose physical science clientele has little use for its statistical functions.

Actually, the electronic statistical machine does not compute statistics; it cross-classifies variables and prints tables—thus combining the functions of the sorter and the tabulator. The statistical function of the 101 can best be described through a simple and concrete example of data analysis. The data used again comes from the master file of members in the Illinois House of Representatives.

Information on education and occupation has been coded into the cards of all members who served in the Illinois House from 1953 through 1961. Suppose it was necessary to discover the distribution of occupations within educational levels for mem-

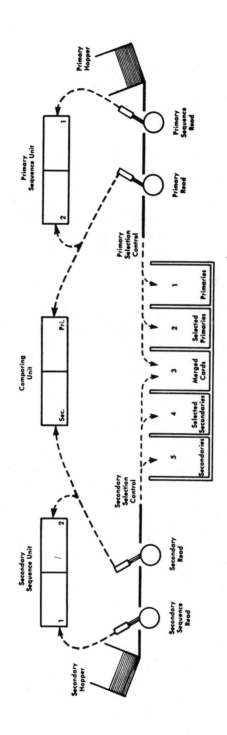

FIGURE III-25
THE IBM 101 ELECTRONIC STATISTICAL MACHINE*

Machine controls

Printing carriages

Control panel

Sorting pockets

* Courtesy of International Business Machines Corporation.

FIGURE III-26
SCHEMATIC OF FEED HOPPERS AND READING STATIONS
ON THE IBM 101*

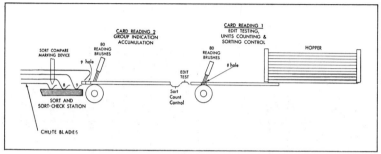

* Courtesy of International Business Machines Corporation.

bers serving during this period. Through proper control panel wiring, the 101 could first be used as a sophisticated sorter to select all cards that contained 1 punches in any columns corresponding to Sessions 68 through 72. The selected deck of cards could then be run through the machine to tally and print the occupational breakdown for Democrats on one printing carriage and the occupations of Republicans on the other carriage. During the same run, the machine could sort the cards according to education. Each educational grouping could then be run through the machine to produce a breakdown of occupation within educational level—separately for Democrats and Republicans. The resulting tables printed by the 101 for this example would be similar to those in Figure III-27.

Cross-classifications can be constructed far more efficiently on the 101 than on the counter-sorter. Moreover, the 101's ability to print tables eliminates the possibility of error from hand-copying totals from the counters on top of the sorter. The researcher still is left with the job of percentagizing his tables and calculating measures of associations for his data. Although (as discussed in Chapter VI) a computer can calculate percentages and correlation coefficients at the same time it prepares cross-classifications, it still has not rendered the 101 obsolete. Those who understand enough control panel wiring to operate the 101 will find it a con-

FIGURE III-27   TYPE OF CROSS-CLASSIFICATION TABLES PREPARED ON THE PRINTING CARRIAGES OF THE IBM 101

DISTRIBUTION OF OCCUPATIONS WITHIN EDUCATIONAL LEVELS —DEMOCRATS — LEFT CARRIAGE

Educational Level	Code	Total Democrats and Republicans	Total Democrats	No Info. 0	Law 1	Farm 2	Insurance 3	Business 4	Labor 5	Clerks 6	News Media 7	Other Prof. 8	Other 9
All Levels		316	154	6	52	12	16	22	11	23	7	2	9
No Information	0	17	8	2	1		2	1	1	1			3
Graduated from high school but went no further	3	17	9		1			3	1	4			
Attended college but did not get a 4-yr. degree	4	6	4			1		1			2		
Attended college and got a 4-yr. degree	5	139	61	1	49	2	2	3	2	2			
Attended high school and may have graduated	7	46	21	2		2	2	1	3	6	3	1	1
Attended college and may have a 4-yr. degree	9	91	51	1	1	7	10	13	4	10	2	1	2

DISTRIBUTION OF OCCUPATIONS WITHIN EDUCATIONAL LEVELS—REPUBLICANS — RIGHT CARRIAGE

Educational Level	Code	Total Democrats and Republicans	Total Republicans	No Info. 0	Law 1	Farm 2	Insurance 3	Business 4	Labor 5	Clerks 6	News Media 7	Other Prof. 8	Other 9
All Levels		316	162	5	47	19	23	36	1	21	3	1	6
No Information	0	17	9		2		1	1		4			
Graduated from high school but went no further	3	17	8	1		2		2	1	1	1		
Attended college but did not get a 4-yr. degree	4	6	2			1		1					
Attended college and got a 4-yr. degree	5	139	78	2	45	5	12	5		6			3
Attended high school and may have graduated	7	46	25	1		5	2	10		4	1	1	1
Attended college and may have a 4-yr. degree	9	91	40	1		6	8	17		6	1		1

venient machine to have around, especially for jobs that are either too short or too urgent for a computer run.

CONCLUDING REMARKS

This chapter has been designed to acquaint the beginner with the functions and operating principles of the basic types of unit record machines. For specific instruction in using these or other machines, write the manufacturer for the reference manual on the machine in question. For the most part, these manuals are written so they can be understood by the uninitiated. After studying a manual, the reader should have little difficulty in operating the machines discussed in this chapter.

In operating any unit record equipment, proper card handling is important. A few hints on this art may be helpful here. Beginners usually find it surprisingly difficult to acquire the simple motor skills for handling cards proficiently. The motions soon become automatic, but some general rules might speed the process.

Before putting cards into a feed hopper on any machine, make sure their edges are smoothly aligned along all four sides. This can be done by holding the cards *loosely* in one hand while lifting and tapping the cards firmly against the joggle plate on top of the machine. (On the sorter, the purpose of the joggle plate is served by the right angle formed between the glass top and metal rim.)

The beginner is likely to make two mistakes in the intricate art of card joggling. He is likely to hold the cards too tightly, causing them to resist alignment from tapping. He also is likely to treat punchcards like ordinary playing cards and try to straighten them out between his hands without using the joggle plate, thus not getting the edges smooth enough. The quickest and surest procedure is to hold the cards loosely while lifting and tapping them smartly against the joggle plate.

After joggling the cards, always check their top and bottom edges to make sure none are nicked or frayed. Duplicating doubtful cards on the keypunch often prevents cards from jamming. Always fan cards before putting them into the feed hopper. This removes static electricity, which causes cards to stick together.

Take care not to nick the cards or disturb their alignment when placing them in the feed hoppers.

Observing these hints and exercising general care while handling punchcards can help avoid card jams and mangled data—experiences that are always frustrating and sometimes costly.

NOTES

1 The "B.C." notation was suggested by Steven G. Vandenberg's reference to "B.E.C."—Before Electronic Computers. See his article, "Some Thoughts about Possible Changes in Research Practices Resulting from the Use of Electronic Computers," *Behavioral Science,* 4 (April, 1959), 163-64.

2 A thorough review of unit record equipment can be found in Alan D. Meacham (ed.), *Data Processing Equipment Encyclopedia: Volume 1, Electromechanical Devices* (Detroit: Gille Associates, Inc., 1961) and in its periodic supplements.

3 International Business Machines Corporation is reported to account for about 80 per cent of the sales in the computing industry. If sales were analyzed for unit record equipment only, the proportion would probably be even higher. Many computer manufacturers have not even developed their own unit record machines. In fact, the sales brochures of competing manufacturers will sometimes picture IBM machines connected to their computers as peripheral equipment.

4 Information for this section was obtained from the IBM publications "An Introduction to IBM Punched Card Data Processing" (White Plains, N. Y.: IBM Data Processing Division, F20-0074, undated) and "Reference Manual for the IBM 24 Card Punch and IBM 26 Printing Card Punch" (White Plains, N. Y.: IBM Data Processing Division, A24-0520-1, 1963).

5 The IBM 1231/2 Optical Mark Page Reader is another means for recording information on punchcards that deserves to be investigated by researchers who gather data through questionnaires. This machine reads pencil marks from specially designed questionnaires, interview sheets, or source documents, and transfers the information to punchcards at up to 1,400 pages per hour. Pencil marks must be placed between lines as on the familiar IBM test scoring sheets, but considerable freedom is permitted in locating these lines on the form.

6 This information was collected from various editions of the *Illinois Blue Book.* The card format has been designed the permit the file to be updated and extended back for sessions before 1933. The legislators have been assigned identification numbers in *tens* instead of *units* to permit the insertion of new names without disturbing the

alphabetical sequence. For more about this coding technique, see Chapter V, p. 141.

7 Information for this section was obtained from the IBM publication "An Introduction to IBM Punched Card Data Processing" (White Plains, N. Y.: IBM Data Processing Division, F20-0074, undated).

8 Information for this section was obtained from the IBM publication "Reference Manual for the IBM 82, 83, and 84 Sorters" (White Plain, N. Y.: IBM Data Processing Division, A24-1034-1, 1962).

9 Cards can be sorted at a speed of 2,000 cards per minute on the IBM 84, which reads holes with a photoelectric eye instead of a wire brush. The IBM 84 has not been included in this discussion both because of its unique operating feature and because it is a relatively uncommon machine in university computing centers.

10Because letters are formed by combining two punches in a single column, alphabetic sorting requires two passes through the machine on each column. The first sort is a normal one. On the second sort, however, a small red alphabetic sorting switch at the front of the machine is moved toward the center of its hub to permit sorting on the *zone punches* only (0, 11, or 12). This process is repeated for each column in the alphabetic field, proceeding from the right to the left.

11Information for this section was obtained from the IBM publication "Functional Wiring Principles" (White Plains, N. Y.: IBM Data Processing Division, A24-1007-0, 1960).

12See the discussion of "study codes" in Chapter V, p. 142.

13Information for this section was obtained from the IBM publication "Reference Manual for the IBM 407 Accounting Machine" (White Plains, N. Y.: IBM Data Processing Division, A24-1011-1, 1959).

14Information for this section was obtained from the IBM publication "Reference Manual for the IBM 557 Alphabetic Interpreter" (White Plains, N. Y.: IBM Data Processing Division, A24-0516-1, 1963).

15Information for this section was obtained from the IBM publication "Reference Manual for the IBM 88 Collator" (White Plains, N. Y.: IBM Data Processing Division, A24-1013-3, 1960).

16Information for this section was obtained from the IBM publication "Reference Manual for the IBM 101 Electronic Statistical Machine" (White Plains, N. Y.: IBM Data Processing Division, A24-0502-0, 1958).

CHAPTER IV **ELECTRONIC COMPUTERS**

This chapter is not intended as a general introduction to electronic computers, a topic too complex to be treated so briefly. Its purpose is to provide some definitions and information important for understanding the use of computers in research. The interested reader can find general and comprehensive introductions to electronic computers in several recent books for the serious researcher.[1]

An initial distinction can be made between two general types of computers: *analog* and *digital*. An *analog* computer represents data as physical quantities instead of numbers and "computes" by measuring these quantities through some physical "analogy" to the phenomenon in point. A thermometer, for example, is an analog device that measures temperature in terms of the height of a column of mercury. An engineer's slide rule is a miniature analog computer that translates lengths into numbers. Analog computers are frequently designed to solve specific types of problems involving measurement of physical quantities.

Digital computers represent data in the form of numbers or "digits" instead of physical quantities. Because numbers can represent an unlimited variety of information, digital computers usually are more flexible in problem solving than are analog computers. The main computer in virtually every university-wide computing center is a digital machine. Throughout this book, the word "computer" will refer to *digital* computers only.

Roughly speaking, analog computers *measure* and digital computers *count*. But a computer counts in a different numbering system from that normally used by Western man. Computers find it easier to count in the *binary* system, using only two digits—0 and 1—than in the ten digit *decimal* system. Binary numbers are far better suited to a computer's electronic circuitry, which operates by sensing the presence or absence of electrical currents. For example, the o digit corresponds to the absence of current and the 1 digit to its presence. Information can be represented in computer circuitry by combinations of absent-present currents (or "off-on" conditions) that conform to the binary numbering system.

In both binary and decimal numbers, the *positions* occupied by the digits are of central importance. In the decimal system, the digits 79 express a different value than the pair 97. This is also true in the binary system, but only the digits o and 1 are available for positioning.

Counting in both systems begins the same: the symbol o is assigned to the value *zero* and the symbol 1 to the value *one*. But in the binary system, no other symbols are available to express the next value—*two*—and a new position must be started. Advancing the 1 and leaving the o to mark the units position results in the expression 10, which means *two* in binary notation. The value *three* is 11 in binary form. A comparison of the binary and decimal systems is given in Figure IV-1.

FIGURE IV-1

COMPARISON OF DECIMAL AND BINARY NUMBER SYSTEMS

Decimal	Binary
0	0
1	1
2	10
3	11
4	100
5	101
6	110
7	111
8	1000
9	1001
10	1010
11	1011
12	1100
13	1101
14	1110
15	1111

Digital computers sometimes are classified as "binary" or "decimal" machines. A *binary* machine uses the straight binary number system. Contrary to the implications of its name, a *decimal* machine also uses binary digits but uses them only to code individual decimal digits. The first ten decimal digits (0 to 9) can be coded with four binary digits (or "bits"). The circuitry of a decimal computer arranges its binary digits into groups of four, each group being used for one decimal digit. The numbering system used by these machines is more accurately called "binary coded decimal" (BCD). A comparison of the binary, decimal, and binary coded decimal systems is given in Figure IV-2.

FIGURE IV-2

COMPARISON OF DECIMAL, BINARY, AND BINARY CODED

DECIMAL SYSTEMS

Binary	*Decimal*	*Binary Coded Decimal*
10000	16	0001 0110
10001	17	0001 0111
10010	18	0001 1000

Technical considerations that do not warrant discussion here are involved in designing a given computer as a binary or BCD machine. Fortunately, the average computer-user needs only a general awareness of the fact that digital computers operate in some form of binary numberings. In normal practice, he need never fuss with binary notation; the computer will accept his decimal data and translate the information into its own numbering system.

Enough groundwork has been laid to permit defining a computer. According to Borko, a computer "is a machine that is able to calculate and perform sequences of arithmetical and logical operations in accordance with preprogrammed instructions."[2] This simple definition masks a very powerful machine. Most digital computers—certainly those to be discussed in this book— are "general purpose" machines. "Special purpose" computers, such those installed in satellites and rockets, are built to perform specialized operations. General purpose computers, however, are designed to handle a wide variety of data processing tasks. A general purpose computer can, in principle, execute *any* definable and finite symbol-manipulation process.[3]

One implication of this general purpose character is that a computer can perform the specialized functions of unit record equipment (see Chapter III). In computer processing, moreover, these functions are integrated and continuous. Data cards do not have to be moved from one machine to the other. Furthermore, the computer performs these operations at a fantastic speed. Unit record machines are limited by the movement of mechanical parts, but the internal operating speed of electronic computers is limited ultimately only by the speed of light. Computers are slowed down considerably, however, when engaging in mechanical tasks such as reading cards or printing results of calculations. In order to use costly computer time most efficiently, physical manipulation of data often is done on unit record machines, even though general purpose computers can perform the same operations much faster.

A discussion of the operating characteristics can be facilitated by making an early distinction between computing "hardware" and "software." *Hardware* is physical apparatus—the computer itself. *Software* refers to methods of instructing the computer— called computer *programming*. The computer user needs to know about both computing hardware and software.

COMPUTING HARDWARE

The first commercial computer, UNIVAC I, was marketed in 1951. Two years later, IBM built its first commercial high-speed computer, the 701. The computing industry has grown tremendously in the relatively brief period since the early 1950's. Literally hundreds of makes and models of computers are currently in use. Although IBM accounts for 80 per cent or more of the computers in operation at educational institutions, there are sufficient differences among types of IBM computers to preclude detailed discussion of any specific model or make. Other publications contain up-to-date reviews of the characteristics of specific machines.[4]

The University of Illinois appears to have been the first university to make a computer available for general research purposes.[5] Today, approximately 300 colleges and universities maintain computing facilities for research.[6] Although the main computers in university computing centers are all general purpose machines, the specific make or model available can make a great deal of difference to a researcher. Any general purpose computer can do whatever another can do, but some can do it faster or with fewer instructions. In some cases, moreover, a computer's capabilities for transferring information in and out of the system are limited by the equipment to which it is connected. The particular hardware available at university computing centers can be an important concern to the researcher.

Surveys of available computing equipment become outdated rapidly because universities continually install newer machines. The changing situation is reflected in two relatively recent surveys conducted in 1961 and 1963 by Thomas A. Keenan, Director of the University of Rochester Computing Center.[7] Relevant data from those surveys are contained in Table IV-1.

Computers can be classified somewhat crudely as "small," "medium," and "large." Two factors—operating speed and storage capacity—are usually involved in this classification, and it often is difficult to classify any particular computer that rates high on one criterion and low on another. Within the IBM family, however, one can tag computers in the 700 or 7000 series as "large," those in the 1000 series as "medium," and those in the 600 series as "small."

University computing centers are, of course, acquiring bigger and bigger machines. Table IV-1 discloses only seven schools in 1963 using the small IBM 650, which once was used by almost half the university computing centers.[8] Although the IBM 1620 clearly emerged as the most common machine on college campuses, it is not apt to be as accessible to political researchers as the IBM 1401, for the 1620 often is at the disposal of engineering schools. The most popular large scale computers in 1963 were in the IBM 709/7090/7094 class.

All general purpose digital computers are alike in their basic design. Each has "input-output" units for moving information into

TABLE IV-1

TOTAL NUMBER OF MAKES AND MODELS OF COMPUTERS REPORTED AT
COLLEGES AND UNIVERSITIES IN 1961 AND 1963

	Total number reported	
	1961	1963
IBM 1620	30	132
IBM 1401	2	41
LGP 30	11	23
IBM 1410	0	14
CDC G-15	5	12
IBM 709	7	8
IBM 7090	4	8
CDC 1604	2	8
IBM 650	39	7
IBM 7094	0	6
Burroughs 220	5	6
Burroughs 204/205	3	6
IBM 7070	4	5
IBM 7072	0	4
IBM 7074	0	3
IBM 7040	0	3
G. E. 225	1	3
UNIVAC 1105	1	2
Burroughs E102	2	2
Gen/Prec. RPC 4000	1	2
UNIVAC SS80	1	1
CDC 3600	0	1
CDC G-20	0	1
2-4 smaller computers[a]	-	51

[a] Small computers of more or less equal value, no one of which could be considered the principal computer at the center; 1963 total reflects some duplication count, all but 3 computers included in other totals above.

and out of the machine. Each also has a "memory" unit for storing the information, an "arithmetic-logical" unit for operating on the information, and a "control" unit for coordinating the operations. These functional units are diagrammed in Figure IV-3.

FIGURE IV-3

DIAGRAM OF FUNCTIONAL COMPONENTS OF AN
ELECTRONIC COMPUTER

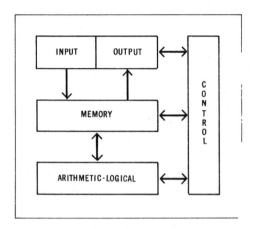

INPUT-OUTPUT

Information can be entered into a computer from a variety of media: cards, magnetic tape, paper tape, typewriter, photographic film, printed matter, and even by the spoken word. Similarly, the computer can send out information by punching cards, punching paper tape, writing on magnetic tape, typewriting, printing, exposing film, televising, drawing graphs, and even by making sounds. Magnetic tape, however, is the most common input-output medium for large scale computers.

Magnetic tape is preferred over cards because of its handling speed. Input-output operations ordinarily are mechanical operations and constitute a drag on computer time. High-speed computers can perform thousands of internal operations in the time taken to read one card. Although magnetic tape is an improvement over cards, a computer can still perform hundreds of internal operations in the time required to read eighty columns of information from tape.

Computer time is normally conserved by doing as much of the input-output functions as possible *off* the computer on auxiliary and printed off-line.

equipment or *off-line* machines. Information contained on punch-cards usually is written on tape "off-line" on a card-to-tape reader. Magnetic tapes that contain computer output usually are printed off-line on tape-to-print equipment. *On-line* machines are input-output devices connected directly to the computer. Input-output devices that can be operated either *off-line* or *on-line* are called "peripheral equipment."

When large computers are available, smaller computers frequently are used off-line to handle input-output chores. The IBM 1401 computer, for example, frequently is used solely as an input-output device for computers in the IBM 700 or 7000 class. The 1401 reads information from punchcards onto magnetic tape. A large number of different "jobs" are "loaded" onto tape to constitute a "batch" of jobs for processing on the main computer. The tape reels are then taken off the 1401 and placed on the tape units of the main computer.

At many large installations, the computer operates under control of a *monitor* system, which processes each job loaded on the *input* tape in sequence and writes the answers to each on a separate *output* tape. If any job fails to execute properly—usually because of a programming error—the monitor system will write one or more error messages indicating the trouble and will automatically terminate the job, moving to the next job in the batch. When the entire batch is finished, the output tape reel is removed

Information is recorded on computer tape in the form of magnetized spots created as the tape moves over a read-write station or "head" (Figure IV-4). These spots can be written and interpreted in a variety of codes. One of the most common codes uses seven recording channels (see Figure IV-5). Numerical information is encoded in the bottom four channels in binary coded decimal. The fifth and sixth channels from the bottom are used for encoding alphabetic information, and the top channel is used as a check or "parity" bit. In "even" parity checking, the number of magnetized bits in any vertical column must add up to an even number. When the recording heads are functioning properly, a bit will be placed in the parity channel when necessary to insure that the sum of bits is even. If the check does not come out even, the computer signals an error. This is all done automatically and need not concern us further.

FIGURE IV-4*

SCHEMATIC OF TAPE UNIT

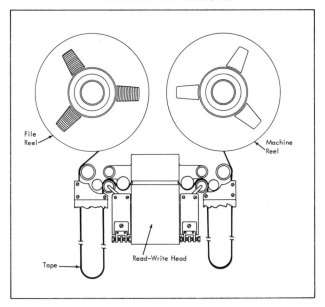

FIGURE IV-5*

SEVEN-CHANNEL CODE ON MAGNETIC TAPE

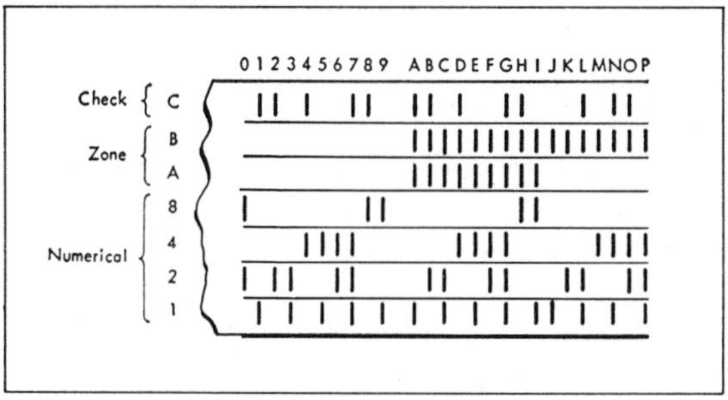

*Courtesy of International Business Machines Corporation.

Information is written on tape in groups of vertical columns called "records." Tape "density" refers to the number of columns that can be recorded on an inch of tape. A density of 200 characters per inch (CPI) is considered "low" density; 556 or 800 CPI is "high" density. An 80 column punchcard is often written as a single record on 80 columns of tape. Records are separated on magnetic tape by a width of blank tape (¾ of an inch on IBM tape) called an "inter-record gap" or more simply a "record gap."

Even on low density tape, less than one-half inch is needed to record the contents of an 80 column punchcard. Because the record gap alone is wider than this, tapes that are loaded with single-card records contain more blank space than information. Tape space sometimes is conserved by "blocking" several records together without separation by a record gap. Without blocking, approximately 25,000 cards can be recorded on one 2,400 foot reel of magnetic tape. By blocking the records in groups of five, more than 50,000 cards can be recorded on a single reel. This information can be read at speeds varying around 100 inches per second.

MEMORY UNIT

Information written on magnetic tape is in *external storage*—it is not directly accessible to the computer for arithmetic and logical operations. For these operations, this information must be entered into *internal storage*—the computer's memory unit. A memory unit can be thought of as a giant matrix of mailboxes, each of which bears a storage location or *address*. Each mailbox or address can hold one computer "word"—a series of binary digits. Some computers have more addressable storage locations or words of storage than others. The number of words of storage is commonly reckoned in units of 1,000. Each unit is symbolized by the letter "K." A computer with 10,000 words of storage is called a 10K machine.

Computers also differ in the speed with which they can retrieve information from storage. The speed of access to the memory unit or "access time" depends on the type of storage the computer possesses. It once was common to store information on a magnetic drum that revolved at high speed under reading and writing heads. Magnetic drums have two disadvantages: they are somewhat limited in storage capacity and relatively slow in access time. The machine must wait until the storage location on the drum revolves under a reading head before information can be retrieved.

Today the most commonly-used internal storage device is a matrix of magnetic cores—tiny rings of ferrous material capable of magnetization by passing currents through electric wires running through their hollow centers. Literally thousands of these tiny cores are threaded on wires to form the core storage of a modern computer. Machines in the IBM 709/7090/7094 series have 32,000 words of magnetic core storage. Because no moving parts are involved, access time to any storage location is almost instantaneous, being limited only by the switching speeds of electronic components and by the speed of light.

ARITHMETIC-LOGICAL UNIT

The computer processes data by doing simple arithmetic and making decisions with the standard logical operators: "and," "or," and "not." These arithmetic and logical operations are accomplished through electronic circuits that open and close when certain conditions are met. In the very first automatic computer— the Mark I completed at Harvard in 1944—these operations were accomplished by electromagnetic relays. The moving parts of electromagnets later were replaced by electronic circuits in vacuum tubes, increasing the operating speed of computers hundreds of times.

Large vacuum tube computers generated tremendous amounts of heat. Powerful air conditioning systems were necessary not only for the comfort of human operators but for the machine to run without burning itself up. Frequent shutdowns also resulted as the thousands of tubes aged and began to burn out.

Transistors have replaced vacuum tubes in modern computer circuitry. The last of the large tube machines—the IBM 709—has been redesigned with transistor components and now is known as the IBM 7090. Transistorized computers not only operate cooler, with less power, in less space, and with greater reliability, but they also operate faster because of transistors' faster switching capabilities.

Modern computers are almost inconceivably fast. Operating speeds on the early electromechanical Mark I were measured in *milliseconds*—thousandths of a second. Operating speeds on vacuum tube computers were measured in *microseconds*—millionths of a second. And the fastest computers today can perform operations in *nanoseconds*—billionths of a second. The relationship is as follows:

> one millisecond = .001 of a second
>
> one microsecond = .000001 of a second
>
> one nanosecond = .000000001 of a second

Computers are beginning to operate so quickly that the length of wires connecting various components is a factor to be considered in machine design. Long wires slow down operations as the computer waits for electricity to travel between components.

The consequence of fast operating speed is, of course, fast data analysis. The electromechanical Automatic Multiplying Punch of the early 1930's was hailed as a great time-saver in computing cross-products used in correlational analysis. Carver praised the ability of the machine to compute the products of heights and weights of 1,000 individuals: "One may therefore place our cards in the machine, press a button, resume other duties, and some fifty minutes later the 1,000 cards will have yielded the total. . . ."[9] This same operation plus the computation of the correlation coefficient itself can be done in a matter of seconds on a modern computer.

CONTROL UNIT

The control unit directs all operations of the computing system, including the input-output devices. It selects the instructions to be performed; obtains, moves, and stores data within the computer; and coordinates all the functions of the system. In effect, the researcher operates the computer by furnishing the control unit a set of instructions to follow. This set of instructions is called a "program."

COMPUTING SOFTWARE

Computers often are referred to as "giant brains." But as Green has observed, computers are more like "giant clerks."[10] A computer has to be told exactly what to do and when to do it. These instructions must be organized in sequence and specified in minute detail. Procedures for preparing computer instructions are referred to as computing "software."

Every computer can perform a relatively small number of basic operations. Some typical operations are "read," "write," "add," "subtract," "compare," "store in memory," and so on. These basic operations are built into the machine circuitry and activated by specific machine *instructions,* one for each operation. Every instruction in a given computer is associated with a binary code number. For example, an instruction to "add" expressed in binary code for a computer with a 36 bit "word" might be 000100000000000000000000000000000000. A complete set of ordered instruction codes is a computer *program.*

Some computer programs for statistical analysis may contain hundreds or even thousands of machine instructions. The above example makes it clear that writing a computer program in binary codes or *basic machine language* is a complex, frustrating, and time-consuming process. Fortunately, programming has been made considerably easier with the development of special *programming* languages to substitute for basic machine language. The computer accepts instructions expressed in a programming language and translates them into equivalent instructions in its own basic machine language.

Programming languages can be divided into "machine-oriented" and "problem-oriented" languages. Machine-oriented languages commonly use mnemonic symbols to represent machine instructions, e.g., SUB for "subtract" and DIV for "divide." Programs written in a symbolic machine-oriented language are *assembled* by the computer into basic machine language. Although a machine-oriented language simply substitutes alphabetic symbols for strings of binary digits, it provides a much easier method of programming than does a basic machine language. Programs written in a symbolic language, however, still must spell out every step and operation the computer must perform. Moreover, because symbolic languages *are* machine-oriented, different symbolic languages are used for different computers. A programmer must learn different languages for different computers.

Problem-oriented languages, on the other hand, are based not on technical features of a particular computer but on types of problems to be solved. A program written in a problem-oriented language can be used on any computer that has a *compiler* program for translating it into machine language. Furthermore, problem-oriented languages employ *macro-instructions*—each of which is translated or "compiled" into more than one basic machine instruction. Macro-instructions relieve the programmer from repeatedly specifying every step the computer must follow in performing fundamental data processing functions. A program written in a problem-oriented language always involves fewer original instruction statements than translated statements.

A variety of problem-oriented programming languages have been developed. COBOL (COmmon Business Oriented Language) has been designed for inventory and bookkeeping problems. COMIT was designed for processing textual information in problems of information retrieval and mechanical translation of foreign languages. The best known problem-oriented language by far is FORTRAN (FORmula TRANslator), which permits writing programs in a form similar to algebraic notation. Many data processing problems in political research can be effectively expressed in FORTRAN programming language, thus making knowledge of FORTRAN a valuable methodological skill.

Some attention should be given here to the question of including computer programming as part of the research training in the behavioral sciences generally and in political science in particular. Several writers have taken strong positions in favor of training researchers in computer programming. Wrigley's position is as follows:

> There seems to be a growing demand for persons who are simultaneously competent researchers, experienced in the use of multivariate methods, and skilled as computer users and programmers. To try to meet this demand, behavioral

science departments should introduce courses in the numerical methods appropriate for computers both for graduate and undergraduate students and should recruit and train good programmers. . . . It is my opinion that [the work of computing centers] . . . should be supplemented by the behavioral departments themselves. All graduate students nowadays should know of the existence and potentialities of computers; many should be given the opportunity of using a computer for the analysis of their own data; some of the more enthusiastic should be encouraged to try their hand at the writing of programs; and occasional ones with the requisite ability, temperament, and mathematical knowledge should be trained specifically as computer specialists. . . .[11]

Freeman reveals a similar attitude:

Very few individuals are trained in computer programming and in a behavioral science discipline. So behavioral scientists often have trouble in communicating the details of their data processing problems to programmers, and programmers are unable to find behavioral scientists who are willing and able to learn the intricacies of programming.

What is needed are individuals trained in both areas; in a behavioral science and in computer programming. In the long run, the best policy might be to encourage—even require—behavioral science graduate students to develop at least the most basic skills in programming.[12]

Those who are opposed to requiring—or even encouraging—methodological training in computer programming are apt to defend their opposition by saying that the researcher can always go to a programmer with his problem. In my opinion, this is the same as saying that training in statistics is not needed because the researcher can always go to a statistician. The analogy, of course, is not perfect, but there are at least two important similarities in the situations. A researcher needs to know something about statistics before he can communicate properly with a statistician. The same is true for researchers and programmers. But even more important, truly imaginative use of statistics and computers in research demands a combination of methodological skills and substantive knowledge in one person.

This point has been emphasized by several writers. Martin and Hall contend:

Effective utilization of many computers is dependent on the ability of the researcher to use the machine himself. Thus it is important that the researcher be able to use the computer, for not only can he more easily make better use of machines that are available, but he is also likely to obtain a better solution to his problem. More important, he is then equipped to use the computer to solve a larger and possibly more important problem.[13]

And Beaton says, "Anyone who has programmed realizes the advantages of encouraging the scholar to program. There is no better way to have him see the power of the machine and to open his eyes to new research approaches."[14]

Researchers do not need to become expert programmers, but they perhaps should know the fundamentals of programming so they can conceptualize the feasibility of their problems for computer processing. In effect, they need a "working knowledge" of the language. This will enable them to write small programs for simple problems and will facilitate interaction with an experienced programmer for complex programs and problems. Contrary to some belief, this level of knowledge in FORTRAN programming ordinarily can be attained in less than one month of occasional study by a person without college mathematics. This is far less than that normally needed to acquire a working knowledge of French or some other foreign language—a standard requirement of doctoral programs in the behavioral sciences.

FORTRAN PROGRAMMING

The purpose of this section is not to teach FORTRAN programming. That requires a book of its own.[15] Instead, this section attempts to provide an insight into the nature of computer programming through an example written in FORTRAN. Hopefully, reading this section will lead to a better understanding of what programming is.

Technically speaking, there are really several versions of FORTRAN. Differences within the language are brought about mainly by differences in machine hardware. But all versions of FORTRAN are quite similar, and a programmer would have little trouble in moving from one to another. The version to be used in this chapter is FORTRAN IV for the IBM 709/7090/7094.

Regardless of the language being used, computer programming requires complete understanding of absolutely every step in the data processing operation. As Rufus Browning points out:

> . . . the computer places heavy demands on the researcher. It constrains him to be absolutely unambiguous, to specify his terms and statements precisely, exhaustively. Vagueness, deliberate or not, is impossible: it is perfectly clear what each instruction in the computer program does.[16]

In order to achieve completeness, precision, and proper execution in computer programming, programs should be written with the use of a "flowchart"—a diagram of the steps to be performed. A flowchart functions in much the same manner as a detailed research design. Both specify exactly what steps are to be taken, in what order, and what is to be done if decisions are made along the way. It is possible to write a successful program *without* making a flowchart beforehand, but programming with vague or nonexistent flowcharts incurs the same risks as doing research with vague or nonexistent research designs.

The nature of computer programming will be illustrated by a flowchart and program for calculating summary statistics from raw election returns. In this example, the raw election data are recorded on punchcards as discussed in Chapter II and illustrated in Figure II-2. Each card contains three items of information: a county identification number, the number of votes cast in the count for the Republican candidate, and the number of votes cast for the Democratic candidate.

The computer is directed to calculate four new items of information for each county: the Republican percentage of the vote cast, the Democratic percentage, the plurality difference between the parties' percentages, and a code signifying the outcome of the election—a Democratic or Republican victory. The computer prepares an output card that contains both old and new information: the county identification, the Republican and Democratic raw election returns, the Republican and Democratic percentages of the vote, the plurality difference between the parties, and the outcome code.

FIGURE IV-6
PROGRAM FLOWCHART FOR COMPUTING ELECTION PERCENTAGES

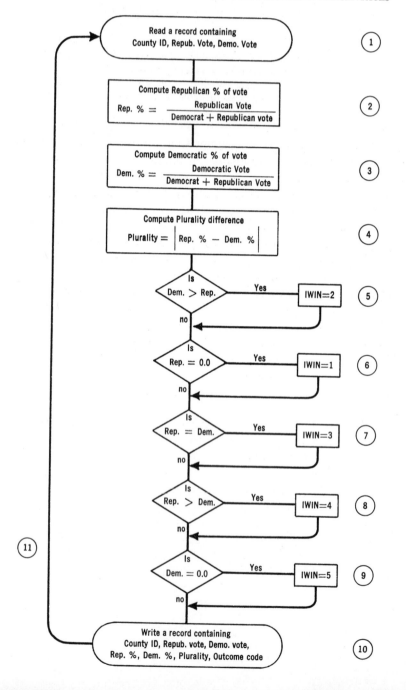

A flowchart depicting the steps in the program is given in Figure IV-6. In the first step, the computer reads the county identification and the raw election returns from an input tape prepared from the cards on off-line equipment. Steps 2, 3, and 4 provide for computing the parties' percentages of the vote and the plurality difference. Steps 5 through 9 provide for assigning an outcome code to each contest according to this scheme:

1 the Democratic candidate won all the votes (was unopposed)
2 the Democratic candidate won a plurality of the votes
3 both candidates received the same number of votes
4 the Republican candidate won a plurality of the votes
5 the Republican candidate won all the votes (was unopposed)

Step 10 directs the computer to write the original data and the computed information in one record on an output tape. In step 11, the process returns to the "read" command and begins again. The steps are repeated until all input records have been read from the tape. The job terminates when the computer runs out of data to be read. The output tape is then removed from the computer and placed on off-line equipment to punch out the information written on the tape.

The actual FORTRAN IV computer program prepared from this flowchart is handwritten on a standard coding form as shown in Figure IV-7. The coding form facilitates punching the FORTRAN statements on cards to form a *program deck* (see Figure IV-8). The computer gets its instructions from the program deck, which it reads before reading the data cards.

The FORTRAN statements in Figure IV-8 are numbered in correspondence with the numbered steps in the flowchart (Figure IV-6). The function of each statement in the program will be described in turn.

Step 1:   1 READ (5, 2) ID, REPVOT, DEMVOT
2 FORMAT (I3, F7.0, F7.0)

The first statement in this pair directs the computer to read a card containing the county identification, the Republican vote, and the Democratic vote. FORTRAN limits the name assigned to

Figure IV-7

Computer program written on FORTRAN coding form

```
C FOR COMMENT

STATEMENT
NUMBER                          FORTRAN STATEMENT

1   5 6 7   10    15    20    25    30    35    40    45    50    55    60    65    70  72

 1    READ (5,2) ID, REPVØT, DEMVØT
 2    FØRMAT (I3,F7.0,F7.0)
      PCTREP = (REPVØT / (REPVØT + DEMVØT)) * 100.0
      PCTDEM = (DEMVØT / (REPVØT + DEMVØT)) * 100.0
      PLURAL = ABS(PCTREP - PCTDEM)
      IF (DEMVØT .GT. REPVØT) IWIN = 2
      IF (REPVØT .EQ. 0.0) IWIN = 1
      IF (REPVØT .EQ. DEMVØT) IWIN = 3
      IF (REPVØT .GT. DEMVØT) IWIN = 4
      IF (DEMVØT .EQ. 0.0) IWIN = 5
      WRITE (6,3) ID, REPVØT, DEMVØT, PCTREP, PCTDEM, PLURAL, IWIN
 3    FØRMAT (1HP,I3,F7.0,F7.0,10X,F6.1,F6.1,F6.1,2X,I1)
      GØ TØ 1
```

FIGURE IV-8

FORTRAN IV COMPUTER PROGRAM FOR COMPUTING ELECTION PERCENTAGES

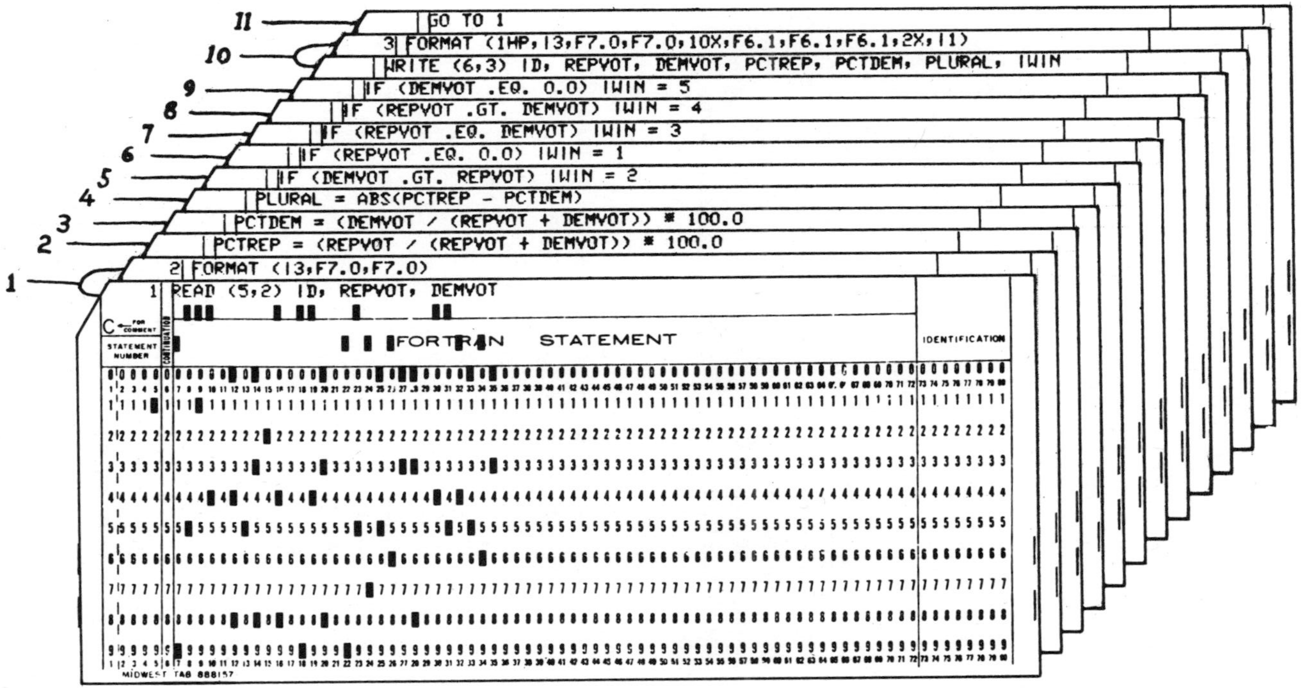
11
GO TO 1
10
3 FORMAT (1HP,I3,F7.0,F7.0,10X,F6.1,F6.1,F6.1,2X,I1)
WRITE (6,3) ID, REPVOT, DEMVOT, PCTREP, PCTDEM, PLURAL, IWIN
9
IF (DEMVOT .EQ. 0.0) IWIN = 5
8
IF (REPVOT .GT. DEMVOT) IWIN = 4
7
IF (REPVOT .EQ. DEMVOT) IWIN = 3
6
IF (REPVOT .EQ. 0.0) IWIN = 1
5
IF (DEMVOT .GT. REPVOT) IWIN = 2
4
PLURAL = ABS(PCTREP - PCTDEM)
3
PCTDEM = (DEMVOT / (REPVOT + DEMVOT)) * 100.0
2
PCTREP = (REPVOT / (REPVOT + DEMVOT)) * 100.0
1
2 FORMAT (I3,F7.0,F7.0)
1 READ (5,2) ID, REPVOT, DEMVOT
C FOR COMMENT
STATEMENT NUMBER
CONTINUATION
FORTRAN STATEMENT
IDENTIFICATION
MIDWEST TAB 888157

each item of information (or "variable") to only six characters, which accounts for the abbreviation. The numbers within parentheses in that expression mean "read this information from tape unit 5 according to the format specified in statement 2." Tape unit 5 is by convention the *input* tape. In this program, statement 2 happens to be the second statement, but statement numbers may be assigned arbitrarily. A FORMAT statement in FORTRAN tells the computer in which columns on the card the information is located. The first term within parentheses—"I3"—states that the county identification (ID) is an *integer* variable located in the first three columns of the card. The "I" stands for "integer" and "3" for the number of columns in the field.

The second term within parentheses—"F7.0"—states that "REP-VOT" is to be considered a *floating-point* number (a number with a decimal point) that occupies the next seven columns on the card and has no digits past the decimal point. The "F" in the term stands for "floating-point," the number "7" stands for the number of columns in the field, and ".0" stands for no digits past the decimal point. The third and final term in the FORMAT expression is also "F7.0" and tells the computer that "DEMVOT" is recorded in the next seven digit field and is also to be considered as a floating-point number. Both REPVOT and DEM-VOT must be treated as floating-point or decimal numbers because percentages are being calculated.

Step 2: PCTREP = (REPVOT / (REPVOT + DEMVOT))
* 100.0

This statement equates a variable called "PCTREP" (for "percent Republican") to the amount obtained by dividing the Republican vote by the two-party vote and multiplying the result by 100.0 to convert the answer to percents. FORTRAN uses the slash symbol to indicate division and the asterisk to indicate multiplication.

Step 3: PCTDEM = (DEMVOT / (REPVOT + DEMVOT))
* 100.0

This statement calculates a variable called "PCTDEM" (for "percent Democratic") as discussed in Step 2.

Step 4: PLURAL = ABS(PCTREP - PCTDEM)

"PLURAL" is the name given to the plurality difference between the parties' percentages of the vote. In FORTRAN IV, the term "ABS" calls out a built-in function that takes only the *absolute* value of the amount resulting from subtracting PCTDEM from PCTREP. Negative signs that might appear are ignored by this function.

Step 5: IF (DEMVOT .GT. REPVOT) IWIN = 2

This states: *If* the number of Democratic votes is *greater than* (.GT.) the number of Republican votes, set "IWIN" equal to 2, signifying a Democratic victory. (In FORTRAN, a variable name that begins with an "I" is an integer variable and carries no decimal point. Naming the variable "WIN" would have required setting it equal to a decimal point number (2.0).) If the Democratic candidate did *not* get more votes than the Republican, nothing is done to the variable IWIN, and the computer proceeds to execute the next statement.

Step 6: IF (REPVOT .EQ. 0.0) IWIN = 1

This states: *If* the number of Republican votes *equals* (.EQ.) zero (0.0), set IWIN equal to 1, signifying that the Democratic candidate won all the votes. Obviously, this condition could not exist unless the Democrat had more votes than the Republican (see Step 5). In this case, the value of 2 in IWIN would be *replaced* with the value of 1. If the Republican vote is not equal to zero, nothing is done to IWIN, and the computer proceeds to the next statement.

Step 7: IF (REPVOT .EQ. DEMVOT) IWIN = 3

This states: *If* the number of Republican votes *equals* (.EQ.) the number of Democratic votes, set IWIN equal to 3, the code for a tie election. (It is conceivable that both candidates for a statewide election could get the same number of votes in a given county.) If the two votes are not equal, nothing is done to IWIN and the computer proceeds to the next statement.

Step 8: IF (REPVOT .GT. DEMVOT) IWIN = 4

This states: *If* the number of Republican votes is *greater than* (.GT.) the number of Democratic votes, set IWIN equal to 4, signifying a Republican victory. If the Republican did not get more votes than the Democrat, nothing is done to IWIN and the next statement is executed.

Step 9: IF (DEMVOT .EQ. 0.0) IWIN = 5

This states: *If* the number of Democratic votes *equals* zero, set IWIN equal to 5, signifying that the Republican won all the votes. If the Republican vote does not equal zero, nothing is done to IWIN and the next statement is executed.

Step 10: WRITE (6, 3) ID, REPVOT, DEMVOT, PCTREP, PCTDEM, PLURAL, IWIN

3 FORMAT (1HP, I3, F7.0, F7.0, 10X, F6.1, F6.1, F6.1, 2X, I1)

The first statement in this pair directs the computer to write out the original variables and the results of its calculations. The numbers in parentheses mean "write this information on tape unit 6 according to the format specified in statement 3." Tape unit 6 is by convention the *output* tape. The very first term within parentheses in the FORMAT statement is "1HP", which—in this example—is a command for the off-line equipment to punch the results on cards instead of printing them on paper. The next three terms that follow are identical to those in statement 2, which specifies the input format.

The next term in statement 3 is "10X", which means "skip ten columns on the card." The letter "X" stands for a skip instruction and "10" indicates the number of columns to be skipped. The term "F6.1" is repeated three times for the three variables, PCTREP, PCTDEM, and PLURAL. All three are punched out in six-column fields with one digit after the decimal point.

The next term, "2X", causes two columns to be skipped before punching out IWIN according to "I1"—a one column integer variable, no decimal point.

Step 11: GO TO 1

This statement returns control to statement 1, which directs the computer to read a card from tape and repeat the process. This program forms a "loop" that is continued until the computer runs out of data cards to read and the job is terminated.

Appendix A-1 describes an election analysis study prepared with a similar but more complex computer program for calculating summary statistics from raw voting returns and census estimates of the total eligible electorate.

The computer program described above involves only thirteen instruction statements in FORTRAN. Each of these statements, however, is a *macro-instruction* that translates into many specific machine language instructions after processing by the FORTRAN compiler. In fact, these thirteen statements were translated into 117 machine language instructions by the FORTRAN compiler for the IBM 709 computer.

Writing a program in a programming language like FORTRAN produces a *source program* that must be compiled into a machine language or *object program* before it can be executed by the computer. The FORTRAN compiler accepts source programs and produces object programs which are punched on cards in binary code. Once a source program has been successfully compiled, the object program deck is used instead of the source deck to avoid the compilation time required each time the program is run. Although the object deck contains many more instruction statements than the source program, the object deck generally contains fewer cards because many binary words can be punched on one card. The cards of a binary program deck are full of holes and are virtually unintelligible to the researcher.

Careful study of this simple example of programming will hardly qualify you as a computer programmer, but it should provide some insight into the art. A far more complex example of a computer program written in FORTRAN IV is contained in Appendix C-2, which produces a tabulator listing of a general and powerful program for preparing cross-classification tables and computing tests of association between cross-classified variables. Chapter VI discusses this program in detail.

A computer cannot do anything without a program, and writing programs for large data processing tasks is a complex and time-consuming enterprise. Fortunately, however, computer programs can be generalized so they can be used repeatedly to perform the same basic operations with different data. This is a feature of the cross-classification program presented in Chapter VI and Appendix C-1. Generalized programs can serve the data processing needs of researchers at other institutions. Programs written in a problem-oriented language like FORTRAN can be run at any computing center that has a compiler for the language.

Every computing center maintains a "library" of programs and detailed descriptions ("write-ups") of their purposes, capabilities, and procedures for use. Programs in the library may have been written by programmers on the computing center staff or they may have come from other universities or from industry. Users of similar computers have also organized into "users groups" for distributing information about new programs for their type of computer. Perhaps the best-known users group is SHARE (Society to Help Avoid Repetitive Effort), which serves those who have IBM 704/709/7090/7094/7040/7044 computers. Information about users groups can be found in the *Communications of the Association for Computing Machinery*, a monthly publication.

Researchers in the behavioral sciences will find information about computer programs and applications in the "Computers in Behavioral Science" section in every quarterly issue of *Behavioral Science*. *Behavioral Research* and *Educational and Psychological Measurement* are two other journals that report computer applications in the behavioral sciences. The Medical Computing Center in the College of Medicine at the University of Cincinnati has developed a set of statistical programs for the IBM 1401. These programs are described in *MEDCOMP: Handbook of Computer Applications in Biology and Medicine.*[17] Some FORTRAN programs for multivariate analysis are contained in *Multivariate Procedures for the Behavioral Sciences.*[18] Users of IBM equipment in general will find computer programs listed in the *Catalog of Programs for IBM Data Processing Systems.*[19]

The Health Science Computing Facility in the Department of Preventive Medicine and Public Health at UCLA's School of Medicine has prepared an extremely valuable set of programs for a variety of statistical analyses on the IBM 709/7090/7094. Write-ups of these programs can be found in *BMD: Biomedical Computer Programs.*[20] A correlation analysis program from the BMD manual is discussed in Chapter VII.

COMPUTERS AS TOOLS OF RESEARCH

The behavioral science community has barely begun to realize the potential value of computers in research. Nevertheless, Wrigley already predicts that

> the electronic computer will prove to be the most versatile and influential scientific instrument so far invented and that it will play a larger role in the scientific histories of the future than even such obvious challengers as the microscope and the telescope.[21]

This prediction assumes that behavioral scientists will take advantage of computers' capabilities. Wrigley points out, however, that some early administrators of university computing centers discouraged the use of computers by behavioral scientists by limiting access to researchers with enormously complex mathematical problems. This policy was geared to the needs of physical scientists and discriminated against behavioral scientists, who often wanted to use the computer only for purposes of manipulating or compiling large masses of data. Viewing the problem from the administrator's position, Wrigley remarks, "The volume of the behavioral scientist's input was often surprising, and that of his output even more so."[22] Some computing center administrators found it difficult to justify the use of a powerful machine for the relatively simple tasks proposed by behavioral scientists.

An incident that occurred during my graduate training at Indiana University might illustrate the differences between computer applications by social and physical scientists. At that time, the university computing center had an IBM 650, one of the most popular models then in use but a slow machine by present standards. The computing center operated on an "open-shop" basis;

researchers were expected to operate the machine themselves and were allowed to reserve machine time for any part of the day or night.

I usually signed up to use the IBM 650 for a half-hour or an hour at most. Before even going on the computer, I spent an hour or more preparing my data on legislators' voting records. Once the job was underway, the computer spent more time reading my data than calculating and punching out the answers, and, as Wrigley indicated, the computer often generated as many cards of output as it read as input.

In contrast, I recall the large blocks of computer time, from six to ten hours, signed for by the physical scientists, who ordinarily fed far fewer cards into the machine. The best example of this was the graduate student in astronomy who signed for the machine from midnight to 6:00 a.m. for more than ten consecutive evenings. He used the computer to construct alternative models of the solar system, and each model required about six hours of machine time. He would stroll in shortly before midnight, place a sizable program in the input hopper of the computer, follow the program with a small deck of cards drawn from his pocket, press the proper buttons, and settle back to read a paperback mystery while the 650 blinked and whirred for six hours of computing. Dawn would come, the machine would grind out a few answer cards, and another solar system would be made.

What was the difference between his use of the computer and mine? For one thing, he knew what he was looking for and he had a sophisticated theory to help him find it. For another, his data and theory permitted the formulation of his problem in precise, albeit complex, mathematics. The theory and data available to me were not amenable to precise mathematical formulation. At that time, I used the computer mainly to compile frequency distributions of "yes" and "no" voting positions on hundreds of roll calls taken by legislators from different types of districts. This job would have been completely unfeasible without the use of punchcard data processing equipment and, even with the use of the counter-sorter, would have been discouragingly time-consuming. The nature of my data and the limitations of my theory produced a data processing problem requiring large input and large output, with little computer manipulation and compilation in between, but the computer still proved to be a tremendous help.

While not denying the advantages of computers in manipulating and compiling information for large masses of data, those who predict a truly important role for computers in behavioral science research do not view this as the greatest contribution of computers. These writers more likely agree with Weeg that the "greatest glory" of a computer "is its ability to do mathematics in a hurry."[23] Speed in computation is valued mainly because it opens the door to the use of complex multivariate models and analytical procedures in research.[24] Multivariate procedures have not been widely used by political scientists, who still tend to design their research in terms of bivariate statistics. Of course, the computer can be of great help in calculating these statistics. "Yet the computer's potential will certainly not be realized," says Cooley, "if all it is asked to do is compute more and more bivariate correlation coefficients."[25]

Any casual observer of political life must be aware of the multiplicity of variables that cause any given phenomenon. Because of the multi-causality of the real world, bivariate models of explanation must necessarily be lacking in explanatory power. Why, then, have not more political scientists used multi-variate techniques? A major reason for the unpopularity of multivariate statistical analysis has been the impractical aspects of their use. Although the use of factor analysis—a prominent and powerful multivariate procedure—was reported in *The American Political Science Review* as early as 1935,[26] the tremendous complexity of the method did not encourage its application in subsequent research. The method did not reappear in the *Review* until 1960, when the work was done on a computer.[27] Pinner has summarized the situation:

> For decades, factor analysis has been the exclusive domain of experts; the mathematical sophistication needed and the inordinate amount of labor often required made it prohibitive to the ordinary researcher in social science. Recently these difficulties have been largely removed. We have now good introductory descriptions of the method written for people of moderate statistical means. Moreover, the presence of high-speed computers on most larger campuses and the

existence of "canned" programs has taken most of the work out of factor analysis.[28]

The tremendous power of the computer is demonstrated not only by its ability to perform factor analyses and to compute other types of multivariate *statistics* but also by its ability to handle multivariate *models* of political processes through stimulation. Arguing for the use of computers in constructing theories of political process through simulation models, Browning says, "The computer is particularly well suited both to keep track of complex relationships and to carry out with great speed the repetitive operations involved in many decision processes."[29]

Without a doubt, the exciting potentiality of computers in data processing lies not merely in their ability to manipulate and compile large masses of information but in their ability to perform complex multivariate analyses. This does not mean, however, that one cannot justify the use of computers merely for manipulating or summarizing data. The appropriate test is whether the computer helps the researcher answer the questions he wants to ask. A computer can be of great value to a researcher even though he may hardly tap the computer's capabilities. One need not always drive research assistants to their limits, and, as Wrigley says,

> To the scientist with limited time and energy, the computer means extra research assistance. Unlike its human counterparts, this assistant is indefatigable, incredibly fast, and remarkably accurate; but it shares, with the humans it is superseding, the need to be given extremely precise instructions. It is moronic in the literalness with which it does what it is told to do.[30]

Within the limits of its abilities, the computer does what it is told to do, and this may lead to the very real danger, of which Marks warns, that "a computer makes it possible to do simply and easily a number of relatively meaningless things." But he continues:

> Although the increased use of computers may lead to increased production of meaningless results, this is not an argument against the use of computers. Important jobs have been neglected in the past because of the difficulties involved in tabulation of computation.[31]

In other words, some questions have gone unanswered because the researcher could not afford to ask all the ones he would have liked. Instead of the researcher's choosing among competing questions, computers have encouraged him, as Borgatta and Robbin have stated, "rather, to ask all relevant questions."[32] Thus the computer can not only help the researcher *answer* questions but can also encourage him to *ask* the questions.

This handbook barely hints at the potential of computers in the analysis of political data. But the utility of punchcards and computers is so great even at the lower levels of data processing that this elementary introduction to the method can still provide considerable payoff for political scientists who see how they can make use of this technology.

NOTES

[1] Harold Borko (ed.), *Computer Applications in the Behavioral Sciences* (Englewood Cliffs, N. J.: Prentice-Hall, 1962) covers computing equipment in the first seven chapters. See also Frederick P. Brooks, Jr. and Kenneth E. Iverson, *Automatic Data Processing* (New York: Wiley, 1963), Bert F. Green, Jr., *Digital Computers in Research: An Introduction for Behavioral and Social Scientists* (New York: McGraw-Hill, 1963), and William H. Desmonde, *Computers and their Uses* (Englewood Cliffs, N. J.: Prentice-Hall, 1964).

[2] Borko, *op. cit.*, p. 60.

[3] A machine that can execute any finite symbol-manipulation process is called a "universal Turing machine"—named after A.M. Turing, who discovered that a machine of sufficient complexity could perform any calculations that could be done by hand. Every general-purpose digital computer with sufficient storage qualifies as a Turing machine. Turing machines and computers are discussed in Green, *op. cit.*, Chapter 15.

[4] See Alan D. Meacham (ed.), *Data Processing Equipment Encyclopedia: Volume 2, Electronic Computers* (Detroit: Gille Associates, Inc., 1961) and periodic supplements. The Commerce Clearing House's new service, *The Automation Reporter*, is another good source of equipment specifications. Also see *Data Processing Systems Encyclopedia* (Detroit: American Data Processing, Inc.).

[5] Charles Wrigley, "Electronic Computers and Psychological Research," *American Psychologist*, 12 (August, 1957), 501-8.

[6] This estimate is based on responses to Thomas A. Keenan's survey of university computing centers (see note 7) and on responses to a similar survey taken by the National Academy of Sciences. The latter

survey had not been published at the time of this writing. It was brought to my attention through personal communication with Thomas Keenan.

[7] These data were made available through the kindness of Dr. Thomas A. Keenan in advance of publication of the findings from the 1963 survey. See his *1963 Survey of University Computing Centers* (in press). The data in Table IV-1 for 1963 conform closely to the findings of a separate survey by Dr. Roy F. Reeves, Director of the Numerical Computation Laboratory, The Ohio State University Research Center (mimeographed, dated August 1, 1963).

[8] The IBM 650 was even a more common machine at university computing centers before 1961. See Albert E. Beaton, "University Data Processing Centers," *Harvard Educational Review*, 31 (Summer, 1961), 243-49; see p. 245.

[9] H. C. Carver, "Uses of the Automatic Multiplying Punch," in G. W. Baehne (ed.), *Practical Applications of the Punched Card Method* (New York: Columbia, 1935), p. 418.

[10]Green, *op. cit.*, p. 3.

[11]Charles Wrigley, "The University Computing Center," in Borko, *op. cit.*, p. 157.

[12]Linton C. Freeman, "The Use of Simplified Programming Systems in IBM 650 Data Processing," *Behavioral Science*, 7 (January, 1962), 117.

[13]E. Wayne Martin and Dale J. Hall, "Data Processing: Automation in Calculation," *Review of Educational Research*, 30 (December, 1960), 523.

[14]Beaton, *op. cit.*, pp. 246-47.

[15]Harry L. Colman and Clarence Smallwood, *Computer Language: An Autoinstructional Introduction to FORTRAN* (New York: McGraw-Hill, 1962), and S. C. Plumb, *Introduction to FORTRAN* (New York: McGraw-Hill, 1964), are two recent "programmed texts" specifically designed for self-study. Daniel D. McCracken, *A Guide to FORTRAN Programming* (New York: Wiley, 1961) presents a more traditional approach to the subject.

[16]Rufus P. Browning, "Computer Programs as Theories of Political Process," *Journal of Politics*, 24 (August, 1962), 582.

[17]T. Sterling and S. Pollack (eds.), Part I, "Statistical Systems." (Cincinnati: Medical Computing Center, College of Medicine, University of Cincinnati, 1963).

[18]W. W. Cooley and P. R. Lohnes, *Multivariate Procedures for the Behavioral Sciences* (New York: Wiley, 1962).

[19]IBM publication C20-8090-3, dated September, 1963, and supplemented monthly.

[20]W. J. Dixon (ed.), *BMD: Biomedical Computer Programs* (Los Angeles: UCLA School of Medicine, Department of Preventive Medicine and Public Health, Health Sciences Computing Facility, 1964). Copies of the BMD manual may be purchased at $5.00 each (postpaid) from the UCLA Student Store, 308 Westwood Blvd., Los Angeles 24, California.

[21]Wrigley, "The University Computing Center," in Borko, *op. cit.*, p. 163.

[22]*Ibid.*, p. 148.

[23]Gerard P. Weeg, "The Electronic Computer," in Richard D. Duke (ed.), *Automatic Data Processing* (East Lansing: Institute for Community Development and Services, Michigan State University, 1961), p. 28.

[24]This is the position taken in Kelly and Lingoes, "Data Processing in Psychological Research"; Wrigley, "The University Computing Center"; Benson, "The Use of Mathematics in the Study of Political Science"; and W. W. Cooley and P. R. Lohnes, *Multivariate Procedures for the Behavioral Sciences* (New York: Wiley, 1962).

[25]William W. Cooley, "Research Methodology and Modern Data Processing," *Harvard Educational Review*, 31 (Summer, 1961), 262.

[26]H. F. Gosnell and N. N. Gill, "A Factor Analysis of the 1932 Presidential Vote in Chicago," *American Political Science Review*, 29 (December, 1935), 967-84.

[27]Duncan MacRae, Jr. and James A. Meldrum, "Critical Elections in Illinois: 1888-1958," *American Political Science Review*, 54 (September, 1960), 669-83.

[28]Frank A. Pinner, "Notes on Method in Social and Political Research," in Dwight Waldo (ed.), *The Research Function of University Bureaus and Institutes for Government-Related Research* (Bureau of Public Administration, University of California, Berkeley, 1960), p. 205.

[29]Browning, *op. cit.*, p. 582. Examples of computer simulation are given in Oliver Benson, "Simulation of International Relations and Diplomacy," in Borko, *op. cit.*, pp. 575-95; and in Harold Guetzkow (ed.), *Simulation in Social Science: Readings* (Englewood Cliffs, N. J.: Prentice-Hall, 1962).

[30]Wrigley, "The University Computing Center," *op. cit.*, p. 163.

[31]Eli S. Marks, "You Can Do It on a Computer, But Should You?" *Public Opinion Quarterly*, 27 (Fall, 1963), 482.

[32]E. F. Borgatta and J. Robbin, "Some Implications of High Speed Computers for the Methodology of Social Research," *Sociology and Social Research*, 43 (March-April, 1959), 262.

CHAPTER V   SUGGESTIONS FOR COLLECTING, CODING, AND MANAGING PUNCHCARD DATA

The beginner in data processing is asked to learn new ideas, mechanics, and procedures that are all somehow related. Unfortunately, everything cannot be discussed at once, and there needs to be some order of presentation. To stimulate interest in the methodology, Chapter II—"Recording Political Data on Punchcards"—was placed immediately after the Introduction to show the relevance of data processing to political research. The present chapter, which deals with collecting, coding, and managing punchcard data, was not given its "logical" place immediately after Chapter II because the equipment's operating principles had to be discussed before these suggestions could be understood adequately. Hopefully, the preceding two chapters provide enough information about the hardware and software of data processing equipment to make this chapter meaningful.

In all aspects of human endeavor, the available technology strongly affects the way we do things. This is especially true with respect to data processing. Technological advances in computing hardware or software can render procedures for collecting, coding, and managing punchcard data obsolete almost overnight. As stated in the Introduction, all how-to-do-it statements in this handbook are subject to early obsolescence. They are suited to computing equipment and programming language currently in use. With today's rapidly changing technology, that is how any instructional handbook for practical use must be written.

The suggestions in this chapter assume a technology associated with a large-scale digital computer with magnetic tape input-output capabilities. These suggestions do not necessarily apply to data processing on a counter-sorter, or even on an early computer like the once-popular IBM 650. In fact, some suggestions about collecting and coding data for processing on the counter-sorter make the data unfit for computer processing. Because the counter-sorter is still widely used in behavioral research, the following discussion will give special attention to incompatibilities between counter-sorter and computer processing.

COLLECTING DATA

LAYING OUT THE FORMAT

Since the early 1930's, the counter-sorter has been the workhorse machine for processing social science data.[1] Even after development of modern computing equipment, many students still designed research and collected information with an eye toward processing the data on the counter-sorter. The abilities and limitations of this machine have clearly affected collection of data and strongly influenced design of the card format.

This "counter-sorter psychology" places a high premium on fitting all data for one case in the 80 columns of one punchcard. This practice not only saves on the number of cards used but also facilitates data analysis by restricting the sorting process to only one deck of cards. Analyses are performed on the counter-sorter by first sorting cards into separate coding categories for one variable and then running *each* of these categories through the machine again to count the punches for a *second* variable.[2] This process can produce a cross-classification or cross-tabulation between any two variables *punched on the same card*. The counter-sorter cannot be used in this way to cross-classify variables punched on *different cards*—hence the pressure for limiting the data to one card.

This psychology still prevails among some researchers. As recently as 1963, Backstrom and Hursh advised readers of *Survey Research* to

> Use columns on the machine card economically. Analysis is far easier if you get your data on one card per respondent. Naturally, you don't want to sacrifice any information you get, but proper planning may permit compressing the data to the 80 columns on the data card . . .[3]

Often considerable ingenuity was demonstrated in fitting all the information onto one card through "proper planning."[4] Several answers given in response to an open-ended question (e.g., "Why did you vote for him?") were sometimes coded in the same column, producing multiple punches in that column. A variation on this practice was that of coding two *different* items of information in the same column, taking care that the codes for each did not overlap (e.g., codes 1-4 for one item and 5-9 for the other). Through skillful use of these techniques, a researcher could compress more than 100 variables into a standard 80 column punchcard.[5]

The concern about the number of cards used for collecting data has indeed been a real one. McCarger recognized as one of the major problems of card design

> that of having too much data for a single card, posing the question of whether to go into a multiple card layout, or whether to drop information and/or squeeze the data onto a single card. There is no hard and fast rule, here, but it is my opinion that the dictum of having all information on one card, sometimes heard in punched-card circles, is vastly over-rated. Cards are not expensive, and punching them is not a terrible problem. Once the cards are punched it is a simple matter to produce new decks. Thus, I would caution you against drastic squeezing designed to achieve processing economy; frequently it turns out to be a false economy.[6]

Some years ago I thought it economical to record as many elections as possible on the same card. I succeeded in squeezing *seven* different elections on one card by lopping off the units digit on each county vote total. The "economy" I had achieved subsequently cost many hours of programming to analyze the votes for individual offices in different years. In order to obtain greater flexibility in analysis, I eventually had to "un-squeeze" the elections so that each election was recorded on a separate card.

Given the capabilities of present technology, it is no longer important to put variables that are to be cross-classified on the same card. The computer can easily relate information on one card to information on another. The card format and the number of cards used to record the data are relatively unimportant considerations when analyzing data with modern computers.[7] Some standardizing of formats, however, can be helpful in *managing* punchcard data (see "identification codes," p. 139).

PREPARING THE DATA FOR KEYPUNCHING

In order to reduce errors that occur in putting data in punchcard form, it is sometimes desirable to have keypunch operators work directly from original documents or sources. McCarger poses the objective in this manner:

> In general, we try to strike a balance here between the requirements of fast, accurate punching and the reduction of the amount of copying of documents which is done by persons other than the punch operator. From the standpoint of the key-punch operator, we try as much as possible to give the puncher a literal document which she merely has to copy, as opposed to one which she has to figure out. We try to reduce the number of documents which the punch operator must handle, the amount of page turning, complex page scanning and other things which detract from rapid and accurate punching.[8]

This objective cannot always be achieved when working with political information which must be assembled from different sources and coded carefully before keypunching. Two types of political data that can often be keypunched directly from original materials, however, are election returns and "pre-coded" interview responses. Figures II-2 and II-3 (in Chapter II) indicate how these data can be punched directly from official election reports and original interview schedules.

Careful planning and editing of materials before they are given to keypunch operators can dramatically improve the operators' speed and accuracy. Gruenberger warns, "If the keypunch operator is expected to code while punching (or even to look around the schedule sheets for the next item) the error level in punching will soar."[9] Backstrom and Hursh suggest rewriting all code numbers on the lefthand side of the interview schedule to help the keypuncher: "Uniform coding alignment allows her eye to travel quickly down the side of each page instead of back and forth across each page."[10] They also suggest writing the code numbers in a color different from the printing on the schedule. Colored lines or markings often can be used to guide the keypuncher's work.

Many types of political data do not lend themselves to direct punching from original materials, and information must be recorded on coding sheets before being punched. Figures II-4 to II-8 (in Chapter II) illustrate how coding sheets are used in recording information found in descriptions of political institutions, biographical sketches, legislative journals, and governmental directories. These coding sheets can be designed and printed for specific data collection projects. Graph paper—5 squares to the inch and 17 inches wide—makes a suitable substitute. This provides 85 squares per line: 80 squares for the information to go into the 80 columns of a punchcard and 5 squares for a margin in which identifying labels can be entered to guide the coder. Graph paper marked by heavy lines every fifth column offers reference markers for coders and keypunch operators.

CHECKING FOR ERRORS

The use of coding sheets provides the flexibility that is often necessary for recording political data, but the price for this flexibility in coding is an extra step in putting the data on cards, causing added effort and additional chance for error. Most *keypunching* errors can easily be detected by "repunching" data on the verifier (see Chapter III). If an erroneous punch is found in the card, a small red light appears on the verifier and the machine stops. The operator thus notes the error and indicates the correction on the card. Errors in punching can also be detected by printing out or "listing" the cards on the tabulator (see Chapter III) and checking the listing against the original code sheets. When applied to numerical data, this method is usually slower and not as fool-proof as verifying by machine. But visual checking is an efficient and effective means for verifying textual information (see Chapter VIII).

Because they are less easily detected, errors caused by inaccurate *coding* are more serious than those caused by inaccurate *punching* of the codes. The following remarks made by Backstrom and Hursh about coding survey data also apply to coding other types of political data:

> Because coding imposes many decisions—into which category does a particular response best fit?—it demands a high level of understanding of the subject matter of the survey. The price of accurate coding is complete uniformity of decision and careful attention to detail through all questionnaires.
>
> Inexperienced people can learn to code survey data, but they should work in a small group assembled around a common table. In this way the study director or his agent constantly can check to be sure that all coders are handling similar responses the same way. He is responsible for all decisions and immediately calls the group's attention to new judgments. If for some reason the director cannot be present during coding, the coders should record any changes they make, or questions they may have left unresolved, on a sheet provided for this purpose and clip it to the front of each questionnaire. These sheets will flag the director's attention to specific problems or erroneous coding.
>
> Double checking the coding is a worthwhile safeguard. It can be done by having coders exchange questionnaires and check each others' decisions. An estimate of how well the coding scheme works (coder reliability) can be obtained by having different coders code a sample of the same questionnaires. By determining how much agreement there is among coders, you have a measure of the system's application. . . .
>
> . . . .
>
> All coding decisions should be assembled and duplicated into a manual for use by coders. The coding manual itself becomes a veritable research document. It provides column-by-column instructions, except for items on which the codes are self-evident. Besides being an instruction booklet for coders, the coding manual serves as a guide to locating material in the survey. Write absolutely everything into it, trusting nothing to memory, which is bound to fail when you come back to this study after doing other things.[11]

Backstrom and Hursh have outlined a system for reducing coding errors by monitoring the ongoing coding process and adjusting to feedback from the coders when they have encountered problems. Such a system is essential to accurate coding of "soft" data gathered from surveys, biographical sketches, and descriptions of political institutions. Errors in coding this type of data may go undetected forever as few, if any, checks can be made once the data are on cards. This is less true for such "hard" data as roll call votes and committee assignments. Accuracy in coding these data can be tested quite easily by checking the distributions of punches in the card columns. If the legislative journal states that a roll call was divided into 54 "yes" votes and 40 "no" votes, the column containing that vote should have 54 "yes" punches and 40 "no" punches. If a legislative committee has 20 members, the column in which its membership is recorded should have 20 "membership" punches. This method of checking the marginals does not insure that the codes are punched correctly for each individual, but it does provide an important check that can be made in a routine manner on a computer or a counter-sorter.

NUMBERING INTERVIEW QUESTIONS

Questions contained in interview schedules or items included in questionnaires usually are numbered serially, i.e., the first question asked is number 1, the next question is number 2, and so on. Occasionally, lower-case letters are used to identify questions with several parts—3a, 3b, and 3c. This numbering system ignores the format to be employed in punching responses to these questions. Because some columns at the beginning of each card will be used to record the respondent's identifying number, the responses to question 1 in the interview schedule might be punched in column 4; responses to question 2 might be punched in column 5; responses to questions 3a, 3b, and 3c might be punched in columns 6, 7, and 8. Notice the lack of correspondence between the number of the question and the location of the information on the punchcard. The researcher must keep in mind—and yet keep separate—the *question* numbers and the *column* numbers. This source of confusion has plagued many a researcher, but it can be avoided easily in most survey studies.

After the interview questions have been formulated and arranged, the punchcard format for recording the responses can be determined. The card layout can usually be made definite at this time. The questions can then be assigned the numbers of the columns in which responses will be recorded. Because the numbers serve only to label and identify questions, there should be no objection to numbering the first question *4* if the responses to that question are punched in column 4. Similarly, a question that generates responses requiring a two-column code might legitimately be numbered 44-45, if the responses are punched in columns 44-45. If the individual's responses extend to more than one card, the question might be numbered 1/21 to indicate column 21 in card 1 or 2/35 for column 35 in card 2. This numbering system is used in the survey data example in Figure II-3 (Chapter II).

This simple method of numbering interview questions pays off handsomely at the analysis stage, for the researcher need not translate the question numbers on the interview schedule into column locations on punchcards. This may seem to be a trivial suggestion, but many data processing difficulties can be avoided through the use of seemingly trivial techniques.

CODING SUGGESTIONS

To reiterate, many coding suggestions or "rules" advanced in this section contradict earlier advice based on use of the counter-sorter. This is especially true of the first three rules. The other suggestions are prompted more by convenience in data analysis than by the computer's technological requirements.

USE ONLY ONE PUNCH PER COLUMN

As stated in the previous section, researchers sometimes punch two or more code numbers in a single column to record all information on one card. The use of multiple punches in a column can facilitate analysis on the counter-sorter, but this practice complicates computer processing. In general, computing equipment and programming languages are designed to handle numerical data or, in some cases, letters of the alphabet and certain special characters. Multiple-punching can produce combinations of holes that are meaningless to the computer and, in fact, are sometimes rejected as "invalid" information. In addition to this fundamental barrier to data processing, Bisco lists six other disadvantages of using multiple punches for coding purposes:

1. Virtually no computer programs exist for doing statistics on multiply-punched data. . . .
2. The increased number of punches per column structurally weakens a card and can increase the probability of card jams on card reading equipment.
3. The simplest error control, a deck listing, takes several times the amount of paper required for cards containing only valid Hollerith characters.
4. Check sums and distributions, more sophisticated error controls, have much more limited applicability—compensating errors are more probable.
5. Because of the more complex editing and manipulating routines, [special] computer programs run much more slowly than do programs for single-punch per column cards. . . .
6. The packing of information using multiple punches is, in some ways, antithetical to having standard coding conventions. . . .[12]

USE ONLY THE DIGITS 0 TO 9 AS CODES; DO NOT USE − AND +

The minus and plus punches (sometimes called the X and Y or 11 and 12 punches) have often been used as distinct coding categories in counter-sorter data processing. In computer processing, however, these punches normally indicate positive or negative values and are not easily interpreted as coding categories. Some standard programs will accept these punches but will interpret them as "positive" or "negative" zeros. The practical result is that a computer often does not distinguish between 0, −, and + codes.

DO NOT LIMIT YOURSELF TO SINGLE-COLUMN CODES

Data processing on the counter-sorter was facilitated by putting all the information on one card as well as by punching all coding categories for a given variable in a single column. This permitted the determination of the complete distribution of codes on a given variable from only one pass on the counter-sorter, which reads only one column at a time. Two or more passes on the machine were necessary if the codes extended to two columns. If the ten codes provided by the 0-9 punches were not enough for some purposes, two additional categories could be obtained by using the plus and minus punches. A thirteenth category could be obtained by recognizing the *absence* of a punch in the column as a legitimate code (see rule on blanks as codes below). And, of course, the number of possible codes would increase tremendously with multiple punches.

It is no longer necessary to force data into the limited coding categories of a single column. Modern computers can easily handle variables coded in two columns, although this capability has not always been capitalized on when writing computer programs for processing behavioral science data. Chapter VI describes in detail a computer program that *will* accept two-column codes in cross-classifying one variable against another. The coding categories can begin with oo and extend continuously to 99. Within wide limits, the researcher can now use as many coding categories as his data require.

PLAN MULTIPLE-COLUMN CODES WITH REGARD TO DATA ANALYSIS

Sometimes analysis is helped by organizing the information into "telescoping" code structures (also called "collapsing" or "range" codes). For example, the Survey Research Center of the University of Michigan uses a three digit telescoping code to record the wide variety of responses to questions concerning individual likes or dislikes about political parties and candidates for public office. The first digit of this code signifies whether the response is positive or negative about the candidate or his party. The second digit of the code signifies the issue referred to by the response—government economy, foreign policy, etc. The third digit identifies the exact character of the response—against Medicare or for a stronger policy in Berlin. This coding technique enables the researcher to analyze responses according to the depth he chooses.

USE "EMPIRICAL" CODING WHEREVER POSSIBLE

A distinction can be made between "empirical" and "analytical" coding: empirical coding means recording the data as closely as possible to its original detail; analytical coding means recording the data according to some preconceived scheme that uses broader categories, thus disregarding original detail. The importance of empirical coding has been stressed and elaborated in Bisco's memo, "Policies and Standards for Coding Data":

> In other words, as much as possible of the original detail elicited by a data collecting process or device should be preserved in machinable form.
>
> One example of the desirability of empirical coding is the age variable. Often coders are instructed to assign a person to some age category, like 18-25. If, as is often the case for political science, it is necessary to restrict analysis to persons twenty-one and over, the researcher must either go back to the original interview schedule and recode the age information or introduce an error or bias factor by some form of estimation. Often, original schedules have been destroyed or are not conveniently available for recoding.
>
> Another example is the variety of verbal material elicited by an open-ended question. This material is rich in perceptual, evaluative, cognitive, and attitudinal materials which are often lost by assigning respondents to one of five or six categories. . . .
>
> Besides making data less useful to other analysts, coding practices tailored to one research criterion may ultimately limit the researcher's own investigation in unfortunate ways. First a category is at the nominal level while the original age gives an interval measure [see Chapter VII for a discussion of levels of measurement]. New statistics have been and will continue to be developed which exploit the fact of more information, and which allow an intermix of nominal and ordinal, nominal and interval, or interval and ordinal data. Second, a particular grouping or categorization may hinder comparison of a distribution or statistic with criterion data, e.g., the Census, or with results of prior analyses. Third, coding error is less, and coding speed can be greater when the coder does not have to evaluate the data or make analytic type distinctions. For example, having a coder decide whether a particular response means the interviewee considered a presidential candidate a "liberal" as opposed to a "conservative" can lead to considerable unreliability and questions about validity. Having the coder assign a numeric code which indicates the actual response . . . can lead to much greater reliability and validity. Finally, present data processing capabilities make the construction of indexes, scales, and groupings more reliable and precise than by human coding.[13]

USE "NATURAL" CODING WHEREVER POSSIBLE

When recording data that is quantitative in fact or in principle, the "natural" values or ordering should be captured in the codes. For example, the number of chambers in a legislature should be coded 1 or 2 respectively for unicameral or bicameral legislatures. Interview responses like "never," "seldom," and "often" should be coded 1, 2, and 3, instead of 3, 2, and 1. A "high" response should be coded with a larger number than a "low" response. The use of natural coding reduces coding error and simplifies subsequent analysis of the data.

AVOID THE USE OF A BLANK SPACE AS A CODING CATEGORY

Statistical programs are commonly written in problem-oriented computer languages (see Chapter IV) that do not make easy distinctions between blank spaces and zero punches. Because these programs interpret blanks as zeros, a blank space ordinarily should not be used as a coding category. There may be exceptions to this rule. The principle of natural coding, as discussed above, suggests using o to code "none" or "zero" when these are the actual values assumed by the variable—such as the percentage of Negroes in an all-white county. However, sometimes the information for these variables is missing, and it is tempting to use a blank space to indicate this lack of information. In fact, some special computer programs *are* designed to handle incomplete data by distinguishing between blanks and zeros in the columns. Unless the researcher intends to process his data with such a program, he is advised to adopt a numerical coding category to indicate "no information."

PROVIDE FOR CONSISTENCY IN CODING

The elaboration of this suggestion is also taken from Bisco's "Policies and Standards for Coding Data";

> There are several advantages in intra-study consistency. First, coders can more easily "know" the code; the coders do not have to look up every code, and coding is more reliable because there is less chance of mis-reading code categories . . .
> In preparing codes it is also useful to make them as compatible as possible with the codes used in other data collec-

tions. . . . Increasingly, analysis requires the combination of
several different types of data—like interview material from
both Congressmen and constituents—or the pooling of several collections in order to have a reliable estimate of some
parameter.

. . . .

The major method of attaining maximum compatibility is
agreement among researchers on a number of coding conventions—e.g., for missing data, for identification, etc.[14]

Appendix B reprints what Bisco describes as "a number of conventions which we have developed, or on which we have found
an already prevailing consensus, in the preparation of the ICPR
archives." They are reprinted in this book to promote the development of consistent procedures among the studies.

The "basic scheme" of the coding conventions in Appendix B
is as follows:

Code Content
0 Inapplicable
1 "Yes" ("good" or most positive)
2
3
4
5 "No" ("bad" or least positive)
6
7 "Other" (not specified in previous coding categories)
8 "I don't know" (offered by the respondent)
9 "Not ascertained" (given by the coder)

This scheme ascribes a "permanent" meaning to codes 0, 1, 5, 7,
8, and 9. If "yes" or "no" answers are the only responses to a
given question, no use is made of codes 2, 3, 4, and 6. This specific assignment of codes may not be desirable for some computer
programs. Chapter VI of this handbook describes a computer
program that processes the data most efficiently when code
numbers are used consecutively, so that "no" should become
code 2; "other," code 3; "I don't know," code 4; and "not ascertained," code 5. (The program treats the 0 code, which is almost
universally regarded as the "not applicable" or "no information"
code, as less than 1 and does not put it in the high order position
after 9.)

Because some researchers may use programs that presume "consecutive" coding, the "jumped" coding in the scheme above may not be suitable. For our purposes, the important feature in that coding scheme lies not in ascribing "permanent" meanings to certain code numbers but in reserving low-order digits (excluding o) for "substantive" categories and following them with the higher code numbers for "other," "don't know," and "not ascertained" categories. This coding practice permits these categories to be excluded from statistical computations, if desired, by exercising an option on some computer programs to "lop off" certain high order digits. The cross-classification program discussed in Chapter VI contains such an option.

SUGGESTIONS FOR MANAGING DATA COLLECTIONS

The idea of "managing" data collections is relatively new in political research. Traditionally, political research has been conducted with library materials and the data collected in the form of notes written or typed on index cards. The form and legibility of these notes depend on the style and temperament of the individual scholar. Insofar as these data collections are "managed," they are managed solely for the *immediate* use of the *original* investigator, who labels and sorts the cards to suit his research. After the study is completed, the note cards are sometimes discarded. If not, they are seldom labeled, sorted, and stored in a manner that facilitates their later use by the same scholar for a different study. It is even more rare for the scholar to concern himself with making his data available for use by others. Data management, as ordinarily practiced with information gathered through library research, is oriented toward the needs of the original investigator. As such, it is a short-run operation of limited scope.

In contrast, collections of punchcard data usually are managed with an eye toward broad, long-run considerations. As mentioned in Chapter I, the *flexibility* and *reproducibility* features of punchcard data promote pooling and sharing data collections. Proper management permits information to be understood and analyzed by scholars not involved at the data gathering stage and it enables the original investigator to return to the data for research on other topics. The suggestions offered in this section are prompted by such broad, long-run considerations.

IDENTIFICATION CODES

A useful but not necessarily iron-clad distinction may be drawn between *identification* and *variable* coding. The distinction hinges on whether the code *identifies the things* being studied (people, objects, or events) or whether it tells the *values* of the variables associated with the things under study. Up to this point, virtually all our discussion of coding has been concerned with variable coding. The distinction between the two types of codes should become clear in the following discussion of the purpose of identification coding.

A straightforward way of recording observations on people, objects, or events is to use a separate card for each unit of observation, organizing the data by individual persons, objects, or events. For example, county election returns for the office of President would be recorded on 100 separate cards for a state with 100 counties. These cards must be identified exactly as to which card contains the votes cast in which county. This is accomplished by an identification code. In the election returns example, the identification can be made by assigning a number from 001 to 100 to each of the counties and punching this number on the card in a three-column field. The information punched in this field is ordinarily not regarded as a variable to be used in analysis but as a means of identifying counties in the study.

In addition to identifying the county for which the vote has been recorded, the researcher may also want to know the election *year* and the *office* being contested. If election data have been collected for many states, he will need to know the *state* in which the election was held. And if there are other types of punchcard data available, he must be able to identify the election *studies* themselves. All this information can be recorded by use of identification codes.

In general, the need for extensive identifying information becomes acute when a library's collection of punchcard holdings grows. Researchers have sometimes identified various studies by punching them on cards of different colors or by varying the corner cuts on cards from two different studies. This method of identification might serve if the number of studies in the library is small and the users of the data few. Supplies of different colored card stock become exhausted, however, and careful markings are easily destroyed when the cards are reproduced.

The answer to this problem lies in punching needed identification directly into the cards themselves. Each card in the library should be uniquely identifiable by means of codes punched in certain columns. Backstrom and Hursh contend that adopting a consistent format for identification items "will make life easier study-to-study with the mere knowledge that case numbers, study numbers, and the like can always be found in the same columns."[15] Although they suggest reserving the last few columns of a card for this identifying information, most computer programs and prominent data-gathering agencies favor using the *first* few fields on a card for identifying information.[16]

Systems of identification codes are always established with some specific collection of data holdings in mind, although certain features are common to all such systems. This discussion of identification codes will be illustrated by studies on file in Northwestern's Political Data Library. Most of the holdings in this library were completed or initiated under a Social Science Research Council grant to Professor Charles S. Hyneman of Indiana University.[17] The amount of punchcard data collected under Professor Hyneman's supervision grew to such proportions that it became necessary to establish identification codes for geographical *areas* to which the data pertained, for *studies* that prompted the collection of the data, for *years* covered by the data, and for governmental *institutions* being studied—in addition to *individual* observational units with the studies.

Approximately the first ten columns of every data card produced in the SSRC project at Indiana were reserved for identification purposes. The proper location of any stray data card in the library could be established simply by examining the identification codes at the left-hand side of the card. Various methods were devised for coding this identifying information. It later was learned that these coding methods had names and were described in the IBM General Information Manual, *Coding Methods*.[18] The following discussion of identification codes used in the Indiana SSRC Project refers to names and descriptions contained in that manual. This identification system is presented as a concrete example of identification coding for a political data library.

SEQUENCE CODES

This is the simplest code to use, for it simply assigns consecutive numbers to items in a list. Assigning identification numbers to counties according to their alphabetical ordering, as in the election returns example, produces a sequence coding. Because it bears no relation to characteristics of the coded items, a sequence code requires a code book to decipher the identification. The sequence code's advantage is its ability to code an unlimited number of items by using the fewest possible digits.

Most of the information collected at Indiana was on state politics. Columns 1-2 of every card in the data library were reserved for a sequence code identifying the *state* for which data had been gathered. A glance at these columns told an important fact about the data. When the data holdings eventually extended beyond the American states to roll call voting in the United Nations, the code number oo was used in these columns.

In a simple sequence code, new items in a list are assigned the next-higher unused numbers. It should be noted, however, that the assignment of next-higher code numbers invalidates whatever order existed in the original listing. In particular, a simple sequence code devised for an alphabetical listing of the members of the United Nations in 1945 would have been disrupted as soon as the first new nation was admitted. By use of a *complete* sequence code, however, it is possible to preserve alphabetical order of the items while keeping the codes originally assigned to items in the list. The idea behind a complete sequence code is to assign original code numbers by *tens* instead of *units*. A complete sequence code established for the United Nations in 1945 might have accommodated the new nations as follows:

Original Member: 1945	*Code*	*Nations admitted later (year)*
	.	
	.	
	.	
	004	Afghanistan (1946)
	.	
	006	Albania (1955)
	.	
	008	Algeria (1962)
	.	
Argentina	010	
	.	
	.	
Australia	020	
	.	
	025	Austria (1955)
	.	
Belgium	030	
	.	
	.	
Bolivia	040	
	etc.	

When using complete sequence coding, thought must be given to the universe from which the listing will be drawn so that enough code numbers are left unassigned to accommodate new entries.

BLOCK CODES

This code divides a series of consecutive numbers into blocks, each block being reserved for groups of items having a common characteristic. This system uses few code digits to identify each item, but expansion of the code to include additional items within each block is limited to those numbers left unassigned when the code was originally established.

Columns 3-4 on every card in the data library are reserved for a block code identifying the type of data gathered. The first digit in this two-digit "study code" indicates whether the data pertain to legislators, other public officials, counties, or public documents. The second digit indicates exactly what type of data have been gathered in these studies.[19]

Meaning of first digit	Code	Description of study
Data gathered on members of the legislature	10	Biographical information
	11	Roll call votes in lower chamber
	12	Roll call votes in upper chamber
	13	Legislative committee assignments
	14	Interviews with legislative candidates
	1-	
	1-	unassigned
	1-	
Data gathered on other public officials	2-	unassigned
	2-	
	25	Survey of county officials
	2-	
	2-	unassigned
Data gathered on counties or other areas	30	Census information
	31	County voting returns
	3-	
	3-	unassigned
Data gathered on public documents	41	Descriptions of votes in lower chamber
	42	Descriptions of votes in upper chamber
	43	Histories of legislative bills
	4-	
	4-	unassigned
unassigned	5-	
	6-	
	7-	unassigned
	8-	
	9-	

Many academic and professional data-gathering organizations organize their studies by means of block codes, which are sometimes referred to as "study numbers" or "project numbers" instead of study codes.

SIGNIFICANT DIGITS CODE

In this system, all or some of the code digits describe some characteristic of the items themselves. The most important advantage of a significant digit code is reduction or complete elimination of the decoding usually required with sequence or block codes. The user familiar with the item characteristics can recognize individual items from the code itself.

Columns 5-6 in some of the Indiana legislative studies provide a simple example of a significant digits code. This field contains the last two digits of the year in which the legislative session was held. Data that pertain to a legislative session held in 1961 are punched *61* in columns 5-6. A similar practice was followed in identifying election years for punchcards containing election returns. Roll call votes taken in the various committees of the United Nations were also identified with significant digit codes: *1* for votes taken in the First Committee, *2* for votes taken in the Second Committee, and so on. As a final example of significant digit coding, *1* is used as a code for the lower chamber of a legislature and *2* as a code for the upper chamber.[20]

GROUP CLASSIFICATION CODES

These designate major and minor data classifications by successive fields on the card. The number of fields required in the code is determined by the number of different classifications necessary to identify the data properly. The examples of sequence, block, and significant digit coding discussed above may all be reconsidered in terms of a "grand" group classification code. The first field in this grand or master code indicates the state to which the data pertain. The second field describes the nature of the data collected. The third field in most of the studies reveals the year for which the data were collected. Additional fields provide further identification about the observational unit, resulting in each data card in the library having a unique identification number. The entire group classification code for the committee assignments held by former State Representative Birch Bayh in the 1959 Indiana General Assembly occupies the first ten columns on the data card:

Column Number	Identification code
1-2	"12" (Identifies the state, Indiana)
3-4	"13" (Identifies the study, Legislative Committee Assignments)
5-6	"59" (Identifies the year of the session, 1959)
7	"1" (Identifies the lower chamber of the legislature)
8-10	"056" (Identifies the member in the legislature, Birch Bayh, now U.S. Senator from Indiana)

The codes and descriptions for the rest of this legislative committee assignment study are contained in Appendix A-5.

IDENTIFICATION OF DIFFERENT CARDS FOR THE SAME CASE

Two or more cards may be needed to record all necessary information about a particular case—be it a person, object, or event. All cards for a given case in the study should carry identical identification codes with the exception of a code disclosing the sequence number of each card within each case: *1* for the first card of a given case, *2* for the second card, and so on. This code is called a "card number" or "deck number."

Most computer programs require that input be arranged so that all cards for a given case are sorted together in sequence, followed by all cards for the next case, and so on. This can be done quite rapidly on the counter-sorter—sorting first on the card number and then on the case numbers. Card sorting is not always a fool-proof operation, however, and a mistake in ordering cards can be crucial, as Figure V-1 illustrates.

In Figure V-1, the second card for the second case is misplaced. Thus the computer will read the *first* card of the *third* case in place of the misplaced card. It will then read the *second* card in the third case as the first one in that case, and so on until the misplaced card is encountered and proper sequencing is restored. Because the information would be read incorrectly into the computer, the results of the analysis would be hopelessly in error.

FIGURE V-1

ONE CARD MISPLACED IN SEQUENCING OF CARDS BY CASE NUMBER

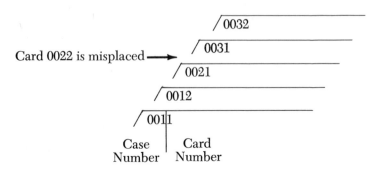

It is, therefore, important that cards be arranged in proper order before being fed into the computer. The collator is the appropriate machine for checking card sequence. But, unfortunately, the collator is not a common piece of equipment in university computing centers, and sequence checks are difficult to make without it. In the absence of a collator, sequence checks are made either by going through the interpreted cards one by one or by examining a listing of the cards prepared by the tabulator (Chapter III describes the collator, interpreter, and tabulator).

But with a little planning, an easy and surprisingly effective check can be made without special equipment each time data are submitted for processing. If the different cards for each case in a given study are reproduced on different colored stock, then the process of sorting cards into sequence within each case will cause colored cards to be alternated, e.g., a blue card for the *first* card in the first case, a yellow one for the *second* card, a pink one for the *third* card, a blue card for the first card in the *second case,* and so on. The result will be a uniform hue across the top of the cards after they have been tapped together and smoothed out. If the cards are all properly arranged in sequence, this hue will be unbroken across the top of the entire study. But if one of the cards is out of order, two cards of different color that ordinarily are separated will be placed together, producing a thin but detectable stripe across the top of the cards.

This seemingly trivial method can help a researcher avoid considerable frustration and can save computer time by detecting errors in card ordering. If it is not feasible to reproduce cards on different color stock, the same effect can be obtained by carefully marking the tops of the separate decks with different colored felt-tip markers.

BASIC VARIABLES AND BLANK COLUMNS

In the days of data processing on the counter-sorter, it was a wise practice to repeat "basic" variables on each card if the study had two or more cards per case. Thus, any variable in the study could be easily cross-tabulated with basic variables. Although this practice has little importance in computer processing, it still has some application. For example, if the variable is of help in checking marginal totals for errors, then it may be useful to repeat the variable across all the cards in a given case. Except for such special instances, this practice is not of much advantage today.

It used to be advantageous to leave some blank columns on a card so that additional variables could be entered later for purposes of cross-tabulation. Today this practice is still useful for accommodating *new* measures constructed from two or more other variables. This is an especially common procedure with survey research data, from which responses to several questions about the same topic might be combined to form a summary measure of attitude. Providing some card columns to contain new measures after they have been constructed eliminates the necessity of constructing them each time the data are analyzed.

HOUSEKEEPING HINTS

The following paragraphs contain a series of miscellaneous remarks. Some may be obvious, but all deserve to be considered in keeping house for a collection of punchcard data. It is, of course, important to exercise some control over the conditions under which cards are stored. They should always be kept under pressure; this helps keep them from curling, which in turn helps prevent card jams in processing operations. Humid conditions also cause curling, and storage rooms should be air-conditioned or dehumidified.

The cards will suffer less from handling if the corner-cuts are observed so that right and left corner-cut cards are not mixed together in processing—life can be made easier in this regard if only *one* type of corner-cut is stocked. In general, information can be retrieved more easily if some description of the data is written across the top of the cards with a felt-tip marker. The amount of handling is reduced as the cards no longer need be pulled out in order to examine identification codes. The first and last cards in the study get the most wear and are most likely to be lost if constantly pulled out. These cards should be marked "first" and "last" so their presence can be detected easily when the cards are removed for processing.

USING PUNCHCARDS IN TEACHING ACTIVITIES

Punchcards can be used in introducing students—especially undergraduates—to political research. The experience of actually doing their own research with punchcard data and data processing equipment is a stimulating one for students at all levels. In making these data available for student use, it is to be expected that mistakes and ruined cards will result, but this is the way learning occurs. To guard against ruined data, students should be given duplicate decks for their own use. If they ruin their data cards, the originals still are available for reproducing. This way only some paper is lost, and paper is cheap.

PUTTING DATA ON MAGNETIC TAPE

Magnetic tape should be considered as an information-carrying medium if the number of cards in a given study is large—more than one box, or 2,000 cards. The tape facilitates handling large numbers of cases and insures that case sequencing cannot be charged through an accident in handling cards.

Magnetic tape has a drawback in teaching data processing methods to beginners. Data cannot be "seen" when they are recorded on tape, and the ability to see the information is an important property of the punchcard when instruction is being given in this new research methodology.

NOTES

¹ An extensive collection of papers describing the applications of mechanical equipment to social science research during the early 1930's can be found in G. W. Baehne (ed.), *Practical Applications of the Punched Card Method in Colleges and Universities* (New York: Columbia University Press, 1935).

² A detailed discussion of data processing on the counter-sorter is given in Appendix C of Herbert Hyman's *Survey Design and Analysis* (Glencoe, Ill.: The Free Press, 1955).

³ Charles H. Backstrom and Gerald D. Hursh, *Survey Research* (Evanston: Northwestern University Press, 1963), p. 162.

⁴ The pressures toward the 80 column standard worked both ways. Researchers not only tried to squeeze down to 80 columns but they also tended to include variables to fill out empty columns. A surprisingly large number of studies happened to fit exactly on one card.

⁵ E. A. Hooton once managed to record 125 items of anthropometric information on an 80 column punchcard. See his chapter, "Anthropology," in G. W. Baehne (ed.), *Practical Applications of the Punched Card Method in Colleges and Universities* (New York: Columbia University Press, 1935), pp. 383-88.

⁶ Robert S. McCarger, "Data Processing and Planning," in Richard D. Duke (ed.), *Automatic Data Processing: Its Application to Urban Planning* (East Lansing: Institute for Community Development and Services, Michigan State University, 1961), p. 81.

⁷ It should be pointed out that some early computers, like the IBM 650, also imposed severe restrictions on the format of data cards. The 650 would normally accept information only in fixed-field widths—e.g., 5, 8, or 10 columns.

⁸ McCarger, *op. cit.*, p. 79.

⁹ Fred Gruenberger, *Computing Manual* (Madison: The University of Wisconsin Press, 1952), p. 4.

¹⁰Backstrom and Hursh, *op. cit.*, p. 154.

¹¹*Ibid.*, pp. 153-59.

¹²Ralph L. Bisco, "Information Services for Political Science: Progress and Prospects," paper delivered at the 1964 Annual Meeting of the American Political Science Association, Chicago, pp. 15-16.

¹³Ralph L. Bisco, "Policies and Standards for Coding Data," Inter-University Consortium for Political Research Memorandum, 1964 (multilith, 10 pp.), pp. 4-6.

¹⁴*Ibid.*, pp. 9-10.

¹⁵Backstrom and Hursh, *op. cit.*, p. 116.

[16]The Inter-University Consortium for Political Research, for example, requires that those who request analysis decks prepared from studies on file in its data repository allow seven columns at the beginning of the analysis deck for identifying information.

[17]Professor Hyneman received the grant in 1957 for a three year study of public policy formation in Indiana. See Charles S. Hyneman, "The Collection and Uses of Political Data," *Citizenship Clearing House Bulletin,* 7 (March, 1959), 2-3. Part of the grant was used to extend the data on legislative personnel collected previously and to pioneer in collecting new types of data relating to other aspects of public policy formation in state government. The Indiana political system provided the laboratory in which research techniques were developed and initially applied. The "data library" that resulted was eventually expanded to include information on other states, but most of the holdings relate to Indiana politics. (I was associated with the project during my graduate study at Indiana University. Professor Hyneman provided me with duplicated sets of the data cards when I moved to Northwestern in 1961.)

[18]International Business Machines Corporation. Data Processing Division, White Plains, N. Y., undated, Form #F20-8093.

[19]See footnote 17 for background information on the data library. The codes and card formats of most studies in the data library are contained in the Appendices to this book. Study 31 is in Appendix A-1; Study 10 in Appendix A-3; Studies 11 and 12 in Appendix A-4; Study 13 in Appendix A-5; and Study 43 in Appendix A-6.

[20]Note the similarity between "significant digits" identification coding and "natural" coding for variables, page 136.

CHAPTER VI

PROCESSING QUALITATIVE DATA:
A GENERAL CROSS-
CLASSIFICATION PROGRAM

Political scientists frequently collect or arrange their data in categories or classes. This often is done because the qualitative nature of some political data will support no form of measurement other than "nominal" or "classificatory" scaling.[1] Only the simplest statistical operations (e.g., counting and tallying) can be performed on such data. Judges' party affiliations and court decisions are examples of *qualitative* political information that invite little more than categorization or classification.

Information that is fundamentally or conceptually *quantitative* in nature is also frequently categorized by political scientists. Classifying nations into "high," "medium," and "low" categories according to military expenditures involves categorization of data that are *fundamentally* quantitative in nature. The classification of nations into similar groupings according to degree of economic development involves categorizing a variable that is *conceptually* quantifiable but is difficult to measure with precision.

CROSS-CLASSIFICATIONS AND COMPUTERS

How can punchcards and computers help process such information? Qualitative data recorded in categories on punchcards can, of course, be rapidly counted and tallied into frequency distributions with the use of a computer, or even a counter-sorter. An example of an elementary statistical table prepared from punchcard data is Table VI-1, which shows, in percentages, the distribution of responses to an interview question on voting preferences asked in a pre-election sample survey of more than one thousand people in California.

Counting the number of code punches in given fields and calculating percentages is a simple operation for any computer. But

TABLE VI-1

PRESIDENTIAL PREFERENCES OF A SAMPLE OF CALIFORNIA
VOTERS, ASKED NOVEMBER 3, 1960[a]

Kennedy	Nixon	Undecided	(N)
50%	44%	6%	(1,157)

[a]Adapted from a table in Lee and Buchanan.[2]

despite its simplicity to the computer, the researcher may find
the operation quite valuable. Although in *calendar time* the researcher literally may find it faster to stand for hours in front of a
hot counter-sorter producing simple frequency distributions of
responses to each of a hundred questions asked in a survey, he
probably will consider it a more expeditious and better use of his
time to use a computer to do the same job with greater accuracy
in one minute or less.

A basic set of frequency distributions for each variable is often
desired at the beginning of a study, but few if any research under-
takings are terminated after merely disclosing a profile of the
data through frequency of percentage distributions. The next
step involves making comparisons among various response-cate-
gories. Many problems of political research involve grouping
cases or responses by categories for one variable and then examining their response distributions on a second variable. The data
presented in Table VI-1 may be re-analyzed in this manner. The
respondents can be grouped according to their party affiliations
and the percentage distributions for "Republicans" and "Democrats" can be examined separately. This is done in Table VI-2.

A tabular presentation of this form is sometimes referred to as
a "cross-classification," "cross-tabulation," or "contingency table."[4]
Because only two variables are cross-classified in the table, it is
also commonly called a "bivariate" distribution. This manner of
presenting data is widely used in the social sciences. Ames has
called it "the mainstay of the sociologist," who, like the political
scientist, asks, "Does any association exist between the variables
determining a cross-classification? Can we say anything about

TABLE VI-2

PRESIDENTIAL PREFERENCES OF A SAMPLE OF CALIFORNIA
VOTERS IN 1960, BY PARTY[a]

Party Affiliation	Kennedy	Nixon	Undecided	(N)
Republican	11%	85%	4%	(470)
Democrat	78	16	6	(687)

[a]From a table in Lee and Buchanan.[3]

the direction of the association? And, finally, how strong is the association?"[5]

The data presented in Table VI-2 clearly show an association between party affiliation and voting preference. Republicans prefer Nixon, and Democrats prefer Kennedy. The *strength* of this relationship must be determined with suitable statistical techniques, which will not be discussed here.

Cross-classifications such as this can be prepared by using a counter-sorter to separate the sample into Republicans and Democrats and to tally the number of "Kennedy," "Nixon," and "Undecided" responses within each category. Again, however, the computer saves time and effort when many tables are needed. The same computer programs that prepare simple frequency and percentage distributions once were used to produce contingency tables. The data were merely sorted into the required classifications before being read into the computer, and the machine calculated a percentage distribution for each classification of cards it read. The researcher was required to make a separate pass on the machine for each variable he wanted to use in cross-classifying his data. If he wanted to introduce a third variable— such as religion—into the analysis, he had to separate his Republican and Democratic sets into such religious subsets as Protestants and Catholics. He then had four physically distinct sets of cards and could instruct the computer to prepare a percentage distribution for each, as shown in Table VI-3.

TABLE VI-3

PRESIDENTIAL PREFERENCES OF A SAMPLE OF CALIFORNIA
VOTERS IN 1960, BY RELIGION AND PARTY[a]

Religion and Party		Kennedy	Nixon	Undecided	(N)
Protestants	Republicans	6%	90%	4%	(345)
	Democrats	70	23	7	(367)
Catholics	Republicans	31	64	5	(81)
	Democrats	91	6	3	(198)

[a]From a table in Lee and Buchanan.[6]

By preparing separate cross-classifications of party and voting
preferences for Protestants and Catholics, "religion" is, in effect,
"held constant" as a third variable. For this sample of voters,
about nine out of ten Protestant Republicans preferred Nixon
and an equal proportion of Catholic Democrats preferred Kennedy. Catholic Republicans, however, showed somewhat greater
preference for the Catholic Kennedy than did Protestant Democrats for the Protestant Nixon, but there were far fewer Catholic
Republicans than Protestant Democrats. The potential value of
studying more than two variables at one time can be seen even
in this elementary example of *multivariate* analysis.

It should be noted that, when the computer is used to prepare
cross-classifications by counting frequencies within sets and subsets in this manner, it is being operated precisely like an over-
grown counter-sorter. However, a large-scale general-purpose
computer has the ability to operate in a grander fashion in making cross-classifications. It can accept data cards in an unordered
form and can sort internally by sets and subsets to hold one or
more variables constant. Moreover, it can handle more than
twelve categories (one column) of information per variable, automatically recode the data to pre-determined categories, automatically collapse tables by rows or columns, calculate a variety
of statistical measures to determine the strength of association
between variables, and clearly label the tables it produces in the
process. All that is needed to put the capabilities of the computer

to better use in constructing cross-classifications in this way is an appropriate program.

As noted in Chapter IV, programming requirements figure prominently in the effective use of computers in research. At least two writers have addressed themselves specifically to problems of developing suitable cross-classification programs for individual research problems. James Farmer has reviewed three alternative methods for using the computer to cross-classify variables: (a) programming each problem separately by hand methods, (b) using one general distribution program on all problems, and (c) using a program generator that provides a different program for each problem.[7]

Farmer has observed that the first alternative offered most efficient use of the computer but wasted programming skills, which most social scientists do not possess, by demanding that basically similar programs be written for every problem. He concluded that the second alternative—the general cross-classification program—probably would not fit the processing requirements of most research problems and would certainly be least efficient in terms of computer time. The program generator, which requires familiarity with programming languages and machine operation, was selected as an acceptable compromise solution.

Farmer's compromise alternative was challenged later by Ames, who wanted to make the computer available for student and faculty research in the University of North Carolina's sociology department. Ames rejected the use of a program generator as an impractical alternative because it requires

> a new orientation on the part of the user. This is not to say that he is incapable of acquiring this knowledge, but that it is outside of the realm of his immediate activity. He is not so much interested in the computer as in what the computer can do for him.[8]

Ames believed that, despite the inefficiencies of running such a program on a computer, a better choice was a general or "unitary program which summarizes as much of the essence of the data as is possible, even though some of the computations will be useless to a particular user."[9] He discussed a unitary program for the UNIVAC 1105 computer that has been used successfully by many researchers untrained in the technical details of machine operation or computer programming.

SOME COMPUTER PROGRAMS FOR CROSS-CLASSIFICATIONS

Some aspects of computer programming were discussed in Chapter IV, which argued that a working knowledge of programming language was essential for a fully effective use of computers in a variety of research problems. The same chapter, however, also acknowledged the definite value of general programs for performing common data processing functions. Fortunately, several general programs for preparing cross-classifications from raw data are now available. When the features of these programs meet the research problem's requirements, they usually provide a ready and satisfying data processing solution to even the uninitiated researcher—if he studies the instructions carefully and asks questions along the way.

Undoubtedly there must be dozens of different cross-classification programs in operation across the country; the problem lies in learning about them. My search through IBM's "Catalog of Programs"[10] and the computer program abstracts published in *Behavioral Science* led to several programs for preparing frequency counts but few constructed contingency tables from raw, ungrouped data fed directly into the machine. Brief descriptions will be presented of those that qualify as general cross-classification programs. They will be followed by a detailed write-up of the cross-classification program in common use for political research at Northwestern University.

NCG09: Contingency Table Analysis with Kendall's Tau-c, in use at the University of North Carolina as of December 15, 1962. This is the program referred to above by Ames. Written for a UNIVAC 1105 computer, it generates thirty contingency tables per pass for single-column data with a maximum of twelve categories for each variable. There apparently is no practical limit to the number of cases that can be processed at any one time. The program will produce only bivariate tables, and cards must be sorted into sub-categories before processing if one wants to introduce a third variable as a constant. The program computes chi-square values, Kendall's tau-c, levels of significance for both statistics, means, medians, and percentages by rows or for the grand total. There are no provisions for labeling the variables on the output.

BMD02S: Contingency Table Analysis, included in the 1964 edition of *Biomedical Computer Programs*, the School of Medicine, UCLA.[11] BMD02S has no practical limit on the number of cases, number of variables, or number of tables it can process. It can compute chi-square, the contingency coefficient, a maximum likelihood ratio and percentages by rows, columns, and grand total. It can recode any given variable up to ten different ways, accommodate two-digit data in 22 x 22 tables, and collapse tables automatically if the number of observations in a given row or column does not exceed a previously established value. There is no provision for either introducing a third variable into the analysis or for labeling output tables with descriptions of the variables.

BMD08D: Cross Tabulation with Variable Stacking, also included in the 1964 edition of *Biomedical Computer Programs*. BMD08D will handle up to 1,500 cases and 100 variables, and there is no practical limit to the number of tables that can be produced on any run. It will compute chi-square, means, standard deviations, and correlation coefficients (presumably product-moment) for each table, but it will *not* compute percentages. It can recode any variable in a variety of ways, accommodate two-digit data in 34 x 99 tables, and collapse tables as instructed. There are provisions for controlling as many as four variables with the use of the variable "stacking" recoding feature. Only six alphanumeric characters can be used for labeling the output tables.

BMD09D: Cross Tabulation for Incomplete Data, also in the 1964 edition of *Biomedical Computer Programs*. BMD09D will handle as many as 2,000 cases and 100 variables, and there is no practical limit to the number of tables it can process. It will only compute a correlation coefficient for the table. It can recode any variable a variety of ways, accommodate two-digit data in a 20 x 20 table, and collapse categories. Missing values can be identified and eliminated from the analysis. There is no provision for introducing a third variable into the analysis and none for labeling output tables with descriptions of the variables.

BIVARIATE STATISTICS: In use as of January, 1964 at the Institute for Social Research, the University of Michigan. The program, also referred to as "Filter-tau," can process an apparently unlimited number of cases and up to 200 variables with no limit on the number of tables that can be prepared, although only 90 are prepared on a single computer pass. It will compute chi-square, Kendall tau-a and tau-b, the contingency coefficient, Goodman-Kruskal gamma, and percentages by row, columns, and grand total. It cannot recode variables, and handles only one column in 12 x 12 tables, but it can eliminate categories at either end of the coding range. There is a provision for introducing a third variable into the analysis as a control variable, and there is one for labeling output tables, but only with 18 alphanumeric characters for each variable. The program provides for *weighting* cases as is sometimes necessary in sample surveys.

CPA114:   IBM 7090 program for four-fold tables published in *Behavioral Science*, 8 (January, 1963), p. 86 (as Computer Program Abstract 114 by Curtis R. Miller, Pacific State Hospital, Pomona, California). It will process 50 variables for 99,999 cases. It produces these four-fold table statistics: chi-square, chi-square with Yates correction, phi coefficient, Fisher's exact test, contingency coefficient, coefficients of concordance, and cosine-phi approximations to the tetrachoric r. It will recode variables according to instructions but will produce *only* four-fold tables, i.e., bivariate distributions of dichotomous data. There is no provision for introducing a third variable into the analysis.

All the preceding programs can prepare cross-classifications from raw data cards read directly into a computer, and each has some special features to recommend its use for a particular purpose. Perhaps many other useful cross-classification programs currently are available, but information about their existence and operation is hard to obtain. Adequate channels for exchanging programs and programming ideas in behavioral research have not yet been developed.

This handbook provides an opportunity for acquainting an audience of potential users with a general cross-classification program that has been helpful in a wide variety of research problems in the behavioral sciences at Northwestern University.

Experienced computer users may be interested in special features
of the program, and beginners in this type of research may find an
extensive discussion of one particular program of help in understanding how a computer can process qualitative political data.

NORTHWESTERN UNIVERSITY'S NUCROS PROGRAM
FOR THE IBM 709

NUCROS was developed from the program description published by Bonato and Waxman in the October, 1961 issue of
Behavioral Science.[12] In one cycle of operation on the IBM 709,
NUCROS will accommodate up to 9,999 cases and 40 variables
in preparing up to 72 *multivariate* tables, with a maximum of four
variables per table. It can compute chi-square, the contingency
coefficient, Kendall's tau (b and c), Goodman-Kruskal gamma,
Somers' d_{xy} and d_{yx}, and percentages by rows and columns.
It can recode any given variable, accommodate two-digit
data in 20 x 99 tables, and eliminate categories at either end of
the coding range. There is also an easily operated provision for
labeling individual output tables with descriptions of every variable involved in each cross-classification.

A typical page of computer output from the NUCROS program appears in Figure VI-1. The data processed for this example
were gathered from student interviews conducted both before
and after the 1962 election in Illinois' 13th Congressional District.
Two of the questions in the interview deal with the respondent's
choice for Congressman and his party identification. The actual
coding categories and distributions of responses to these questions are given below.

Number of
Respondents Code *Who did you vote for?* (*Congressional race*)

74	0	Not applicable: did not vote at all or *not* in-terviewed *after* election
71	1	John A. Kennedy, the Democratic candidate
165	2	Donald Rumsfeld, the Republican candidate
3	3	Robert Cosbey, the "Voters for Peace" candidate
11	4	Did not vote for Congressman
14	5	Don't remember; refused to say
338		

Number of Respondents	Code	Party Identification
2	0	No information: interview terminated before asking question
48	1	Democrat: strong
38	2	Democrat: weak
34	3	Independent: leans to Democrats
31	4	Independent: leans to neither party
36	5	Independent: leans to Republicans
56	6	Republican: weak
85	7	Republican: strong
3	8	Apolitical: never follows politics, doesn't vote, etc.
5	9	Refused to say
338		

Figure VI-1 shows the table produced by the NUCROS program used to cross-classify the respondents' voting choices by their party identifications. The computer output consists of three separate sub-tables. The first one is a complete cross-classification of the total frequencies over all the coding categories for each variable. The six coding categories for the question about voting choice are arranged across the top of the table, and the total number of responses for each category can be found at the bottom of the *columns* across from the word "TOTAL." The ten coding categories for the question about party identification are arranged down the extreme left-hand side of the table. The total number of responses for each of those categories can be found in the *rows* under the word "TOT." At the bottom of that column and to the right of the word "TOTAL" is the total number of cases in the table—338.

The second sub-table expresses cell entries as percentages of the individual *column* totals *less* the frequencies in the 0 coding categories. The third sub-table expresses the cell entries as percentages of the *row* totals less the frequencies in the 0 codes. Note that the 0 codes for the rows and columns do not appear at all in the two percentagized sub-tables. Note also that when the 0 categories are excluded from these sub-tables the total number of cases drops from 338 to 262. The 76 cases "lost" in the percentagizing process had been in one or the other of the 0 categories.

The NUCROS program was designed to drop 0 codes in computing percentages (and in calculating statistics of association) in order to facilitate data analysis. It often is desirable to exclude cases of "no response" from analysis. If the 0 code is reserved for such "no information" or "not applicable" categories (as in the example), these cases are automatically kept out of statistical computations but are available for inspection in the frequency

FIGURE VI-1

NUCROS COMPUTER OUTPUT: CROSS-CLASSIFYING

VOTING CHOICE BY PARTY

```
TABLE NO.  33              VARIABLE NO. 33  WHO DID YOU VOTE FOR
                     VRS.  VARIABLE NO. 17  PARTY IDENTIFICATION
TABLE SIZE =   6  BY  10

                TOT     0    1    2    3    4    5

     0           2      0    0    1    0    0    1
     1          48     10   30    4    0    3    1
     2          38     10   19    6    0    1    2
     3          34      6   13    8    2    2    3
     4          31      7    5   14    0    1    4
     5          36      8    1   26    1    0    0
     6          56     14    2   36    0    3    1
     7          85     16    0   69    0    0    0
     8           3      0    0    1    0    1    1
     9           5      3    1    0    0    0    1

   TOTAL       338     74   71  165    3   11   14


PERCENTS BY COLUMN FROM THE ABOVE MATRIX

     1          38            42.3   2.4  0.   27.3   7.7
     2          28            26.8   3.7  0.    9.1  15.4
     3          28            18.3   4.9 66.7  18.2  23.1
     4          24             7.0   8.5  0.    9.1  30.8
     5          28             1.4  15.9 33.3  0.    0.
     6          42             2.8  22.0  0.   27.3   7.7
     7          69             0.   42.1  0.   0.    0.
     8           3             0.    0.6  0.    9.1   7.7
     9           2             1.4   0.   0.    0.    7.7

   TOTAL       262            71   164    3   11   13
```

PERCENTS BY ROW FROM THE ABOVE MATRIX

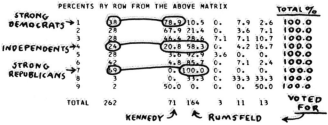

```
STRONG
DEMOCRATS   1    38    78.9 10.5  0.    7.9  2.6  100.0
            2    28    67.9 21.4  0.    3.6  7.1  100.0
            3    28    46.4 28.6  7.1   7.1 10.7  100.0
INDEPENDENTS 4   24    20.8 58.3  0.    4.2 16.7  100.0
            5    28     3.6 92.9  3.6   0.   0.   100.0
            6    42     4.8 85.7  0.    7.1  2.4  100.0
STRONG      7    69     0. 100.0  0.    0.   0.   100.0
REPUBLICANS 8     3     0.  33.3  0.   33.3 33.3  100.0
            9     2    50.0  0.   0.    0.  50.0  100.0

   TOTAL       262    71  164    3   11   13
```

TOTAL %

VOTED FOR

KENNEDY   RUMSFELD

table. If it is desirable to include these categories for any variables in the computations, they can be included automatically through the recoding process by adding the value *1* to the codes for those variables. Although it was not used in the example, the NUCROS program also provides a method to exclude from analysis the eight respondents who could not be assigned a meaningful party identification (codes 8 and 9) and the twenty-eight respondents who did not report voting for the major party candidates (codes 3, 4, and 5).[13]

The NUCROS program produces neatly printed tables that are easy to read and interpret. The strong relationship between party identification and voting choice can be seen clearly in the data of Figure VI-1. Democrats (codes 1 and 2) preferred the Democratic candidate John A. Kennedy (code 1), and Republicans (codes 6 and 7) favored the Republican candidate Donald Rumsfeld (code 2). Because we expect a person's party identification to affect his vote (not the other way around), "party identification" is referred to as an *independent* variable and "voting choice" as a *dependent* variable. Percentages usually have more meaning for the researcher if they are computed from the totals of the independent variable—in this case "party." When the data are percentagized by rows as in the third sub-table, we find that 78.9% of the strong Democrats in our sample voted for Kennedy, and 100% of the strong Republicans voted for Rumsfeld. Rumsfeld also did better with the pure Independents, getting 58.3% of their vote to Kennedy's 20.8%. (Our sample gave about 69% of the reported choices to Rumsfeld, who really got only about 62% of the total vote in the election. We were aware, however, that the sampling procedures used in this class project favored interviewing Republicans.)

Only two variables are involved in Figure VI-1. The NUCROS program, however, permits use of three- and even four-variable cross classifications. Figure VI-2 shows a portion of the computer output for a cross-classification of "voting intention" (asked before the election) by "voting choice" (asked after the election) with "party identification" held constant. Holding party identification constant means cross-classifying voting intention by voting choice for *each* coding category in the party identification variable. That is, the relationship between voting intention and voting choice is examined first for "strong Democrats" (code 1), then for "weak Democrats" (code 2), then "Independents leaning Democratic" (code 3), and so on. Once again, the "no information" category is excluded from analysis. If there are n categories in a third variable used as a "constant" or "control" variable, there will be n separate cross-classifications. If there are n categories in a third variable and m categories in a fourth variable, the number of separate cross-classifications that will be produced is $n \times m$. Regardless of the number of separate cross-classifications produced when third or fourth variables are used, all will be considered by the computer as sub-tables of only *one* main table.

FIGURE VI-2

NUCROS COMPUTER OUTPUT: CROSS-CLASSIFYING VOTING INTENTION
BY VOTING CHOICE WITH PARTY HELD CONSTANT—
ONLY FOR STRONG REPUBLICANS

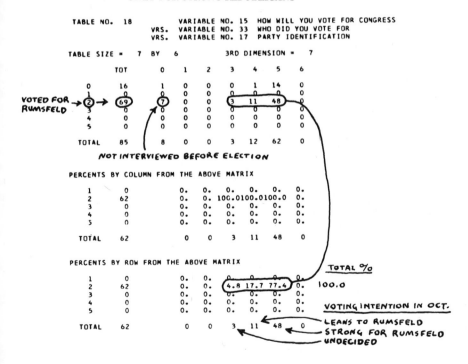

In order to interpret Figure VI-2, it is necessary to know the coding categories used in the survey to record voting intentions as expressed one month before the November election.

Code   Voting intention during the first week of October

0   No information: includes those *not* interviewed before the election
1   Strong preference for John A. Kennedy, the Democrat
2   Leans toward Kennedy, the Democrat
3   Undecided between the candidates
4   Leans toward Donald Rumsfeld, the Republican
5   Strong preference for Rumsfeld, the Republican
6   Refused to answer; rather not say

Because of space limitations, Figure VI-2 shows the cross-classification of voting intention by voting choice for only one category of party identification—the strong Republicans (code 7). It should be recalled from Figure VI-1 that 100% of the 69 strong Republicans interviewed *after* the election reported voting for Rumsfeld. The data in Figure VI-2 reveals that 7 of the 69 had not been interviewed *before* the election. But for the 62 who were asked their voting intentions in October, only 4.8% were undecided as to how they were going to vote. The remainder intended to vote for Rumsfeld and did. This left the Democratic candidate little opportunity to win votes from strong Republican voters during the campaign.

The other sub-tables for voting intention cross-classified by voting choice with party held constant are not given here, but the sub-table for strong Democrats discloses only about two-thirds intending to vote for Kennedy in October. The remainder either favored the Republican Rumsfeld or were undecided. Kennedy improved his support among strong Democrats only slightly by election time. This three-variable analysis clearly indicates that the Republican candidate for Congress from Illinois' 13th District in 1962 obtained his impressive victory by winning early and firm commitments from Republican voters while also attracting support from the Democrats—the minority party in the district.

The brief analyses of the data in these tables were carried out only to aid in interpreting computer output from the NUCROS program. The important point here is the potential value of the computer for processing qualitative or categorized data. These cross-classifications are easily, accurately, and swiftly prepared. Literally hundreds can be prepared in minutes on a large scale computer. To give a time estimate for a typical computer run using the NUCROS program, the IBM 709 required less than five minutes to produce 36 two-variable and 6 three-variable tables from 40 different variables collected on 338 cases. In the process, the computer automatically recoded three variables according to instructions specified by the researcher; computed percentages by columns and rows for each cross-classification; and neatly labeled every table and sub-table with one-line descriptions of the variables involved. Needless to say, this is considerably less than the amount of time required for humans to accomplish the same tasks—even when aided by a counter-sorter and a desk calculator.

The Northwestern University cross-classification program has been discussed at length to furnish an insight into computer processing of qualitative or categorized data. For those who are interested, an even more detailed discussion of the operating instructions for NUCROS is given in Appendix C-1, and the actual program as written in FORTRAN IV programming language is reproduced in Appendix C-2.

NOTES

[1] For a discussion of the different types of data and types of measurement see Chapter VII.
[2] Eugene C. Lee and William Buchanan, "The 1960 Election in California," *Western Political Quarterly*, 14 (March, 1961), Part II, 309-30; see p. 315.
[3] *Ibid.*, p. 318.
[4] Cross-classifications can be prepared on the counter-sorter by first sorting cards into different coding categories for one variable and then running *each* of these categories through the machine again to count the punches for a *second* variable. A detailed discussion of data processing on the counter-sorter is given in Appendix C of Herbert Hyman's *Survey Design and Analysis* (Glencoe, Ill.: The Free Press, 1955).

[5] Richard G. Ames, "Computer Programming Philosophy in a Sociology Department: Theory and Application," *Behavioral Science*, 8 (July, 1963), 257-59; see p. 257.

[6] Lee and Buchanan, *op. cit.*, p. 319.

[7] James E. Farmer, "Automated Programming for Multinominal Distribution Problems on the IBM 650," *Behavioral Science*, 6 (April, 1961), 164-66; see p. 164.

[8] Ames, *op. cit.*, p. 258.

[9] *Ibid.*

[10] IBM, *Catalog of Programs for IBM Data Processing Systems*, Document C20-8090-3, September, 1963. Monthly supplements are issued to update the catalog.

[11] See footnote 20 in Chapter IV.

[12] Roland R. Bonato and Bruce D. Waxman, "A General Cross-Classification Program for Digital Computers," *Behavioral Science*, 6 (October, 1961), 347-57. Many people at Northwestern have contributed to the development of this program. Among them are Betty Benson, David Kaufman, Charles Ladd, Malcolm Spector, and Al Wolfson.

[13] This shows the practical advantage in using low-order digits for "substantive" coding categories as discussed in Chapter V.

CHAPTER VII

PROCESSING QUANTITATIVE DATA:
A SIMPLE CORRELATION PROGRAM

The preceding chapter discussed a general cross-classification computer program for processing *qualitative* information coded into a relatively small number of discrete classes or categories. As pointed out in the introductory comments to that chapter, political data that are fundamentally *quantitative* in nature sometimes are also coded into a limited number of categories to facilitate analysis.

Cross-classifications—the "mainstay" of political research—are easier to construct and interpret if the variables have few categories. But this convenience in dealing with simple cross-classifications is achieved at a loss of information when the original values of the variables are smothered in a "high," "medium," and "low" trichotomy. In previous years, such loss of information may have seemed a reasonable price to pay for convenience in data processing. But the capabilities of modern computers now make processing truly quantitative data as easy as processing qualitative or categorized data. In fact, the analysis of quantitative data sometimes is even simpler because more powerful statistical methods are applicable.

This chapter will discuss computer processing of quantitative information in the context of a standard computer program for calculating simple Pearson product-moment correlation coefficients between two variables. Many other types of computer programs for analyzing quantitative information are available, but a program calculating the product-moment correlation was chosen to illustrate the point because of its presumed familiarity to political scientists.[1] The application of this correlational technique to a concrete problem of political research will be reserved for the end of this chapter. It will be preceded by (1) a discussion of different types of data measurement and types of analysis appropriate to each and (2) some comments on tendencies in political research to use *less* powerful statistical techniques than the data might support. These sections will be followed by an application of correlational analysis to electoral research.

TYPES OF DATA AND TYPES OF MEASUREMENT

Textbooks in statistics commonly recognize four "levels" of measurement—beginning with the lowest—in the *nominal, ordinal, interval,* and *ratio* scales. Each of these scales describes a type of relationship among numerical values in the data. The types of mathematical operations permitted with these numbers depend on the type of scale underlying the data. Before drawing distinctions among these scales or levels of measurement, it is useful to point out another distinction—that between *parametric* and *nonparametric* statistics.

The distinction between types of statistics is certainly relevant to this chapter, but a careful elaboration would draw us far afield. The reader is referred to several statistics books for a comprehensive discussion.[2] Only the essentials will be discussed here.

A *parameter* is a value of some well-defined population. The percentage of votes cast for the Democratic Presidential candidate in a given county in 1964 is a parameter. *Parametric* tests make certain assumptions about the parameters of the population. *Nonparametric* tests, obviously, do not make the same assumptions about population parameters. Another difference between the two is that parametric tests assume that the data are truly quantitative: that the values of the variables can be added and subtracted. Because nonparametric tests do not always make this assumption, they often are extremely useful in political research. Parametric tests, however, almost always are more "powerful" than nonparametric tests. In essence, this means that parametric tests are more sensitive to the existence of relationships within the data.[3] Furthermore, most multivariate techniques and other advanced methods of analysis are based on parametric rather than nonparametric statistics. Therefore, if the data meet the required assumptions, parametric statistics are to be preferred.

NOMINAL SCALES

When numbers are used merely to identify objects, people, or events, the data are said to constitute a nominal or sometimes a "classificatory" scale. As an example of nominal scale data in political research, the numbers *1* and *2* are used to identify Democrats and Republicans respectively. This is measurement at its weakest level, for the only relationship involved is that of *equivalence*. In this context, the number 1 does not mean that Democrats are valued less than Republicans but only that they are not the *same* as—i.e., not *equal* to—Republicans. All people bearing the number 1, however, are equal in the sense that they are all Democrats. Nominal scale data will support only the simplest mathematical operations, such as counting and tallying. But some nonparametric statistics—such as chi-square—can be used with nominal scale data to test hypotheses on how observations or cases are distributed in cross-classifications of categorized variables.

ORDINAL SCALES

The ordinal scale represents measurement at one higher level. Data conform to an ordinal scale when "greater than" or "less than" relationships can be established among the numbers they carry but when "how much" difference exists between them cannot be specified. Responses to questionnaire items regarding conservatism can produce an ordinal scale on which individuals might be ranked from "1" to "3" according to their conservatism. A person assigned number 3 would rank higher in conservatism than a person assigned number 2, and he, in turn, would rank higher than someone assigned the number 1. We could not, however, say anything about the "distance" in conservatism "units" between each of these men. We would not know whether a person scoring 3 or a person scoring 1 was "closer" to the man who scored 2. Ordinal scores cannot be added together and averaged meaningfully because the intervals between the scores are not of known size. These scores are suitable, however, for calculating some nonparametric correlation coefficients, such as Spearman's rho and Kendall's tau. Because these correlation coefficients are based on *ranked* or *ordered* data, they are often called *rank-order* correlations. This term hereafter will be used to refer to non-parametric measures of correlation.

INTERVAL SCALES

Data can be measured on an interval scale when equal distances between numbers in the data represent equal distances in the property being measured. Because these distances or intervals are known, they can be added together, subtracted, or averaged. But an interval scale lacks a known zero point; therefore, the mathematics that can be performed on observed values are limited. The most commonly mentioned example of an interval scale is a household thermometer, which measures temperature in equal units called degrees. Because the size of the intervals is known, it is possible to state not only that the temperature on one day is warmer or colder than the temperature on another day, but also to specify the number of degrees of difference in temperature. However, one day cannot be described as *twice as warm* as another since there is no absolute zero point from which a comparison can be made. One is hard-pressed to find a genuine example of an interval scale in political research. Thurstone's paired-comparison methodology attempts to measure attitudes (e.g., liberalism-conservatism) on a derived interval scale, but few applications of this technique exist in political science literature.[4] After reviewing the first three levels of measurement, Siegel observes: "The interval scale is the first truly *quantitative* scale that we have encountered. All the common parametric statistics (means, standard deviations, Pearson correlations, etc.) are applicable to data in an interval scale, as are the common parametric statistical tests (*t* test, *F* test, etc.)."[5]

RATIO SCALES

Ratio scale measurement applies when the numbers in the data are related as required by an interval scale *and* a true zero point exists. When this additional requirement is also met, the numbers in the data can be expressed meaningfully in terms of their *ratios*. If temperature were measured on a ratio rather than an interval scale, it would be legitimate to describe one day as 10% warmer than another. Many political variables conform to ratio scale measurement. One very common variable that satisfies the necessary requirements is election returns. If the Democratic candidate receives 1,000 votes and the Republican candidate 2,000 votes, we can say not only that the Republican got 1,000 votes *more* than the Democrat but also that he got *twice* as many votes. The ratio scale constitutes the "highest" level of measurement we have discussed, and any statistical test or method of analysis can be legitimately performed on ratio scale data.

POLITICAL RESEARCH AND STATISTICAL ANALYSIS

Statistics texts warn against performing mathematical operations on data that do not meet the assumptions underlying those operations. One common "error" lies in calculating product-moment correlations between two sets of ordinal data, for this correlation coefficient assumes that the data at least conform to interval scale measurement. In actual practice, this error may involve calculating a product-moment correlation coefficient between a three-point measure of social class and a three-point measure of conservatism. Both measures produce ordinal scale data and thus fail to meet the equal interval assumptions of the product-moment correlation coefficient. Because the numbers associated with the data in this example are operated on as if they represented specific "values" of social class and conservatism when they do not, the resulting correlation coefficient provides an ambiguous, if not meaningless, expression of the relationship between the variables.

Injunctions against using more powerful statistics than the data will support are prominently displayed in the statistical literature, and properly so. This literature, however, does not give equal time to warnings against the opposite failing: using methods that do not make full use of the available data. Statisticians probably are less concerned with this problem since no statistical assumptions are violated. Although parametric statistics cannot be used with nominal or ordinal data, it *is* legitimate to reverse the procedure and apply nonparametric tests to interval or ratio data. Moreover, statisticians may be less concerned with the use of "weak" methods for "strong" data because the consequences depend on the nature of the research problem, and research problems vary greatly. From the standpoint of the statistician, procedures may be *legitimate*. But, from the standpoint of the researcher, they may not be *wise*.

The state of statistical analysis in political research has been greatly affected by the nature of the data that interest students of politics. Because most political data have not lent themselves readily to quantitative treatment, there has not been much pressure for political scientists to acquire thorough training in mathematics and statistics. Many of us who do employ statistical methods in research have learned our trade on the job. Relatively few political scientists have had the benefit of extensive formal study in statistics, and even fewer keep up with current developments in statistics.

It is understandable, therefore, that the methodologies underlying published studies often set the pattern for subsequent research on similar topics. Sometimes too little attention is given to the fit between methodology and content. Certain types of data become handled in conventional ways; specific techniques or methods of analysis become accepted as "standard" procedures; and the question of the suitability of these procedures to the research problem often goes unasked.

Useful and important as it is in behavioral research, the simple cross-classification of variables perhaps has been used too much in analyzing political data. A cross-classification is easy to conceptualize and execute, and it is well suited to the nominal and ordinal variables so common in political research. Truly quantitative variables—those that can be measured on an interval or ratio scale—can easily be reduced into groupings or categories and then cross-classified. If a quantitative variable is transformed into only two categories—"high" and "low"—it is said to be *dichotomized*. If it is transformed into three or more groups, it is said to be *trichotomized* or *polychotomized*. Much of the empirical research reported in political science journals consists of cross-classifications of dichotomous, trichotomous, or polychotomous variables. Sometimes these cross-classifications are analyzed with nonparametric statistics; sometimes they have been analyzed only by referring to cell frequencies or percentages. If nominal or ordinal data are involved, these may be the only methods of analysis available to the researcher. On the other hand, if these cross-classifications have in fact been constructed from interval or ratio data, the same methods may be "under-analyzing" the information in the original data.

Sometimes "under-analysis" occurs because of the greater work required by more powerful methods of analysis. It is far easier to hand-calculate percentages and rank-order correlations for cross-classifications of categorized variables than to compute product-moment correlations for the data in their original quantitative form—even if the arithmetic can be done on a desk calculator. Modern computers, however, have suddenly made some of these more powerful statistical techniques as easy to use as their simpler substitutes. Nevertheless, the research literature still neglects these techniques when they might be used to great advantage. In large part, this must be caused by unfamiliarity with computers, but inertia behind conventional methods of analysis is also to blame. Some sophisticated researchers skilled in data processing methodology have occasionally under-analyzed their data by allowing the design of earlier studies to define the research problem.

One can achieve a more adequate analysis of quantitative data by acquiring greater familiarity with computer techniques of data processing. Better analysis of these data can, of course, have important consequences for research. Categorizing and cross-classifying quantitative variables both throws away data and introduces arbitrary judgments in ascribing categories. Both problems in under-analyzing quantitative political data have been exhibited in the analysis of election returns.

Cross-tabulations and occasionally rank-order correlations still are commonly used in investigating the correlation between voting returns and census-type data. For most research questions, however, product-moment correlational techniques would be far better suited for investigating these relationships. All the data would be used; no arbitrary judgments need be made; and the relationship could be expressed more succinctly. In some cases, moreover, the different methodologies might produce different findings from the same data.

CORRELATIONAL ANALYSIS AND ELECTORAL RESEARCH

In his *Primer of Statistics for Political Scientists*, V. O. Key addressed himself specifically to the question, "Why correlate?"

The process of correlation constitutes one of the most valuable tools for the analysis of political data. Whenever the data relative to an hypothesis can be put into the form of a number of paired variables, the technique of correlation may be used in reasoning about the relationships involved. These limits of applicability exclude many types of problems of interest to the political scientist, such as phenomena of which few instances are available, phenomena comprising many more or less imponderable factors that can be disentangled by no mathematical procedure, *phenomena about which the recorded or obtainable data are inadequate*, and so forth. Nevertheless a wide range of problems remain to which the procedure is adaptable, and often baffling and complex phenomena can be broken down into components susceptible of correlational analysis.[6] [Emphasis added]

Key goes on to say that correlational analysis (and he is talking specifically about product-moment correlations) is valuable because it gives a precise statement about the relationship between variables. But, as indicated in the emphasized portion of his answer, correlational analysis is not applicable to all types of political data. The product-moment correlation coefficient assumes that the data are truly quantifiable, i.e., that they are susceptible to ratio scale or at least interval scale measurement.[7]

Research in electoral processes is aided by the quantitative nature of the variables involved. This is to be distinguished from research on voting behavior based on sample survey data, as illustrated in Chapter VI, which discussed analyzing such data through a general cross-classification program. Electoral research, as the phrase will be used here, is based on analysis of *aggregate* data, which are derived from observations on groups of people.[8] These data are often expressed as either simple counts or percentages of objects, people, or events within a given geographical area. Some specific examples of aggregate data in electoral research are the total number of people voting in an election and the total number of votes cast for the Democratic candidate. This information is often related to census-type aggregate data, such as the average number of people living within a square mile and the percentage of the total population living in an urban area.

From a statistical standpoint, one of the most important things about this information is that it is all ratio scale data, suitable for correlational analysis and other advanced parametric statistics. Nevertheless, some researchers have suppressed the quantitative nature of electoral information by grouping data into discrete categories and using simpler cross-classifications or rank-order correlational techniques in their analysis. The quality of the fit between the nature of the data and the methodology employed in electoral research will be investigated by examining three studies of urbanization and interparty competition.

CROSS-CLASSIFYING URBANIZATION AND
INTERPARTY COMPETITION

In 1957, Heinz Eulau reported the results of a study designed to test the hypothesis that "urban structures are conducive to the existence of competitive party systems and that there is a progressive transition to semi-competitive and non-competitive (one party) systems as areas are located along an urban-rural ecological continuum."[9] Eulau tested his hypothesis in Ohio, using county election returns for State Representative from 1946 to 1956, and 1950 census data for the proportion of urban population in each county. On the basis of the election returns, he trichotomized his counties into "competitive," "semi-competitive," and "safe" party systems. On the basis of the census data, he classified the counties into five categories from "rural" to "metropolitan." After cross-classifying these variables, Eulau concluded that "some kind of party competition, either of the complete or modified kind, is a quality of metropolitan and urban ecological areas, while non-competitive systems are predominantly small town and rural phenomena."[10]

In 1960, David Gold and John R. Schmidhauser published a study "designed to test the validity of Eulau's *specific* hypothesis in the case of the 99 counties of Iowa during the same period chosen by him."[11] Gold and Schmidhauser used county election returns for seven different county offices, the office of State Representative, and the office of Governor. Four types of census data were used to construct a measure of urbanization: "(1) per cent employed in industry other than agriculture, mining and forestry, (2) per cent urban population, (3) per cent of population in centers of 5,000 or more, and (4) population of largest center in each county."[12] On the basis of election returns for each office level, the authors trichotomized the counties into straight one-party, generally one-party, and two-party, and they classified the counties into five categories according to rank on the urbanization index. They then cross-classified party competition with urbanization and concluded: "Contrary to the Eulau hypotheses, the Iowa data indicate that among the 99 counties of the state there was *not* a simple positive association between the degree of urbanization and the intensity of party competition."[13]

In 1963, Phillips Cutright published an article that examined the relationship between urbanization and two-party competition at the county level in ten states. He stated, "The primary stimulus for this research stems from the apparently contradictory findings of Gold and Schmidhauser in their study of Iowa and the Ohio case as presented by Eulau."[14] Cutright used county voting returns for one state-wide office in each of ten states for the 1950 or 1952 elections. He dichotomized all counties in each state into competitive and non-competitive categories. The counties were also dichotomized into "high" and "low" categories on the basis of per cent living in urban areas as determined by census figures. Cross-classifying these variables for each of the ten states, Cutright concludes that his data *support* Eulau's hypothesis that "urbanization is positively associated with competitive party politics."[15]

How can these contradictory findings be explained? In some respects, this is an almost hopeless task. All three studies are aimed at investigating the relationship between urbanization and interparty competition, but the research designs employed almost defy comparison, despite their common use of cross-classifications. There are some obvious differences in the offices chosen for study. While Eulau used only election returns for State Representative in Ohio, Gold and Schmidhauser studied election returns for several different offices in Iowa, and Cutright studied only one state-wide office for each state. However, the most im-

portant differences between the studies clearly lie in the way the
authors categorize the raw data available on the two major variables—urbanization and party competition.

In these and other studies, urbanization and party competition
have been measured in a variety of ways. The data used in
measures of urbanization are universally derived from the U.S.
Census, and the data for measures of competition virtually always come from election returns. More specifically, the percentage of the county's population living in census-defined urban
areas is almost always involved in measures of urbanization, and
the difference in the two parties' percentages of the vote cast is
often—but not always—involved in measures of party competition.
Both of these are quantitative variables amenable to correlational
analysis, but students of electoral processes frequently fail to
capitalize on their quantitative nature.

Instead of using these variables directly to test hypotheses
about urbanization and party competition with the powerful
techniques of correlational analysis, researchers have dichotomized, trichotomized, and otherwise categorized the data for
purposes of simple cross-classification. Not only have they thrown
away data in the process, but they also have frustrated attempts
to cumulate research findings by categorizing the variables in
different and arbitrary fashions.

The following scheme reviews the manner in which Eulau,
Gold and Schmidhauser, and Cutright operationalized the two
major variables—urbanization and party competition.

Urbanization

Eulau: Classified the counties into five categories: *Metro,*
Standard Metropolitan Area counties; *Urban,* those with
more than 80% of the population as urban and non-farm;
rurban-rural, between 70-80% urban and non-farm; *rural-
rurban,* less than 70% urban and non-farm; *rural,* no city of
2,500.

Gold and Schmidhauser: Classified the counties into five
categories or "quintiles" according to their ranking on an
urbanization index composed of four factors: (1) % employed in industry other than agriculture, mining, and forestry; (2) % urban population; (3) % living in cities of

5,000 or more; and (4) population of the largest city in
each county.

Cutright: Dichotomized the counties into "high" or "low"
categories according to whether or not 40% or more of the
population lived in urban areas, cities of 2,500 or more.

Party Competition

Eulau: Trichotomized the counties into *competitive* districts,
each party won at least 25% of the elections during the
period studied; *semi-competitive,* one party won less than
25% of the elections but won more than 40% of the *vote* in
at least four of the elections; *non-competitive,* the remainder.

Gold and Schmidhauser: Trichotomized the counties as *one-
party,* if all the elections at the same level were swept by
the same party; *generally one-party,* if the same party carried all but one of the offices during the period studied;
and *two-party,* if the elections were split any more evenly
between the parties.[16]

Cutright: Dichotomized the counties as *one party:* one party
won more than 63% of the vote at the last election; or *competitive:* the winning party got 63% or less of the vote.

Although these authors all begin with basically the same raw
data, they categorize and cross-classify the variables in a manner
that frustrates inter-study comparison. It is hard to tell whether
Eulau's findings on Ohio differ from Gold and Schmidhauser's
in Iowa because of differences in methodologies or in the states
themselves. This problem was commented on by Cutright:

Whether the contradictory findings of the two case studies
we examined are the result of a lack of standardized mea-
surements by the authors of either the dependent or the independent variable we do not know, but what is clear is that
when standardized measures are applied, urbanization is
positively associated with competitive party politics.[17]

But Cutright's "standardized measures" are quite arbitrary di-
chotomizations of quantitative data varying in value over a very
wide range. His method of analysis is consistent across the ten
states, but it throws away data and cannot express the relationship between the variables in a general and efficient manner.

CORRELATING URBANIZATION AND COMPETITION

The interrelationships between these quantitative variables could have been studied more effectively and efficiently through correlational analysis. This would have avoided comparing fundamentally different classification systems, would have disclosed the relationship along the full range of variation within the data, and would have expressed the relationship in a simple coefficient of correlation instead of the cumbersome cross-classifications reported in the articles. Although the use of correlational analysis may have been considered by Eulau in 1957 and rejected as too laborious, the ready availability of computing equipment now makes calculation of correlation coefficients an inexpensive and routine matter.

Any hypothesis stating a simple relationship between two variables should be tested, at least initially, by the most straightforward method possible. Probably the most straightforward test for the relationship between urbanization and party competition would be the computation of a simple correlation coefficient between a standard measure of urbanization and a standard measure of party competition. The percentage of population residing in an urban area and the difference in percentage points of the vote won by each party are likely candidates for these measures. Both commonly are involved in studies on urbanization and party competition and both are quantitative variables that can be used legitimately in calculating product-moment correlations.

Many computer programs exist for calculating correlations between these variables, once they have been punched on cards. One of the most widely available is the BMD02D correlation program.[18] This program will compute a correlation matrix for as many as 150 variables on as many as 99,999 cases. It also will automatically plot out scatter diagrams of the correlations between any pairs of variables specified in advance. These diagrams provide an important visual view of the correlation, linearity of the relationship, and deviant cases. This important information and the correlations—once obtained only after considerable labor—now are produced in minutes by the computer. The researcher's job is limited to familiarizing himself with preparation of program control cards.

A write-up of the BMD02D correlation program has been published in *Biomedical Computer Programs* and will not be reprinted here. The purpose of this chapter is not to show how this program operates but to exemplify the special capabilities of computers in processing quantitative data. The example is drawn from correlational analysis of urbanization and party competition at the county level. This relationship will be examined by correlating quantitative measures of urbanization and party competition for the Presidential, Secretary of State, and Prosecuting Attorney elections in Indiana from 1946 to 1956. The state, offices, and years were chosen simply because the data were already available.[19] The objective here is not to resolve the differences in the three studies cited but to illustrate a straightforward method of analyzing the data through correlational techniques executed on the computer.

The data for this study were voting returns recorded on punchcards according to the format given in Appendix A-1. Columns 66-70 of each card contains the plurality difference between the percentages of votes captured by the two major parties. If the Republican candidate received 55.0% of the vote and the Democratic candidate 45.0%, the plurality difference expressed in percentage points would be 10. This served as the measure of competition: the *closer* the two parties approached a 50-50 division of the vote, the *smaller* the plurality difference in percentage points, representing an increase in competition. The measure of urbanization was simply the percentage of the county's population that resided in urban areas of 2,500 or more as of the 1950 Census. This information was included among several items of census data for each county recorded on a separate set of cards.

The computer was instructed to read first the plurality difference in the percentages of the vote won by each party and then the per cent of urban population for each of the state's 92 counties. This was done for each office examined and for each election year studied. Product-moment correlations were computed between the election plurality and the per cent urban population over all 92 counties for each office in each election year. The

computer also automatically plotted the variables against each
other in scatter diagrams. All this was done in less than two
minutes on the IBM 709 computer.

If a simple relationship between urbanization and party competition in the counties did in fact exist, one would find negative
correlations between the two variables: as urbanization *increased*,
the plurality difference would *decrease*—indicating a closer election and more competition. Figure VII-1 shows the scatter diagram for the highest correlation observed between the variables
in the fourteen elections studied. This was a correlation of −.20
for the 1952 Presidential election. Table VII-1 reproduces the entire set of correlation coefficients for all fourteen elections.

TABLE VII-1

URBANIZATION CORRELATED WITH PARTY COMPETITION FOR THE
PRESIDENTIAL, SECRETARY OF STATE, AND PROSECUTING ATTORNEY
ELECTIONS IN 92 INDIANA COUNTIES: 1946-1956[a]

	1946	1948	1950	1952	1954	1956
President of U.S.		−.13		−.20		−.12
Secretary of State	−.10	−.06	−.15	−.14	−.09	−.12
Prosecuting Attorney	−.05	+.11	−.17	−.03	−.02	
	(N=59)	(N=57)	(N=68)	(N=61)	(N=50)	

[a] Elections for Prosecuting Attorney were frequently uncontested in
some of Indiana's 92 counties. These uncontested elections were
excluded from the analysis, and the number of cases underlying
the correlation is given in parentheses under the coefficient.

With a single exception, all correlation coefficients reported
in Table VII-1 are negative, thus supporting the hypothesis, but
all also are rather small in magnitude.[20] An examination of all
fourteen scatter diagrams discloses no evidence of a curvilinear
relationship that would not be captured in the product-moment
correlation. This evidence suggests that some relationship exists
between the variables in Indiana politics, but the relationship is
at best a weak one.

FIGURE VII-1

BM02D COMPUTER OUTPUT: SCATTER DIAGRAM PLOTTING PERCENTAGE PLURALITY FOR WINNING PARTY BY THE PERCENT OF THE COUNTY'S POPULATION LIVING IN URBAN AREAS—FOR THE 1952 PRESIDENTIAL ELECTION IN ALL 92 COUNTIES IN INDIANA, r = −.20

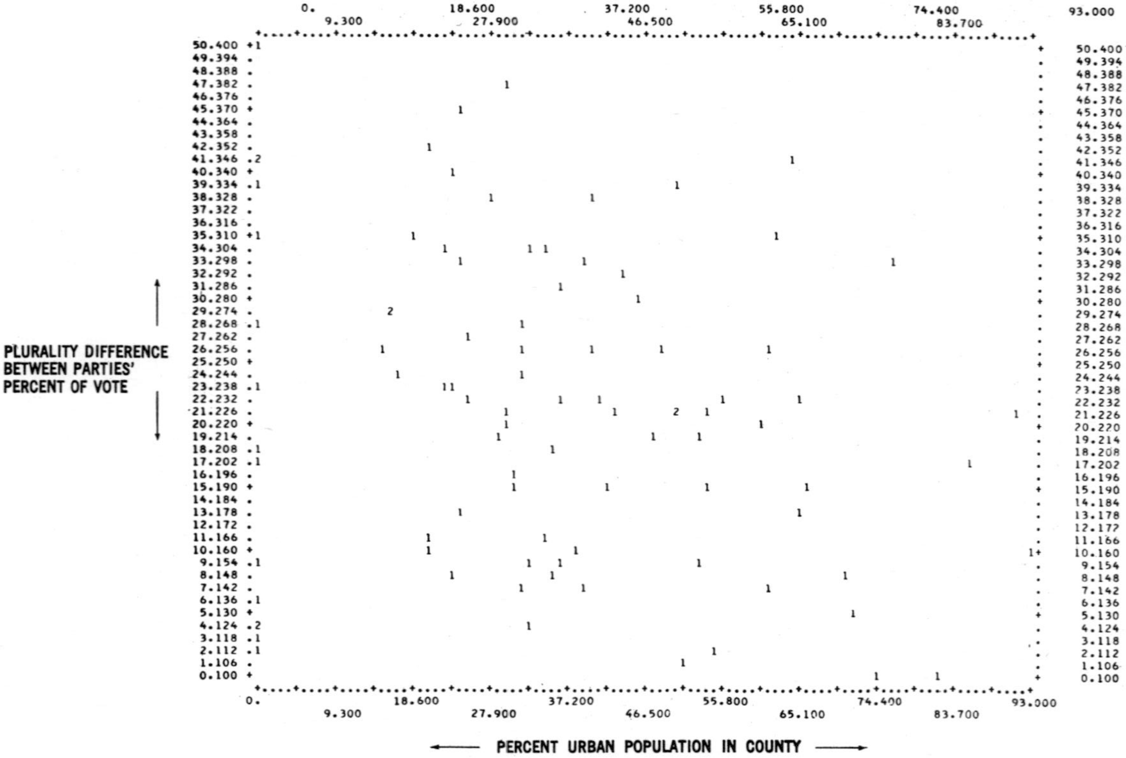

This method of analyzing the relationship between urbanization and competition is both direct and simple. It employs all
information in each variable and summarizes the relationship in
one coefficient for each election. It avoids the problems of categorizing variables and interpreting cross-classifications. It is well-
suited to the data and—with a computer—is easily carried out.

The role of computers in processing quantitative data actually
only begins with these simple correlation coefficients. If the
analysis is to be refined by introducing additional variables (as
the authors cited did in fact do), the computer becomes even
more valuable. The complex procedures and countless calculations involved in multivariate methods—such as multiple correlations and factor analysis—are done routinely with available computer programs. If the political scientist is fortunate enough to
be dealing with truly quantitative variables, a whole new cabinet
of powerful analytical tools can be applied to the research
problem. Familiarity with computer methods of data processing
enables the researcher to analyze quantitative data more adequately.

NOTES

[1] The Pearson product-moment correlation coefficient is discussed in
almost all statistics texts. For a simple treatment with special attention to problems of concern to political scientists see V. O. Key, Jr.,
A Primer of Statistics for Political Scientists (New York: Crowell,
1954), especially Chapter Four. Key also provides a bibliography of
applications of correlational analysis to political research. It might
be pointed out that this method of analysis had been used in political
research as early as 1919. See W. F. Ogburn and Inez Goltra, "How
Women Vote," *Political Science Quarterly*, 34 (1919), 413-33, and
also Stuart A. Rice, "Some Applications of Statistical Method to
Political Research," *American Political Science Review*, 20 (May,
1926), 313-29.

[2] Clyde H. Coombs, "Theory and Methods of Social Measurement," in
Leon Festinger and Daniel Katz (eds.), *Research Methods in the
Behavioral Sciences* (New York: Dryden Press, 1953), pp. 471-535;
Sidney Siegel, *Nonparametric Statistics for the Behavioral Sciences*
(New York: McGraw-Hill Book Company, 1956), pp. 21-30; and
Hubert Blalock, *Social Statistics* (New York: McGraw-Hill, 1957),
pp. 11-16. For a recent re-thinking and re-formulation of his ideas

on data and measurement see Clyde H. Coombs, A *Theory of Data* (New York: Wiley, 1964).

3 The meaning of the "power" of a test is discussed in most statistics texts. An especially thorough discussion is given by Keith Smith, "Distribution—Free Statistical Methods and the Concept of Power Efficiency," in Leon Festinger and Daniel Katz (eds.), *Research Methods in the Behavioral Sciences* (New York: Dryden Press, 1953), pp. 536-77.

4 Perhaps the best—if not the only—example of an attempt to devise an interval scale for measuring political attitudes is Herman C. Beyle's thirty-three-year-old article, "A Scale for the Measurement of Attitude Toward Candidates for Elective Governmental Office," *American Political Science Review*, 26 (June, 1932), 527-44.

5 Siegel, *op. cit.*, p. 28.

6 Key, *op. cit.*, p. 124.

7 Some books on methodology have begun to take a more pragmatic view toward the assumption of interval data. Fred N. Kerlinger's recent and thorough text in methodology, *Foundations of Behavioral Research* (New York: Holt, Rinehart and Winston, 1964), holds:

> The best procedure would seem to be to treat ordinal measurements as though they were interval measurements, but to be constantly alert to the possibility of *gross* inequality of intervals. As much as possible about the characteristics of the measuring tools should be learned. Above all, we need to be particularly careful with the interpretation of ordinal data to which statistical analysis suitable for interval measurement has been applied. Much useful information has been obtained by this approach, with resulting scientific advances in psychology and education. In short, it is unlikely that the . . . researcher will be seriously led astray by heeding this advice, if he is knowledgeable and careful in applying it. [p. 428]

8 Correlations between different sets of aggregate data cannot be translated directly into correlations between the attributes shared by the *individuals* in the group. Perhaps the best known statement of the dangers in correlating aggregate data in the study of individual behavior is W. S. Robinson's "Ecological Correlations and the Behavior of Individuals," *American Sociological Review*, 15 (June, 1950), 351-57. For a defense of the method in answering some questions—especially those about electoral *processes*—see Herbert Menzel, "Comment on 'Ecological Correlations and the Behavior of Individuals,'" *American Sociological Review*, 15 (October, 1950), 674.

9 "The Ecological Basis of Party Systems: The Case of Ohio," *Midwest Journal of Political Science*, 1 (August, 1957), 125-35; see p. 126.

[10]*Ibid.*, p. 133.

[11]David Gold and John M. Schmidhauser, "Urbanization and Party Competition: The Case of Iowa," *Midwest Journal of Political Science*, 4 (February, 1960), 62-75; see p. 63.

[12]*Ibid.*, p. 65.

[13]*Ibid.*, p. 74.

[14]"Urbanization and Competitive Party Politics," *Journal of Politics*, 25 (August, 1963), 552-64; see p. 552.

[15]*Ibid.*, p. 563.

[16]This statement does not square completely with their procedure, but the differences are too minor to warrant reporting their procedure in detail.

[17]Cutright, *op. cit.*, p. 563.

[18]This program is described completely in W. J. Dixon (ed.), *Biomedical Computer Programs* (Los Angeles: Health Sciences Computing Facility, Department of Preventive Medicine and Public Health, School of Medicine, University of California, 1964), pp. 49-59.

[19]These data were collected and analyzed by Mary Frase and Alan Wyner, former undergraduates at Northwestern now pursuing graduate study in political science at Yale University and Ohio State University, respectively.

[20]The question of the statistical significance of these correlation coefficients will not be raised because we are more interested in the *strength* of the relationship. See David Gold, "Some Problems in Generalizing Aggregate Associations," *American Behavioral Scientist*, 8 (December, 1964) 16-18, for an interesting discussion of significance levels computed for *populations* instead of samples.

CHAPTER VIII

PROCESSING TEXTUAL
INFORMATION: TWO
INFORMATION RETRIEVAL
PROGRAMS

This chapter is less instructional than the previous ones. Computer programs for retrieving information from political science materials have not been in existence long enough to warrant giving instructions in their use. The probability of any of these methods becoming obsolete in the very near future is certainly higher than for the data processing techniques discussed in preceding chapters. But because so much important political information exists in textual materials—books, articles, speeches, and newspapers—it is important to know of developments in computer techniques of information processing.

Several specific computer programs for information retrieval deserve to be brought to the reader's attention, although they will not be discussed in this chapter. The use of the General Inquirer program for content analysis of speeches and documents in international relations has been thoroughly treated by Holsti in *Content Analysis*, the first volume in this handbook series.[1] The *American Behavioral Scientist* devoted its entire June, 1964, issue to applications of information retrieval techniques to behavioral science materials. This valuable issue includes some general observations on problems and prospects for information retrieval as well as reports on specific computer programs. Scheuch and Stone describe their use of the General Inquirer to locate survey questions relevant to a specific research problem from hundreds of interview questions asked in past surveys.[2] Bisco proposes a retrieval system that pulls together survey questions and supporting data from archive files.[3] Morrison presents a computer program for indexing the vast amount of material in the Human Relations Area Files.[4] Gardin reviews the progress of the French-developed SYNTOL model for document retrieval.[5] Garfield shows how citation indexing can be used with behavioral science literature.[6]

This chapter will not summarize and evaluate these different techniques; that would be out of place in an introductory book on data processing. Instead, it will discuss at greater length two computer programs—EIKWIC and TRIAL—that have been applied specifically to problems of retrieving information from political science materials. EIKWIC is a general keyword indexing program that has been used to prepare the *Cumulative Index to the American Political Science Review*[7] and to retrieve roll call votes in legislative bodies on the basis of their substantive content. TRIAL is a method for retrieving propositions and findings from political science literature. Each of these programs will be discussed in turn.

KEYWORD INDEXING[8]

To many students in the behavioral sciences, information retrieval schemes involving the use of computers probably appear interesting and ambitious but still of dubious utility for present-day research. While it is true that much of the exciting work being done by information retrieval specialists is still experimental, some of their techniques have long been operational and have already been applied to practical problems of scientific research. Computer-generated keyword indexes to current research literature, for example, have found standard usage within the physical sciences, at least as a partial solution to the problem of keeping abreast of publications in one's field. The success of this general method of using computers to prepare keyword indexes to bibliographical material within the physical sciences has been amply proven; the practical applications of keyword indexing within the behavioral sciences are no less promising.

Keyword indexing in any discipline operates on the assumption that certain terms or "keywords" constitute useful handles for pulling out or retrieving information of interest to the researcher. An ordinary book index serves as a good example of this assumption.

The preparation of any index involves many mechanical tasks: scanning pages for important terms, recording page numbers, cross-listing, and alphabetizing. Familiarity with the subject is undoubtedly an asset in preparing an index, but a good job can ordinarily be expected from any thorough, accurate, and efficient research assistant who is instructed in advance about terms to be included in the index. Computers, which are notoriously thorough, accurate, and efficient, possess the requisite virtues for routinized keyword indexing, and only need instruction in how to do the job.

Computer programs providing these instructions have been available now for some time.[9] By means of the proper program, a computer can be instructed to read natural language material, search the material for the appearance of pre-defined keywords, alphabetize the keywords found, and print out the alphabetized keywords along with some of the "context" in which they occur. Two basic versions of these keyword indexing computer programs have become standard in the field of information retrieval. One version prints the keywords embedded in the original context; this method is commonly called "KWIC" indexing, for "Key-Word-In-Context." The other prints the keywords alongside the original context and has become known as "KWOC" indexing, for "Key-Word-Out-of-Context." Both KWIC and KWOC indexing can now be regarded as operational information retrieval techniques within both the physical and behavioral sciences.

THE NATURE OF A KWIC INDEX

The current capabilities of KWIC indexing can be illustrated by reference to a computer-generated cumulative index to the *American Political Science Review*.[10] A total of 2,614 articles had appeared in the *Review* from its first issue in 1906 through its 57th volume in 1963. These articles were punched on cards as in Figure VIII-1, with different "classes" of cards reserved for different types of information—author, title, and facts of publication.[11] Thousands of these cards were fed into an IBM 709 computer, and the machine produced three types of output: an alphabetical listing of all keywords found in the titles of the

Figure VIII-1

punchcards prepared for KWIC processing: class 1 cards for authors, class 2 cards for titles, and class 3 cards for publication facts

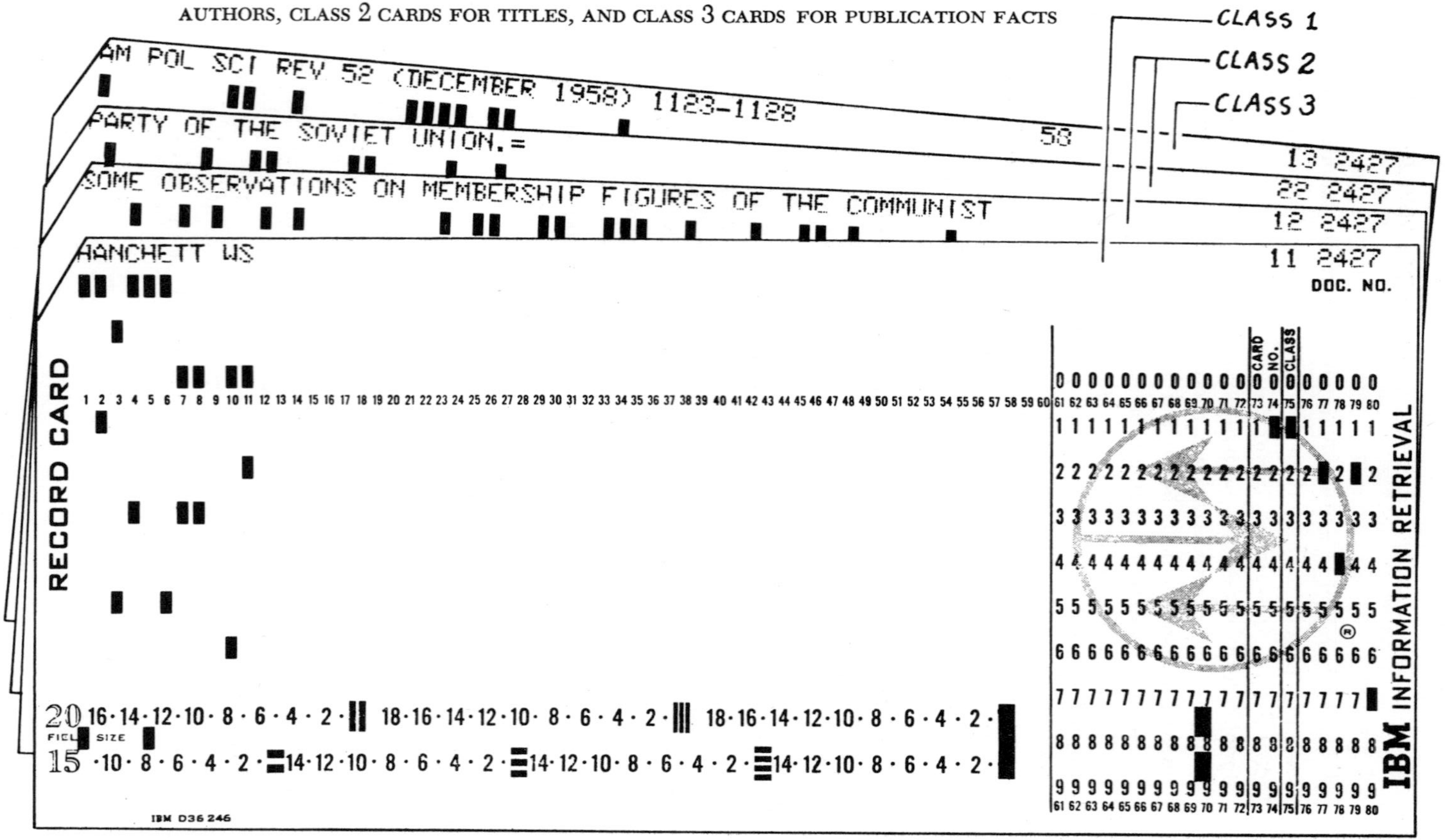
CLASS 1
CLASS 2
CLASS 3
AM POL SCI REV 52 (DECEMBER 1958) 1123-1128
58
13 2427
PARTY OF THE SOVIET UNION.=
22 2427
SOME OBSERVATIONS ON MEMBERSHIP FIGURES OF THE COMMUNIST
12 2427
HANCHETT WS
11 2427
DOC. NO.
RECORD CARD
CARD NO.
CLASS
IBM INFORMATION RETRIEVAL
FIELD SIZE
IBM D36 246

articles along with part or all of the titles in which the keyword occurred (Figure VIII-2), an alphabetical listing of complete citations by first-named author (Figure VIII-3), and an alphabetical cross-listing of all authors, senior and junior (not shown). In Figure VIII-2, the keywords are arranged in alphabetical order to the immediate right of the blank column. The computer decides what constitutes a keyword in one of two ways. It can be instructed either to refer to a list of keywords prepared in advance by the researcher, or to a list of words that are *not* to be considered keywords. In the first case, the computer looks at every word contained in the title of the publication and compares it with its own stored list of keywords. The words in the titles found on the list are then selected for indexing. The process operates in a comparable way when a list of *non-keywords* is used: the computer includes the word in the index only when the word does *not* appear in the list. The latter procedure was used in the preparation of the cumulative index of the *Review*. Sample *non-keywords* (words not indexed) are "an," "of," "the," and "other."

To use the index in Figure VIII-2, scan the vertical column of keywords for one that is of interest to you. Then read the context of the title printed on the same line as the keyword. There is room provided on the line for only 78 character-spaces, though this proved adequate for printing in full 86% of the 2,614 titles from the *Review*. A title with no more than 78 characters and spaces prints out in full, although a portion of the title may be "wrapped around" and printed before or after the keyword, depending on where the keyword appears in the title. Some of the words in longer titles do not print out, again depending on the position of the keyword in the title.

Once an interesting title has been located in the keyword listing, the user of the index looks at the reference code given on the same line in the right-hand column. This code gives the first six letters of the senior author's last name, his initials, the year of publication of the article, and the identification number of the article. The code enables the user to locate the complete citation in the author-alphabetized bibliography shown in Figure VIII-3.

This type of index is also known as a "permuted" keyword index, for an article will appear as many times as the number of

FIGURE VIII-2

KWIC COMPUTER PRINTOUT: KEYWORD LISTING FROM THE
Cumulative Index to the American Political Science Review

KEYWORD / TITLE	AUTHOR	I.D.#
REPUBLICAN AND DEMOCRATIC NATIONAL COMMITTEES (PARTIES).= PERSONNEL OF	SAYRE WS32	1117
ADVISORY COMMITTEES IN BRITISH ADMINISTRATION.=	FAIRLI JA26	826
ARLIAMENTARY ROLE OF JOINT STANDING COMMITTEES IN SWEDEN.=	ELDER NC51	2069
CONFERENCE COMMITTEES IN THE NEBRASKA LEGISLATURE.= THE P	BURDET FL36	1365
SUB- COMMITTEES OF CONGRESS.=	FRENCH BL15	315
MINISTRATION).= PERMANENT ADVISORY COMMITTEES TO THE BRITISH GOVERNMENT DEPAR	PERKIN JA40	1514
LEGISLATIVE INVESTIGATING COMMITTEES.=	MCCART L 22	648
LEGISLATIVE INVESTIGATING COMMITTEES.=	BLAIR JH24	718
N INTRODUCTION TO THE SENATE POLICY COMMITTEES.= A	BONE HA56	2299
ESTION TIME IN THE BRITISH HOUSE OF COMMONS (PARLIAMENT).= QU	MCCULL RW33	1202
A TEST FOR CABINET AUTOCRACY (OVER COMMONS IN BRITAIN).= WOMAN SUFFRAGE IN P	CLARK E 17	423
).= AMENDMENTS IN HOUSE OF COMMONS PROCEDURE SINCE 1881 (PARLIAMENTS	PORRIT E 08	033
Y OF THE PARLIAMENTS OF THE BRITISH COMMONWEALTH .= THE COMMUNIT	HALL HD42	1654
BRITISH EMPIRE (DEVELOPMENT OF THE BRITISH COMMONWEALTH).= THE TREND WITHIN THE	BOGGS TH15	357
BRITISH DOMINIONS AND NEUTRALITY (COMMONWEALTH).=	CLOKIE HM40	1540
THE BRITISH IMPERIAL CONFERENCE (COMMONWEALTH).=	SMELLI KB27	857
FOREIGN POLICY AND THE DOMINIONS (COMMONWEALTH).= BRITISH	DENNIS AL22	643
L STATUS OF THE BRITISH DOMINIONS (COMMONWEALTH).= INTERNATIONA	ALLIN CD23	684
EREIGNTY OF THE BRITISH DOMINIONS (COMMONWEALTH).= THE SOV	ELLIOT WY30	1030
THE BRITISH COMMONWEALTH OF NATIONS.=	HALL HD53	2190
IS THE BRITISH COMMONWEALTH WITHERING AWAY.=	WHEARE KC50	2027
THE NATURE AND STRUCTURE OF THE COMMONWEALTH.=	WHEARE KC53	2191
NALISM AND DEMOCRACY IN THE BRITISH COMMONWEALTH-- SOME GENERAL TRENDS.= NATIO	BRADY A 53	2192
SEARCH).= INTER-AMERICAN SCHOLARLY COMMUNICATION IN THE HUMANITIES AND SOCIAL	BURKHA F 60	2491
OCTRINAL CONFLICT (CATHOLICISM AND COMMUNISM).= DEVIATION CONTROL-- A STUDY	BRZEZI Z 62	2547
SLAVIA').= HOW DIFFERENT IS TITO'S COMMUNISM (COMMENT ON 'THE COMMUNIST PART	DRAGNI AN57	2335
REVOLUTIONARY COMMUNISM IN THE UNITED STATES.=	WATKIN GS20	542
THE NEW STRATEGY OF INTERNATIONAL COMMUNISM.=	KAUTSK JH55	2265
THE FRENCH PEASANT AND COMMUNISM-- A PROFILE.=	EHRMAN HW52	2101
WESTERN EUROPEAN COMMUNISM-- THE CURRENT SCENE.=	EINAUD M 51	2061
STATE LEGISLATURES AND COMMUNISM-- THE LIMITS OF DIVERSITY.=	PRENDE W850	2028
SOVIET POLICY TOWARD NATIONAL COMMUNISM, NATIONALISM, AND THE GROWTH OF	MORRIS B 59	2435
ITY OF NATIONS AFTER WORLD WAR II.= COMMUNISM, NATIONALISM, AND THE GROWTH OF	SHOUP P 62	2584
CURRENT 'MASS LINE' TACTICS IN COMMUNIST CHINA.=	STEINE HA55	2245
CONSTITUTIONALISM IN COMMUNIST CHINA.=	STEINE HA51	2066
NATIONALISM, AND THE GROWTH OF THE COMMUNIST CHINA.= MAS	SHOUP P 62	2584
WAR.= COMMUNIST COMMUNITY OF NATIONS AFTER WORLD	BURIN FS63	2604
E AS A FACTOR IN THE RECRUITMENT OF COMMUNIST DOCTRINE OF THE INEVITABILITY OF	HOLT RT54	2220
D MODERATION.= THE TWENTIETH CPSU (COMMUNIST LEADERSHIP.= AG	KENNEY CD56	2316
S ORGANIZATIONS IN MAINLAND CHINA (COMMUNIST PARTY) CONGRESS-- A STUDY IN CA	KUOCHU C 54	2228
YOUTH UNDER DICTATORSHIP (RUSSIAN COMMUNIST PARTY).= THE KOMSOMOLS-- A STUD	FAINSO M 51	2053
RECENT LITERATURE ON CHINESE COMMUNIST PARTY HISTORY.=	STEINE HA52	2126
PPARATUS' OF THE CENTRAL COMMITTEE, COMMUNIST PARTY OF THE SOVIET UNION.= THE	NEMZER L 50	2006
S OF A SOCIAL MOVEMENT.= THE COMMUNIST PARTY OF THE U.S.A.-- AN ANALYSI	MOORE B 45	1757
THE COMMUNIST PARTY OF YUGOSLAVIA.=	NEAL FW57	2334

FIGURE VIII-3

KWIC COMPUTER PRINTOUT: AUTHOR-ALPHABETIZED BIBLIOGRAPHY
FROM THE
Cumulative Index to the American Political Science Review

YEAR

I.D.#   AUTHOR / AUTHOR   JOURNAL & VOL.

```
1929  ABBOTT RS48   ABBOTT RS
                    THE FEDERAL LOYALTY PROGRAM-- BACKGROUND AND PROBLEMS.=
                    AM POL SCI REV 42 (JUNE 1948) 486-499   DATE & PAGES
2024  ABBOTT RS50   ABBOTT RS          SICARD R
                    A POSTWAR DEVELOPMENT IN FRENCH REGIONAL GOVERNMENT-- THE
                    'SUPER PREFET'.=
                    AM POL SCI REV 44 (JUNE 1950) 426-431
2068  ABBOTT RS51   ABBOTT RS
                    THE ROLE OF CONTEMPORARY POLITICAL PARTIES IN CHILE.=
                    AM POL SCI REV 45 (JUNE 1951) 450-463
1120  ADAMS  GW32   ADAMS GW
                    THE SELF-GOVERNING BAR ( LAW ).=
                    AM POL SCI REV 26 (JUNE 1932) 470-482
2155  ADAMS  JC53   ADAMS JC          BARILE P
                    THE IMPLEMENTATION OF THE ITALIAN CONSTITUTION.=
                    AM POL SCI REV 47 (MARCH 1953) 61-83
2134  ADRIAN CR52   ADRIAN CR
                    SOME GENERAL CHARACTERISTICS OF NONPARTISAN ELECTIONS.=
                    AM POL SCI REV 46 (SEPTEMBER 1952) 766-776
1825  AFROS  JL46   AFROS JL
                    LABOR PARTICIPATION IN THE OFFICE OF PRICE ADMINISTRATION.=
                    AM POL SCI REV 40 (JUNE 1946) 458-484
 932  AHL    FN28   AHL FN
                    REAPPORTIONMENT IN CALIFORNIA.=
                    AM POL SCI REV 22 (NOVEMBER 1928) 977-980
1052  AIKIN  C 31   AIKIN C
                    THE MOVEMENT FOR REVISION OF THE CALIFORNIA CONSTITUTION.=
                    AM POL SCI REV 25 (MAY 1931) 337-342
1291  AIKIN  C 35   AIKIN C
                    A NEW METHOD OF SELECTING JUDGES IN CALIFORNIA.=
                    AM POL SCI REV 29 (JUNE 1935) 472-474
1470  AIKIN  C 39   AIKIN C
                    THE BRITISH BUREAUCRACY AND THE ORIGINS OF PARLIAMENTARY
                    POLICY, I AND II.=
                    AM POL SCI REV 33 (FEBRUARY 1939) 26-46 AND (APRIL 1939)
                    219-233
1537  AIKIN  C 40   AIKIN C
                    STATE CONSTITUTIONAL LAW IN 1939-1940.=
                    AM POL SCI REV 34 (AUGUST 1940) 700-718
1587  AIKIN  C 41   AIKIN C
                    STATE CONSTITUTIONAL LAW IN 1940-41.=
                    AM POL SCI REV 35 (AUGUST 1941) 683-700
1631  AIKIN  C 42   AIKIN C
                    STATE CONSTITUTIONAL LAW IN 1941-42.=
                    AM POL SCI REV 36 (AUGUST 1942) 667-688
1983  AIKIN  C 49   AIKIN C          KOENIG LW
                    INTRODUCTION ( TO THE HOOVER COMMISSION SYMPOSIUM ).=
                    AM POL SCI REV 43 (OCTOBER 1949) 933-940
2489  AKZIN  B 60   AKZIN B
                    ELECTION AND APPOINTMENT.=
                    AM POL SCI REV 54 (SEPTEMBER 1960) 705-713
2607  ALBINS HS63   ALBINSKI HS
                    THE CANADIAN SENATE-- POLITICS AND THE CONSTITUTION.=
                    AM POL SCI REV 57 (JUNE 1963) 378-391
1547  ALBRIG SD40   ALBRIGHT SD
                    THE PRESIDENTIAL SHORT BALLOT.=
                    AM POL SCI REV 34 (OCTOBER 1940) 955-959
2609  ALGER  CF63   ALGER CF
                    COMPARISON OF INTRANATIONAL AND INTERNATIONAL POLITICS.=
                    AM POL SCI REV 57 (JUNE 1963) 406-419
1883  ALLEN  EP47   ALLEN EP
                    THE TEACHER OF GOVERNMENT.=
                    AM POL SCI REV 41 (JUNE 1947) 527-534
```

keywords it contains. The first title listed in Figure VIII-2, for example, will be found in five other places in the index: under "REPUBLICAN," "DEMOCRATIC," "NATIONAL," "PAR-TIES," and "PERSONNEL." A total of 10,089 keyword lines were produced for the 2,614 articles from the *Review*. Therefore each title appears in the index on an average of 3.9 times.

THE NATURE OF A KWOC INDEX

Conventional KWIC indexes are "double-entry" indexes; after the user has found a title of interest, he must check the reference code and then enter the author-alphabetized bibliography to get complete information on journal, volume, month, year, and pages. Although it would be possible to develop a KWIC index that would give this information in abbreviated form in the reference code, the purpose of a "single-entry" index is perhaps better served by the KWOC version of keyword indexing, which prints out the complete citation for each appearance of a keyword in the title.

A reproduction of a page of KWOC computer output is given in Figure VIII-4. The punchcard format for the input to the KWOC program is identical to the KWIC format (Figure VIII-1). The input to the KWOC example in Figure VIII-4, however, consisted of 928 titles on "Africa" and "The Middle East" that were reported in the "Foreign and Comparative Government" bibliography published in the back pages of the *American Political Science Review* during the past four years.

Both the KWIC and KWOC programs identify the keywords by searching the title cards for the existence of previously defined keywords or non-keywords. But when the KWOC program finds a keyword, it is reprinted out of context to the left of the complete citation. KWIC, by printing only one line per index entry, is definitely more economical in its use of space and is possibly easier to use in retrieving titles of interest. KWOC, on the other hand, does provide a single-entry look-up and does allow for printing the complete title regardless of length.

ADVANTAGES OF KEYWORD INDEXING

The advantages of automatic indexing of bibliographical material by the keywords contained in their titles are those generally

FIGURE VIII-4

KWOC COMPUTER PRINTOUT: PARTIAL KEYWORD LISTING FROM
928 TITLES ON AFRICAN POLITICS

I.D.#

KEYWORD   AUTHOR

TITLE

PUBLICATION & DATE

```
1140   KENYA    BENNETT G
                 KENYA'S FRUSTRATED ELECTION.=
                 WORLD TODAY JUNE, 1961
1142   KENYA    AUTHOR NOT GIVEN
                 DESPATCH FROM GOVERNOR, KENYA, TO SECRETARY OF STATE FOR THE
                 COLONIES -- RELEASE OF JOMO KENYATTA.=
                 LONDON, HMSO, 1961 ( CMD. 1459 )
1168   KENYA    AUTHOR NOT GIVEN
                 TRANSITION IN KENYA -- A CONTINENT IN REVOLUTION.=
                 ROUND TABLE BRITISH COMMONWEALTH AFFAIRS JUNE, 1961
1316   KENYA    ROSBERG CG
                 REPORT FROM KENYA.=
                 AFRICAN REPORT APRIL, 1961
1530   KENYA    ALTORFER A
                 FINANCIAL OFFICERS IN THE MINISTRY OF LOCAL GOVERNMENT,
                 KENYA.=
                 JOURNAL OF AFRICAN ADMINISTRATION JANUARY, 1961
1537   KENYA    GOLDS JM
                 AFRICAN URBANIZATION IN KENYA.=
                 JOURNAL OF AFRICAN ADMINISTRATION JANUARY, 1961
1961   KENYA    HILL MF
                 THE WHITE SETTLER'S ROLE IN KENYA.=
                 FOREIGN AFFAIRS JULY, 1960
2012   KENYA    BENNETT G
                 THE DEVELOPMENT OF POLITICAL ORGANISATIONS IN KENYA.=
                 POLITICAL STUDIES, 5 (JUNE 1957)
2029   KENYA    BENNETT G          ROSBERG C
                 THE KENYATTA ELECTION-- KENYA 1960-1961.=
                 NEW YORK-- OXFORD UNIVERSITY PRESS, 1961 (REVIEWED IN AM
                 POL SCI REV 56 (JUNE 1962) 484
2031   KENYA    KILSON ML,JR.
                 LAND AND POLITICS IN KENYA-- AN ANALYSIS OF AFRICAN POLITICS
                 IN A PLURAL SOCIETY.=
                 WESTERN POLITICAL QUARTERLY 10 (SEPTEMBER 1957) 559
2035   KENYA    SMITH TE
                 ELECTIONS IN DEVELOPING COUNTRIES ( GAMBIA, GHANA, KENYA,
                 MAURITANIA, NIGERIA, RHODESIA AND NYASALAND, SIERRA LEONE,
                 SOMALIA, SUDAN, TANGANYIKA, TOGOLAND, UGANDA, AND ZANZIBAR )
                 NEW YORK-- ST. MARTIN'S PRESS, 1960
2145   KENYA    MBOYA T
                 KENYA AND THE DEATH OF COLONIALISM.=
                 THE NEW LEADER APRIL 25, 1960
2149   KENYA    AUTHOR NOT GIVEN
                 REPORT OF THE KENYA CONSTITUTIONAL CONFERENCE HELD IN
                 LONDON IN JANUARY AND FEBRUARY, 1960.=
                 LONDON, HMSO, 1960 ( CMD 960 )
2240   KENYA    AUTHOR NOT GIVEN
                 AFRICAN GOVERNMENT IN KENYA.=
                 AFRICA REPORT (JUNE 1963)
2242   KENYA    VENNET G
                 POLITICAL REALITIES IN KENYA.=
                 WORLD TODAY (JULY 1963)
2259   KENYA    AUTHOR NOT GIVEN
                 KENYA CONSTITUTION.=
                 JOURNAL OF LOCAL ADMINISTRATION OVERSEAS (JULY 1963)
2304   KENYA    AUTHOR NOT GIVEN
                 KENYA. SUMMARY OF THE PROPOSED CONSITUTION FOR INTERNAL SELF
                 - GOVERNMENT.=
                 LONDON. HMSO, 1963 CMD 1970
2307   KENYA    RENISON P
                 THE CHALLENGE IN KENYA.=
                 OPTIMA (MARCH 1963)
2361   KENYA    MBOYA T
                 KENYA AT THE CROSS-ROADS.=
                 AFRICA SOUTH (JULY-SEPTEMBER 1959)
2380   KENYA    BLUNDELL M
                 MAKING A NATION IN KENYA.=
                 AFRICAN AFFAIRS (JULY 1959)
2402   KENYA    BLUNDELL M
                 MAKING A NATION IN KENYA.=
                 JOURNAL OF THE ROYAL COMMONWEALTH SOCIETY (JULY-AUGUST
                 1959)
2403   KENYA    BRANNEY L
                 COMMENTARY ON THE REPORT OF THE WORKING PARTY ON AFRICAN
                 LAND TENURE IN KENYA.=
                 JOURNAL OF AFRICAN ADMINISTRATION (OCTOBER 1959)
```

associated with the use of computers in most data processing operations. First of all, the indexes are easily and inexpensively prepared. The input to the KWIC index of the *Review* was prepared by a girl keypunching directly from the title pages of the bound library volumes. It took less than 200 hours for her to punch and correct all the titles in 57 volumes of the *Review*. It took the 709 computer less than 12 minutes to process the 2,614 titles—searching a 418 non-keyword list for each word in every title, preparing 10,089 KWIC index lines, and producing a cross-reference listing for 2,801 senior and junior authors. Another 29 minutes were required to sort the output into alphabetical order, and about 30 minutes were needed to print the output on the IBM 1401.

In addition to the advantages of speed and economy, computer-generated keyword indexes are easily updated with new material and readily reproduced. Once a comprehensive bibliography is punched on cards, it becomes a simple matter to prepare specialized bibliographies by instructing the computer to index the literature only on a smaller number of previously identified keywords, such as "legislator," "legislature," "parliaments," "representation," etc.

For some people, a keyword index also has the advantage of convenience in use. Some users report that an alphabetized list of keywords provides a more efficient means of locating articles of interest than the conventional subject-heading index, where articles are alphabetized by authors within subjects. It must be noted, however, that others have found keyword indexes less convenient than conventional subject-heading indexes.[12] Perhaps it takes time to adjust to using the computer output.

THE DESCRIPTIVENESS OF TITLES

Obviously the *major* disadvantage in computer methods of keyword indexing lies in the "descriptiveness" of the titles fed into the computer. Keyword indexing was originally developed for application to "technical" literature, and indeed the longer and more descriptive titles of journal publications in the physical and biological sciences seem better suited to this technique than titles in the behavioral sciences. Lane has investigated the variation within different fields concerning the suitability of indexing titles solely by their keywords.[13] He points out that the reader interested in "duck shooting" probably would have missed an article entitled "Good Day in Bad Marsh" if he had consulted a keyword index, but he would have found the article under the above subject-heading in the Readers' Guide to Periodical Literature.

The evidence indicates, however, that the professional journals in the behavioral sciences have a higher proportion of "descriptive" titles than periodicals reported in the Readers' Guide.[14] Furthermore, the problem of inadequate titles can be solved largely through editorial supervision during the preparation of the computer input. Scanning the texts of articles whose titles seem unclear or literary in nature will usually disclose some terms or phrases which might be enclosed in parentheses and added to the titles. Keywords added in this manner will be indexed as if they had been in the title. This procedure was followed in preparing the index to the Review, and the first line in Figure VIII-2 shows how the word "PARTIES" was entered as a keyword addition. Keywords were added to 604 of the 2,614 Review titles, indicating that original titles were considered suitably "indexable" in about 77 per cent of the cases.

Thus, considerable improvement can be made in the quality of an index if some editorial supervision can be exercised in recording titles before processing them on the computer. This is relatively easy to do when the input is punched directly from journals as in the preparation of a cumulative index, but it is impossible to do when the input is punched from a bibliography. Although it is faster and usually more convenient to punch from bibliographies, the cumulative index approach will undoubtedly provide a greater pay-off in the long run in terms of more exhaustive coverage, more accurate reporting, more detailed publication information, and improved descriptiveness of titles. The cumulative indexes prepared for individual journals within a given discipline could then be merged to form a comprehensive master cumulative index.[15]

FUTURE APPLICATIONS OF KEYWORD INDEXING

As originally developed and applied within the physical sciences, keyword indexing has been limited to the retrieval of bibliographic items, but the method has also shown definite, albeit limited, uses in genuine problems of *information* retrieval. The American Bar Foundation, for example, has applied KWIC indexing techniques to legislation recently enacted in the 50 states.[16] This index makes it possible for lawyers, legislators, and other interested persons to keep abreast of the enactment of state legislation by searching keyword listings obtained from brief descriptions of the statutes.

KWOC indexing, in particular, can be used to great advantage in identifying legislative votes for use in roll call analysis. Appendix A-4 describes a punchcard format for recording roll call votes in legislative bodies. Systematic collections of punchcard data on voting in state legislatures, Congress, or the United Nations often grow so extensive that it becomes a major project to find all votes that deal with the substantive issues being researched, such as "labor," "foreign policy," and so forth. Keyword indexing provides a method for locating relevant votes out of hundreds of issues on which votes have been taken.

Some 259 roll call votes were taken in plenary sessions and committee meetings of the 15th United Nations General Assembly. Important information about these votes was punched on cards for computer processing with the same EIKWIC program used for bibliographic information. Nations sponsoring the resolutions were treated as "authors"; descriptions of the substance of the votes were recorded as "titles"; and the "source" information consisted of page numbers in the U.N. *Official Records* (where the votes are reported) and column locations on punchcards (where the votes are recorded). The computer read the cards and produced output as reproduced in Figure VIII-5. This shows a KWOC keyword listing accompanied by complete description of the vote, nations sponsoring the resolution, page references for the vote in the *Official Records,* and location of the vote in the punchcards containing actual voting positions of individual na-

FIGURE VIII-5

KWOC COMPUTER PRINTOUT: PARTIAL KEYWORD LISTING OF ROLL
CALL VOTES TAKEN IN THE 15TH SESSION OF THE UNITED NATIONS

BUDGET
NETHERLANDS   NEW ZEALAND   UK
NEWLY INDEPENDENT STATES. AMENDMENT BY NETHERLANDS,
NEW ZEALAND, AND UK TO 18 POWER RESOLUTION ON ASSISTANCE TO
FORMER TRUST TERRITORIES AND OTHER NEWLY INDEPENDENT STATES,
APPROVED IN PRINCIPLE THE PROPOSALS OF THE SECRETARY-GENERAL
FOR INCREASED ASSISTANCE TO THESE STATES FROM THE REGULAR
BUDGET OF THE UN. PASSED, COMMITTEE II, 18 IN FAVOR, 9
AGAINST, 49 ABSTENTIONS (2 DEC 60).
GA/XV...A/C.5/SR. 701--PAGE 338   SET 21 COL 23

BUDGET
ARGENTINA   BOLIVIA   CHILE
COLOMBIA   COSTA RICA   ECUADOR
EL SALVADOR   HONDURAS   MEXICO
PANAMA   PARAGUAY   PERU
URUGUAY   VENEZUELA
UN OPERATIONS IN THE CONGO, 14 POWER AMENDMENT REPLACING
PREAMBULAR PARAGRAPH 4 WHICH RECOGNIZED THAT CONGO EXPENSES
SHOULD BE APPORTIONED DIFFERENTLY FROM THE REGULAR BUDGET
PASSED, COMMITTEE 5, 37 IN FAVOR, 30 AGAINST, 14 ABSTENTIONS
(20 APR 61).
GA/XV...A/C.5/SR. 845--PAGE 91   SET 51 COL 22

BUDGETARY
COLOMBIA   MEXICO   PERU
VENEZUELA
EXAMINATION OF ADMINISTRATIVE AND BUDGETARY PROCEDURES,
VOTE ON 4 POWER AMENDMENT ADDING A FOURTH PREAMBULAR
PARAGRAPH STATING THAT PROCEDURES FOR MEETING CONGO EXPENSES
MUST BE DIFFERENT FROM REGULAR BUDGETARY PROCEDURES.
PASSED, COMMITTEE 5, 30 IN FAVOR, 23 AGAINST, 20 ABSTENTIONS
(20 APR 61).
GA/XV...A/C.5/SR. 845--PAGE 93   SET 51 COL 28

BUDGETARY
CANADA
EXAMINATION OF ADMINISTRATIVE AND BUDGETARY PROCEDURES,
CANADIAN RESOLUTION, AS A WHOLE, AS AMENDED. PASSED,
COMMITTEE 5, 26 IN FAVOR, 24 AGAINST, 29 ABSTENTIONS (20
APR 61).
GA/XV...A/PV. 979--PAGE 239   SET 51 COL 29

BYELORUSSIA
BYELORUSSIA
CONTRIBUTIONS. AMENDMENT BY BYELORUSSIA TO 9 POWER
RESOLUTION ON CONTRIBUTIONS TO THE UN SPECIAL FUND AND TO
THE UN EXPANDED PROGRAM OF TECHNICAL ASSISTANCE, PRELACED
THE WORDS ''STATES MEMBERS OF THE UN OR MEMBERS OF ANY OF
THE SPECIALIZED AGENCIES OR THE INTERNATIONAL ATOMIC ENERGY
AGENCY'' WITH THE WORDS ''ALL STATES.'' DEFEATED
COMMITTEE II, 23 IN FAVOR, 40 AGAINST, 16 ABSTENTIONS (10
DEC 60).
GA/XV...A/C.5/SR. 712--PAGE 418   SET 21 COL 26

CADRES
ARGENTINA   BURMA   CANADA
CEYLON   GHANA   INDIA
INDONESIA   IRAN   IRAQ
IRELAND   MEXICO   MOROCCO
NEPAL   NIGERIA   PAKISTAN
SENEGAL   SOMALIA   SWEDEN
NON-SELF-GOVERNING TERRITORIES, TRAINING OF CADRES.
RESOLUTION URGES MEASURES AIMED AT RAPID TRAINING OF
INDIGENOUS CIVIL AND TECHNICAL CADRES. PASSED, COMMITTEE
4, 73 IN FAVOR, 0 AGAINST, 9 ABSTENTIONS (26 OCT 60).
GA/XV...A/C.4/SR. 1024--PAGE 141   SET 41 COL 17

tions. This index greatly facilitates roll call analysis by providing a tool for retrieving votes relevant to the research question.

RETRIEVING PROPOSITIONS FROM LITERATURE[17]

Several important objectives should be served by an adequate system for retrieving information from any body of literature: (1) The system should have a powerful searching procedure for retrieving information closely relevant to the needs of the scholar. (2) It should handle natural language text. (3) It should place retrieved information in the context of the original study to facilitate interpretation. (4) It should accept abstracts composed of the authors' own words and accompanied by complete page and bibliographic citations. (5) It should be able to accommodate vast quantities of input. (6) It should provide for periodic updating and easy revising of the master input file. (7) Finally, the system should be both economical and easy to use.

TRIAL, an acronym for "Technique to Retrieve Information from Abstracts of Literature," is the title of an information retrieval system that attempts to meet the above objectives in retrieving propositions from political science literature. The title not only is descriptive of the method, but it also reflects the exploratory nature of the effort. Some day, automated information retrieval systems will be commonplace aids to scholars, but many exploratory steps must be taken first. New developments in TRIAL will doubtless improve on the system described here, and technological breakthroughs may make the TRIAL approach to the problem altogether obsolete. In the meantime, the system should be able to provide some valuable experiences in the methodology of information retrieval while giving some assistance to scholars in managing their literature.

PREPARING THE TRIAL INPUT

The input to TRIAL consists of abstracts of articles and books in political science. Although there is no technical obstacle to using complete texts as input, it certainly is less expensive in material, keypunching time, storage space, and computer time to include only the "essential" information. In addition to achieving these economies, abstracting also promises to improve the

effectiveness of the retrieval process itself. Findings and propositions sometimes are camouflaged in the literature and escape
detection by machine searches. A skillful abstracter can often
expose this information for retrieval.

Every TRIAL abstract is physically divided into a "summary"
section describing the study as a whole, and one "statement"
and one "elaboration" section for each proposition or finding
identified in the study. The "summary" section of the abstract
attempts to describe the article in terms of the following headings
—"the problem," "research design," "conclusions," and "suggestions for research." These headings do not apply to every article,
and the abstracter may omit reference to them if they are in-
appropriate. They are intended mainly to give some structure to
the information in the summary.

Each proposition or finding identified in the article is represented in the abstract by a "statement" and an "elaboration." The
statement contains the proposition or finding. Initially, direct
quotations from the source were used whenever the original language was suitable. It was found, however, that retrieval was
aided considerably by having the abstracter translate the author's
words into a basic political science "language" with the use of a
thesaurus of terms. The author's original words *are* repeated immediately below the statement in the "elaboration," which also
contains additional information relevant to understanding the
proposition or finding. This information might include the operational or conceptual definitions employed as well as the evidence
behind the statement.

The quality of the abstract is, of course, affected by the skills
and knowledge of the persons doing the abstracting. The abstracter must know the literature in which he is working. Someone
who is thoroughly familiar with the subject can make better decisions about what to include and exclude and can do a far
better job of translating the author's words into the basic political
vocabulary.

Several steps are involved in preparing abstracts for input to
the TRIAL system. The original material is first read through in
order to identify propositions and to take notes for the summary.
The article is then reread and the abstract typed on erasable

paper with typewriter margins adjusted for a 60 space line. This corresponds exactly to the TRIAL input format, which uses 60 columns of the card. Words at the end of a line are not hyphenated and agreed-upon substitutions are made for characters not available on computer printers. This procedure produces copy that keypunch operators can reproduce exactly, one punchcard per line.

THE COMPUTER SEARCHING PROCESS

The first 60 columns of each punchcard are reserved for the text of the abstracts. In column 75 of each card, the keypunch operator adds a "class" number, which indicates whether individual cards contain information about the *author, title,* or *journal* of the article (classes 1, 2, and 3 respectively) or whether the cards represent lines in the *summary* (class 4), in a *statement* (class 7), or in an *elaboration* (class 8). These numbers are used by the program to tell the machine what class of cards should be searched.

The keypunch operator also assigns a number i in columns 73-74 to every card in the ith statement and in its accompanying elaboration. This results in identifying all cards relevant to the first proposition or finding with 01 punched in columns 73-74, all cards for the second proposition or finding with 02 in columns 73-74, and so on. After all the cards for an abstract have been punched and corrected for errors, they are numbered sequentially in four columns (76-79) beginning with 0001. Column 80 is punched 0. In effect, this produces a sequencing by *tens* instead of *units,* which facilitates editing the abstracts once they have been read from punchcards onto magnetic tape. Sample input to the TRIAL system is shown in Figure VIII-6, which reproduces a tabulator printout of some propositions and findings abstracted from Angus Campbell's article, "The Passive Citizen," *Acta Sociologica,* 6 (1962), 9-21.

Magnetic tape is used instead of punchcards for the search and retrieval operations because tape provides a much more efficient and convenient input medium for computers. Once the information has been put on magnetic tape, however, it is removed from direct human observation and manipulation. When cards are

FIGURE VIII-6

TABULAR LISTING OF TRIAL INPUT: PARTIAL ABSTRACT OF AN
ARTICLE BY ANGUS CAMPBELL, "THE PASSIVE CITIZEN,"
Acta Sociologica, 6 (1962), 9-21

```
CAMPBELL A                                                         100010
THE PASSIVE CITIZEN.                                               200020
ACTA SOCIOLOGICA. 6 (1962) 9-21.                                   300030
    PROBLEM-- INTERESTED IN THE PSYCHOLOGICAL FACTORS              400040
INVOLVED IN PASSIVE OR ACTIVE POLITICAL BEHAVIOR. ''THE            400050
BULK OF THIS PAPER IS DEVOTED TO A CONSIDERATION OF THOSE          400060
CHARACTERISTICS OF THE PERSON AND HIS ENVIRONMENT WHICH MAY        400070
BE THOUGHT TO UNDERLIE POLITICAL PASSIVITY.'' (P.10)               400080
CONSIDERS PERSONALITY TRAITS, BASIC PREDISPOSITIONS, AND           400090
SHORT-TERM ATTITUDES.                                              400100
    RESEARCH DESIGN-- NO SPECIFIC RESEARCH DONE FOR THIS           400110
PARTICULAR ANALYSIS. CITES MANY DIFFERENT ARTICLES AND             400120
BOOKS ON THE SUBJECT OF POLITICAL BEHAVIOR.                        400130
    CONCLUSIONS-- TOO LITTLE IS KNOWN OF THE BASIC                 400140
PERSONALITY NEEDS OF THE ELECTORATE FOR THE POLITICAL              400150
SCIENTIST TO MAKE MUCH PROGRESS IN THIS AREA. THE MOST             400160
IMPORTANT BASIC PREDISPOSITIONS ARE SOCIAL DETACHMENT AND          400170
POLITICAL ALIENATION. SHORT-TERM ATTITUDES ARE CONSTANTLY          400180
CHANGING.                                                          400190
''...THE RELATIONSHIP BETWEEN OUR MEASURE OF PERSONAL              01700200
EFFECTIVENESS AND THE PERSON'S EXPRESSION OF DEGREE OF             01700210
INVOLVEMENT IN POLITICS IS MUCH HIGHER AMONG PEOPLE OF             01700220
LIMITED FORMAL EDUCATION THAN IT IS AMONG THOSE OF COLLEGE         01700230
TRAINING.'' (P.12)                                                 01700240
    CITES ARTICLE BY E. DOUVAN AND A.M. WALKER, THE                01800250
SENSE OF EFFECTIVENESS IN PUBLIC AFFAIRS, =PSYCHOLOGICAL           01800260
MONOGRAPHS=, 70, NO. 22, 1956-- 1-19.                              01800270
''...POLITICAL DETACHMENT AND IRREGULARITY ARE                     02700280
DISPROPORTIONATELY HEAVY AMONG INDIVIDUALS AND GROUPS              02700290
ISOLATED FROM THE LARGER SOCIETY.'' (P.13) (ANOMIA)                02700300
    CITES WORK OF W. KORNHAUSER, =THE POLITICS OF MASS             02800310
SOCIETY=. GLENCOE, ILLINOIS-- FREE PRESS, 1959.                    02800320
''...IN URBAN POPULATIONS THE DEGREE OF POLITICAL                  02800330
INVOLVEMENT IS HIGHLY RELATED TO THE ACTUAL NUMBER OF GROUP        02800340
MEMBERSHIPS WHICH A PERSON REPORTS.'' (P.13) ALSO FOUND            02800350
VERY LOW LEVELS OF POLITICAL INVOLVEMENT AMONG U.S. FARMER.        02800360
ALIENATION SCALE INDICATES THAT ALIENATION ''.../IS/ ABOUT         03700370
AS FREQUENT IN ONE RELIGIOUS, RACIAL, OR ECONOMIC GROUP            03700380
AS ANOTHER.'' (P.14) HOWEVER, ALIENATION DOES RELATE TO            03700390
POLITICAL INTEREST AND INVOLVEMENT.. THOSE WHO ARE MOST            03700400
INACTIVE ARE FREQUENTLY ALIENATED.                                 03700410
    CITES D.E. STOKES, POPULAR EVALUATIONS OF GOVERNMENT--         03800420
AN EMPIRICAL ASSESSMENT IN HARLAN CLEVELAND AND HAROLD D.          03800430
LASSWELL (EDS.), =ETHICS AND BIGNESS=, NEW YORK, HARPER,           03800440
1962.                                                              03800450
''IN THE UNITED STATES WHERE NEITHER CLASS NOR RELIGION IS         04700460
THE BASIC DIMENSION OF DIFFERENCE BETWEEN THE TWO PARTIES,         04700470
STRENGTH OF IDENTIFICATION WITH THE PARTIES THEMSELVES IS          04700480
ASSOCIATED WITH POLITICAL INTEREST. THE MOST STRONGLY              04700490
PARTISAN INDIVIDUALS BEING THE MOST INVOLVED AND ACTIVE            04700500
PARTICIPANTS.'' (P.15)                                             04700510
THE INTEREST GENERATED BY AN ELECTION WILL DEPEND ON HOW           05700520
LARGE THE DISCREPANCY IS BETWEEN WHAT THE ELECTORATE WANTS         05700530
```

used, changes and corrections in the data are easily made by replacing the card in error with a correct one. Errors cannot be corrected so readily when the information is represented by magnetized spots on a plastic ribbon.

The TRIAL system includes a special program for providing greater flexibility in editing abstracts after they have been put on tape. This program, which will not be discussed in detail here, provides for automatically inserting, replacing, or deleting whole abstracts or individual lines without handling the original cards. Because the cards had been numbered in tens instead of units when read onto tape, as many as nine new lines may be inserted between cards 00040 and 00050 by numbering the new ones in column 80, making them 00041, 00042, and so on.[18] These sequence numbers are used only in editing operations and are not involved in search and retrieval functions.

A search of the tape containing the abstracts is initiated when a card bearing information identifying the search is placed after the program deck.[19] The information on this card only labels the printout for identification purposes. If a search were to be made for propositions about the effect of education on likelihood of voting, this card might be labeled, "SEARCH FOR EDUCATION AND POLITICAL PARTICIPATION."

As all instruction cards in TRIAL are virtually free of format restrictions, this label could begin anywhere on the card. The program only tells the machine to begin scanning in column 1 for a non-blank column and to regard the contents of that column and the following 58 columns as the identifying label. The machine considers the identification label terminated when it encounters a comma, wherever it appears. Identifying information that extends past a comma, or is more than 59 columns in length, is ignored by the machine.

The comma serves to end the identification label and to instruct the machine to be alert for the designation of the card "classes" which the user intends to search for keywords. For example, let us assume that the user does want to search for findings or propositions relevant to the relationship between "education" and "political participation." The program itself is designed to permit searching any or all classes of input cards. In this example, however, the search probably would be made only within the "statement" cards, class 7. The machine would be instructed to ignore the author, title, journal, summary, and elaboration cards and to search only the statement cards.

The search command is communicated to the computer by specifying within parentheses certain keywords and logical connections that must exist between the keywords in order for a statement to qualify for retrieval. After reading the code number or numbers of the card classes to be searched, the machine senses that it is receiving a search command when it reads a left parenthesis. Because any given command may contain more than one combination of keywords arranged in a "nest" of parentheses, the machine continues to read until the number of *right* parentheses read equals the number of *left* ones. It will then evaluate the logic of the command, working outward from the innermost set of parentheses.

The researcher or user of the system must specify the keywords he wants the machine to use in its search. In the example given, the words "education" and "political participation" would certainly be used, but the search might also include "college," "school," "schooling," "vote," "voting," "turnout," and "involvement." All these possibilities can be incorporated in a TRIAL search by means of special word commands and logical operators.

Merely enclosing a word within parentheses will involve that word in the searching process. Enclosing any word between slashes (e.g., "/SCHOOL/") will define the first six characters of that word as the *root* word and will cause the machine to retrieve any word containing the same combination of characters. The command "/SCHOOL/" therefore will retrieve "schooling" as well as "school." Joining any pair of words with an asterisk (e.g., "POLITICAL*PARTICIPATION") will define the words as a *phrase* and will cause the machine to search for exactly the same phrase.

The real power of the search command lies in the use of standard logical operators expressed on the punchcard as follows: .NOT., .OR., and .AND. Perhaps the use of these operators can best be conveyed by constructing a sample command for the education and voting turnout search. Figure VIII-7 shows the command punched on cards.

This command will cause the machine to select only those statements containing *both* one or more keywords specified within the first nest of parentheses *and* one or more keywords spe-

FIGURE VIII-7
PUNCHCARDS PREPARED FOR TRIAL SEARCH FOR PROPOSITIONS
OR FINDINGS ABOUT "EDUCATION" AND "POLITICAL PARTICIPATION"

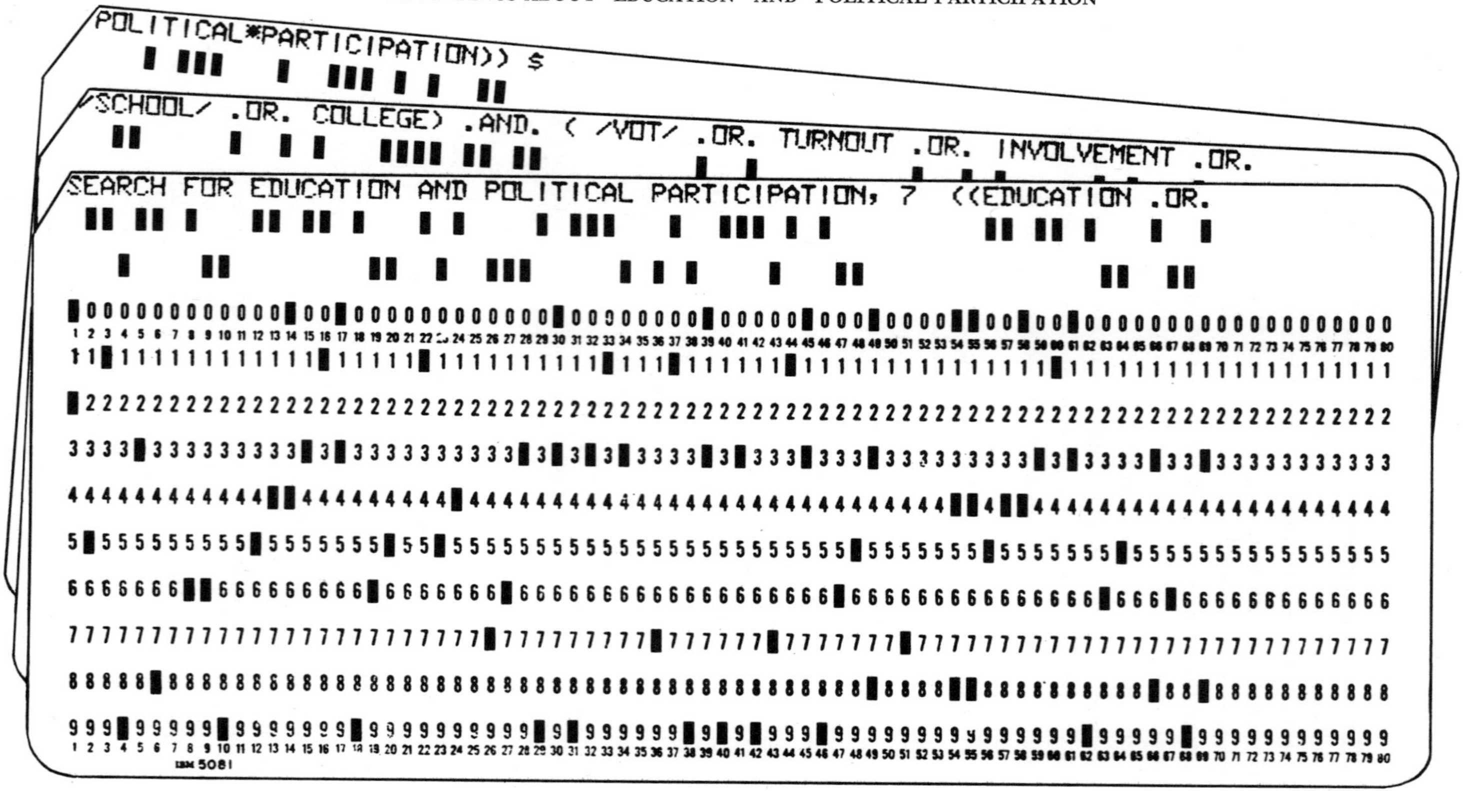

cified within the second nest. If the machine finds any statement of a proposition or finding that satisfies this logical combination of keywords, it will print out the *statement* and its supporting *elaboration* along with the *summary* of the study. A portion of the computer output produced in response to the above command is reproduced in Figure VIII-8. The dollar sign after the last right

FIGURE VIII-8

TRIAL COMPUTER OUTPUT: INFORMATION RETRIEVED FROM THE ABSTRACT IN FIGURE VIII-6 AFTER SEARCHING ACCORDING TO THE COMMAND IN FIGURE VIII-7

```
NORTHWESTERN UNIVERSITY TRIAL SEARCH        08/24/64      PAGE      27


CAMPBELL A

THE PASSIVE CITIZEN.

ACTA SOCICLCGICA, 6 (1962) 9-21.

        PROBLEM-- INTERESTED IN THE PSYCHOLOGICAL FACTORS
    INVOLVED IN PASSIVE OR ACTIVE POLITICAL BEHAVIOR.  ''THE
    BULK OF THIS PAPER IS DEVOTED TO A CONSIDERATION OF THOSE
    CHARACTERISTICS OF THE PERSON AND HIS ENVIRONMENT WHICH MAY
    BE THOUGHT TO UNDERLIE POLITICAL PASSIVITY.'' (P.10)
    CONSIDERS PERSONALITY TRAITS, BASIC PREDISPOSITIONS, AND
    SHORT-TERM ATTITUDES.
        RESEARCH DESIGN-- NO SPECIFIC RESEARCH DONE FOR THIS
    PARTICULAR ANALYSIS.  CITES MANY DIFFERENT ARTICLES AND
    BOOKS ON THE SUBJECT OF POLITICAL BEHAVIOR.
        CONCLUSIONS-- TOO LITTLE IS KNOWN OF THE BASIC
    PERSONALITY NEEDS OF THE ELECTORATE FOR THE POLITICAL
    SCIENTIST TO MAKE MUCH PROGRESS IN THIS AREA.  THE MOST
    IMPORTANT BASIC PREDISPOSITIONS ARE SOCIAL DETACHMENT AND
    POLITICAL ALIENATION.  SHORT-TERM ATTITUDES ARE CONSTANTLY
    CHANGING.

STATEMENT OF PROPOSITION...

    ''...THE RELATIONSHIP BETWEEN OUR MEASURE OF PERSONAL
    EFFECTIVENESS AND THE PERSON'S EXPRESSION OF DEGREE OF
    INVOLVEMENT IN POLITICS IS MUCH HIGHER AMONG PEOPLE OF
    LIMITED FORMAL EDUCATION THAN IT IS AMONG THOSE OF COLLEGE
    TRAINING.'' (P.12)

        CITES ARTICLE BY E. DOUVAN AND A.M. WALKER, THE
        SENSE CF EFFECTIVENESS IN PUBLIC AFFAIRS, =PSYCHOLOGICAL
        MONOGRAPHS=, 70, NO. 22, 1956-- 1-19.

STATEMENT OF PROPOSITION...

    ''PERHAPS THE SUREST SINGLE PREDICTOR OF POLITICAL
    INVOLVEMENT IS NUMBER OF YEARS OF FORMAL EDUCATION.''
    (P.20)

        ''EDUCATIONAL LEVELS ARE RISING AND WILL RISE MUCH
        FURTHER.  IN TIME THIS TREND WILL CHANGE THE CHARACTER OF
        THE ELECTORATE, INCREASING ITS CAPACITY TO COMPREHEND
        POLITICAL AFFAIRS AND ITS CONCERN WITH THEM.'' (P.21)
```

parenthesis on the punchcards in Figure VIII-7 starts the machine looking for another identification label for the next search command. Many different searches can be made during one run on the computer.

There is no guarantee that the TRIAL system offers the best approach to the problem of managing information in political science literature. But it does have potential and deserves to be considered by those who sense a close fit between its capabilities and their needs. The long range usefulness of a system like this can be judged only by the experiences of a variety of scholars. In any case, instructing political scientists in the use of this particular system is far less important than introducing them to the whole range of possibilities in computer processing of political science information.

NOTES

[1] Robert C. North, Ole R. Holsti, M. George Zaninovich, and Dina A. Zinnes, *Content Analysis* (Evanston: Northwestern University Press, 1963), Chapter 8. The original article describing the computer program was by Philip J. Stone, Robert F. Bales, J. Zvi Namenwirth, and Daniel M. Ogilvie, "The General Inquirer: A Computer System for Content Analysis and Retrieval Based on the Sentence as a Unit of Information," *Behavioral Science,* 7 (October, 1962), 484-98.

[2] Erwin K. Scheuch and Philip J. Stone, "The General Inquirer Approach to an International Retrieval System for Survey Archives," 23-28.

[3] Ralph L. Bisco, "Information Retrieval from Data Archives: The ICPR System," 45-48.

[4] Donald Morrison, "Indexing the Human Relations Area Files," 48-50.

[5] Jean-Claude Gardin, "A European Research Program in Document Retrieval," 12-16.

[6] Eugene Garfield, "Citation Indexing: A Natural Science Literature Retrieval System for the Social Sciences," 58-61.

[7] Kenneth Janda (ed.), *Cumulative Index to the American Political Science Review* (Evanston: Northwestern University Press, 1964).

[8] The discussion of keyword indexing is reprinted with slight revision and some additions from Kenneth Janda, "Keyword Indexes for the Behavioral Sciences," *The American Behavioral Scientist,* 7 (June, 1964) 55-58.

[9] The earliest application of keyword indexing by computers to be published seems to have been the IBM bibliography, "Literature on

Information Retrieval and Machine Translation," September, 1958. H. P. Luhn discussed the indexing technique in "Keyword-in-Context Index for Technical Literature (KWIC Index)," IBM Advanced Systems Development Division Report RC-127, August, 1959. *Chemical Titles*, which appeared in 1960, seems to have been the first published application of KWIC indexing outside of the computing industry. Various keyword indexing programs for comupters are now in operation across the country. A thorough discussion of one such program for the popular IBM 1401 computing system is contained in "Keyword-in-Context (KWIC) Indexing Program for the IBM 1401 Data Processing System," Reference Code 1401-CR-02X (White Plains, N.Y.: International Business Machines, 1963). A recent revision of earlier KWIC programs for computers in the IBM 700 series has been prepared by Professor James S. Aagaard of Northwestern University's Department of Electrical Engineering. This program, available through SHARE, is supplied as a series of relocatable subroutines and is designed for use in conjunction with IBM's Basic Monitor IBSYS. The indexes reported on in this paper were prepared with the use of Professor Aagaard's EIKWIC revision.

[10]The cumulative index to the *Review* was processed on an IBM 709 computer with the EIKWIC program in use at Northwestern University (see footnote 9). Dr. Evron M. Kirkpatrick, Executive Director of the American Political Science Association, arranged for the Association's financial support of the indexing project. Miss Louise Cowen, Supervisor of the Northwestern University Computing Center, extended many kindnesses during both the sponsored and unsponsored phases of the project.

[11]There is no practical limit to the number of authors, length of titles, or amount of publication information that can be recorded on punchcards for input to the computer. Additional cards within a given "author," "title," or "source" classification can be used as needed. The standard format for recording bibliographic information on punchcards for keyword indexing is given in the IBM General Information Manual E20-8091, "Keyword-In-Context (KWIC) Indexing."

[12]See C. W. Hanson's review of a KWIC publication in the *Journal of Documentation*, 19 (September, 1963), 137-38.

[13]B. B. Lane, "Key Words in—and out of—Context," *Special Libraries* (January, 1964), 45-46.

[14]Donald H. Kraft, "A Comparison of Keyword-In-Context (KWIC) Indexing of Titles with a Subject Heading Classification System," *American Documentation*, 15 (January, 1964), 48-52. Kraft's analysis of 3,248 entries in an issue of *The Index to Legal Periodicals* and an issue of *The Index to Legal Theses and Research Projects* disclosed that 89.5% had titles judged suitable for keyword indexing.

[15]A computer-generated cumulative index has been prepared by Murray A. Straus and Susanne C. Graham for *Marriage and Family Living*, volumes 1 to 24 (1939-1962). A comprehensive KWIC index to publications in the field of social welfare from 1924 to 1962 has been prepared by Joe R. Hoffer, Executive Secretary of the National Conference on Social Welfare. The social welfare index has both cumulative and bibliographical characteristics, as does *The Index to Legal Theses and Research Projects,* first prepared with the use of a computer in 1962.

[16]*Current State Legislation Index* (American Bar Foundation, Indianapolis: Bobbs-Merrill Company, beginning publication in 1962).

[17]This discussion is extracted from Lester W. Milbrath and Kenneth Janda, "Computer Applications to Abstraction, Storage, and Recovery of Propositions from Political Science Literature," a paper delivered at the 1964 Annual Meeting of the American Political Science Association, Chicago.

[18]Note that this is similar to the complete sequence coding discussed in Chapter V, page 141.

[19]The TRIAL programs were written in MAP—a machine-oriented programming language for the IBM 709—by Mr. William Tetzlaff of the Northwestern University Computing Center.

APPENDIX A-1 **COUNTY ELECTION RETURNS**

This study (31) contains county election returns for selected offices, an estimate of the total eligible electorate, percentage of total vote won by each of the major parties, plurality difference in percentage points, and percentage turnout in election.

Column
Number *Contents of Columns*

1-2   State identification code: *12* (Indiana)

3-4   Study code: *31* (County-by-county election returns)

5-7   County identification number: 001 to 092, numbered alphabetically

8-9   Office for which votes are recorded: 01 President
02 U. S. Congressman
03 Governor
04 Secretary of State
05 Prosecuting Attorney
*06 State Senator
*07 State Representative

10-12   *Legislative district in which the county is located; these columns are blank except for office codes "06" and "07".

13   *Urban-rural code of the legislative district; these columns are blank except for office codes "06" and "07". (See code for column 68 in Study 10, Appendix A-3.)

14-17   *Legislator's identification number assigned to victorious candidate in the election; these columns are blank except for office codes "06" and "07".

18-21   The year in which the election was held

22-29   Total eligible electorate in the county: For 1950 and 1960, calculated as the population 21 and over. For the 1920, 1930, and 1940 censuses, calculated as native-born population 21 and over plus naturalized citizens. Straight-line interpolations were made for inter-census years.

30-36   Vote cast for *Republican* candidate

37-43   Vote cast for *Democratic* candidate

44-50   Other vote

51-55   *Republican* percentage of total vote cast

56-60   *Democratic* percentage of total vote cast

61-65   Percentage of vote cast for other parties

66-70   Plurality difference between percentages of votes captured' by the two major parties

71-75   Percentage turnout in election: calculated by dividing total vote for all parties by the total eligible electorate

76   Outcome of election: 1-Democratic candidate won unopposed
2-Democratic candidate won a plurality of votes
3-Tie election
4-Republican candidate won a plurality of votes
5-Republican candidate won unopposed

Availability of Data: Offices and Election Years

01   *President:* available for all Presidential elections from 1924 to 1960

02   *Congressman:* available for all elections from 1924 to 1960

03   *Governor:* The Governor of Indiana is elected at Presidential elections; availability of data is the same

04   *Secretary of State:* Indiana's Secretary of State is elected for a two-year term; available for all elections from 1924 to 1960

05   *Prosecuting Attorney:* Prosecuting Attorneys were elected for a two-year term until 1954, when their terms were extended to four years; data available from 1924 to 1954 and for 1958

06   *State Senators:* Approximately half the State Senators are elected at each general election for a four-year term; data available from 1922 to 1960

07   *State Representatives:* elected for a two-year term; data available from 1924 to 1960

POLITICAL VARIABLES FOR NATIONAL GOVERNMENTS

The Dimensionality of Nations Project is designed to study the dimensions of variations of 82 nations across 236 economic, political, social, and cultural characteristics and the standing of each nation on each of the resulting dimensions. The principal investigator of the DON Project is Professor Rudolph Rummel, now at Yale University. The main publication of the project will be *Dimensions of Nations* (forthcoming). Professors Harold Guetzkow (Northwestern), Jack Sawyer (University of Chicago), and Raymond Tanter (Northwestern) are co-authors of the book with Rudolph Rummel. The data for all nations and all variables can be obtained through the Inter-University Consortium for Political Research. Only the codes for the fifteen "political" variables are given below.

Variable Name and Number	Code	Information
FREEDOM OF OPPOSITION, #65	0	Political opposition not permitted; groups not allowed to organize for political action (e.g., interest groups, political parties)
	1	Restricted political opposition allowed (groups free to organize in politics, but oppositional role limited and they may not campaign for control of government)
	2	Political opposition mostly unrestricted (groups can organize for political action and may campaign for control of government)

Data sources: *Statesman's Yearbook*, 1955 and 1956; *The Worldmark Encyclopedia of the Nations*, 1960; *Political Handbook and Atlas of the World*, 1955 and 1956. Rating of the nations is for 1955.

VOTING SYSTEM, #66

0 No voting at all
1 Plebescite-type voting only, with single party and no effective primary
2 Single party with effective primary
3 Multi-party system with ban on extreme parties
4 Multi-party system without limitation on parties

Data sources: See variable #65.

POLITICAL CENTRALIZATION, #67

The code value consists of the sum of the following two ratings, whose wording and categories are formulated in terms of the classifications in the data source given below.

Centralization in municipalities
0 Council and executive appointed by higher units, or council indirectly elected and executive appointed from above
1 Council indirectly elected and executive appointed or elected by council, or council directly elected but executive appointed from above; or council indirectly elected or appointed from above while executive is popularly elected
2 Council directly elected and executive elected by council or people, or appointed by council

Centralization in intermediate governmental structures
0 Council advisory and appointed or elected indirectly and executive elected by council or appointed from above, or there is no council and the executive is appointed
1 Council advisory and elected and executive appointed from above, or executive elected by people and council appointed from above
2 Council directly elected and governing authority and executive appointed or elected by council or people

Data source: Samuel Humes and Eileen M. Martin, *Structure of Local Governments Throughout the World* (The Hague: M. Nijhoff, 1961).

FEDERALIST-
UNITARY,
#68

0 Country has a federal government system
1 Country has a unitary government system
Data sources: See variables #65 and #67. Federal and unitary governments are distinguished by the existence or nonexistence of a constitutional division of powers between central and local governments.

TAX REVENUE
FROM INCOME
AND WEALTH
DIVIDED BY
TOTAL REVENUE,
#69

Actual amounts were entered in the cards. Revenue from income and wealth includes "mainly general and specific taxes on individual and corporate income, excess profits taxes, stamp duties on dividends, death and gift taxes, etc." (*United Nations Statistical Yearbook, 1957,* p. 517) Total revenue refers to the "total receipts" figures in the national account tables. Grants received from foreign governments, and "proceeds of loans and surpluses from previous years" are excluded from this total. Domestic currency figures were used in calculating the ratio.

Data sources: United Nations Statistical Yearbook, 1959, Table 178, pp. 492-539.

CUSTOMS TAX
REVENUE
DIVIDED BY
REVENUE,
#70

Customs tax refers to the import and export duties classified in the receipts section of the national account tables in the *United Nations Statistical Yearbook.* See variable #69 for the definition of "revenue." Domestic currency figures were used in calculating the ratio.

Data sources: The same as for variable #69.

PRESS
CENSORSHIP,
#71

0 Complete or fairly complete censorship of news
1 Some censorship of news
2 No censorship, other than usual laws about libel and the controlling of news of a national security nature.

Data source: Ratings are based on a United Press survey of censorship conditions around the world as of December, 1954, published in *The New York Times,* January 9, 1955. *The Worldmark Encyclopedia of the Nations* (1960) was also consulted.

LEGALITY OF
GOVERNMENT
CHANGE,
#72

0   Last *and* present government came into being through non-legal means (e.g., illegal elections, revolutions), or if there has been only one government since independence, present government came into being illegally

1   Last *or* present government came into being through non-legal means, or if there has been only one government since independence, present government came into power legally

2   Last and present government came into being through legal means

Data sources: Government refers to the executive head of the government; legality refers to the constitutional provisions for transferring power, or in the absence of a constitution, the traditional practice of a country (e.g., hereditary transference of power). Rating is for 1955. These sources were consulted: *The Worldmark Encyclopedia of Nations* (1960); *The Statesman's Yearbook; Political Handbook and Atlas of the World;* and *Britannica Book of the Year.*

LEGITIMACY
OF PRESENT
GOVERNMENT,
#73

0   Present government came into being through means other than revolution

1   Present government came into being through revolution

Data sources: See variable #72. The distinction between the variables is that the concern here is with only the present government and with only revolutionary means of power transference. Rating is for 1955.

TENURE OF
LAST TWO
GOVERNMENTS,
#74

Actual number of years entered in the cards. Data refer to the average tenure of the last two governments. "Government" is defined as the executive head. The present government is counted only if it has been in office for four years or more.

Data sources: See variable #72. Rating is for 1955.

DEFENSE
EXPENDITURES
DIVIDED BY GNP,
#75

Actual amounts are entered in the cards. "Defense expenditures" includes total current and capital outlays. They are generally budgeted figures for fiscal years ending in 1955 and are given in domestic currency. GNP (gross national product) is based on the total value of goods and services produced in a country in a year's time.

Data sources: The "defense" classification in the national account tables in the *United Nations Statistical Yearbook, 1959,* Table 178, pp. 492-539. Other sources for defense expenditures: *Moody's Municipal and Government Manual; Statesman's Yearbook;* and the *Yale University Data Program.* GNP figures were acquired from the International Cooperation Administration as reported in a U.S. Senate Foreign Relations Committee working paper prepared by the Research Center in Economic Development and Cultural Change of the University of Chicago, *The Role of Foreign Aid in the Development of Other Countries* (Washington: Government Printing Office, 1957); and from Norton Ginsburg, *Atlas of Economic Development* (Chicago: University of Chicago Press, 1961), p. 16.

AMOUNT OF
GOVERNMENT
EXPENDITURES
DIVIDED BY GNP,
#76

Actual amounts are entered in the cards. Government expenditures refer to the budgeted current and capital outlays of the national government. Redemption of debt is excluded as are also certain capital transfers. Grants to foreign governments are included. Domestic currency figures were used in calculating the ratios.

Data sources: Government expenditure figures were taken from the national accounts tables in the *United Nations Statistical Yearbook, 1959,* p. 490. Sources of defense expenditures are the same as for variable #75.

GOVERNMENT
REVENUE
DIVIDED BY
GOVERNMENT
EXPENDITURES,
#77

Actual amounts entered in the cards. See variables #69 and #76 for definitions, year, and sources of revenue and expenditure data, respectively. Ratio was calculated using domestic currency figures.

NUMBER OF
POLITICAL
PARTIES,
#78

Counted as given in the data sources. Parties with a membership less than 1% of the population were not counted.

Data source: Statesman's Yearbook, 1956; Political Handbook and Atlas of the World, 1956; and *The Worldmark Encyclopedia of the Nations* (1960).

POLITICAL
DEVELOPMENT,
#78a

A rating given in the source below and based on party competitiveness in the legislature and executive responsibility within a multi-party system for the years 1940-1960. A low rating indicates low political development.

Data source: Phillips Cutright, "National Political Development: Measurement and Analysis," *American Sociological Review,* 28 (April, 1963), 253-64. The ratings of 77 countries in this article were used by the project through the courtesy of Phillips Cutright.

APPENDIX A-3 **BIOGRAPHICAL INFORMATION ON STATE LEGISLATORS**

The information contained on the cards in these decks (1 for House members and 2 for Senate members) refers to personal data about individual legislators and designates the specific sessions since 1925 in which each legislator served. (These codes were constructed several years ago for "counter-sorter" data processing. Consequently, they do not conform to the coding suggestions in Chapter V.)

Card
Column
Number   CATALOG OF CONTENTS

  1-2   State identification code: *12* (Indiana)

  3-4   Study code: *10* (Legislative Personnel Study)

    5   Deck number: 1 (House members)
                             2 (Senate members)

  6-10   Legislator's identifying number

11-12   Legislative district the man represented

13-14   Number of sessions he served in legislature

15-16   Number of sessions he served in this chamber at any time

17-18   Number of sessions he served in this chamber beginning with 1925

19-20   His first session in legislature

21-22   His first session in this chamber

23-24   His *last* session in this chamber

   25   *1925* session: membership status in terms of legislative service

   26   His status during *next* session of legislature

   27   *1927* session: membership status in terms of legislative service

28   His status during *next* session of legislature

59   *1959* session: membership status in terms of legislative service
60   Status during *next* session of legislature
61   *1961* session: membership status in terms of legislative service
62   Status during *next* session of legislature
63   *1963* session: membership status in terms of legislative service
64   Status during *next* session of legislature
65   Legislator's experience in other chamber of legislature
66   His continuity of service in this chamber
67   Cause of his final retirement from this chamber
68   Urban-rural category into which his district falls
69   Number of counties in legislator's district
70   Number of members elected from that district
71-72   Year of birth
73   Age category into which legislator falls at entry into legislature
74   Age category into which legislator falls at entry into this chamber
75   Age category into which legislator falls at last session in chamber
76   Occupation of legislator
77   Educational background
78   Religious affiliation
79   Party affiliation
80   Flag column — irregularities in legislative service which require special attention

Card Column Number	*Contents of Columns*
6-10	Legislator's identifying number: These numbers, which are different for House and Senate members, are used throughout the Studies of the Data Library to identify individuals who have served in the Indiana legislature.

Card
Column
Number   *Contents of Columns*

11-12   Legislative district the man represented: This is a two digit
        code referring to House and Senate legislative districts. The
        House and Senate district codes are not the same.

13-14   Number of sessions he served in the legislature: This includes
        the total number of sessions the legislator served in *both*
        houses, up to and including his last session in this chamber.
        If he served in the other chamber *after* retiring from this one,
        that post-chamber service is *not* added to this total.

15-16   Number of sessions he served in this chamber at any time

17-18   Number of sessions he seved in this chamber, beginning with
        1925

19-20   His first session in the legislature: This column contains the
        last two digits of the year in which he served his first session
        in the legislature, either chamber. Therefore, if he served his
        first session in 1925 − 25 is entered in these columns.

21-22   His first session in this chamber: (last two digits of year)

23-24   His *last* session in this chamber: (last two digits of year)

25   *1925* session: membership status in terms of legislative
        service:
        0 The man was *not* a member of this chamber during this
          session.
        1 He *was* a member and was in his *first* session of service.
        2 He was a member with *one* previous session of experience,
          and that experience may have been in either chamber.
        3 He was a member with *two* previous sessions of experience,
          etc. Therefore, this is his *3rd* session in the legislature.
        4 He was a member in his *4th* session of the legislature.
        5 He was a member in his *5th* session of the legislature.
        6 He was a member in his *6th* session of the legislature.
        7 He was a member in his *7th* session of the legislature.
        8 He was a member in his *8th* session of the legislature.
        9 He was a member of this chamber during this session and
          was serving *at least* his *9th* session. He may have had more
          than eight previous sessions of experience. If concerned
          about this possibility, refer to column 80, which contains a
          code designed to flag all such occurrences.

63   *This code is used in ALL columns catalogued* "membership
        status in terms of legislative service"—the odd-numbered ones
        from 25-63.

*Card
Column
Number*   *Contents of Columns*

26   His status during the *next* session of the legislature:

0   *Not applicable*; he was not a member of this chamber this session

1   He returned to this chamber to serve in the next session

2   He served in the other chamber the next session

3   He was defeated in the *primary* election for the House

4   He was defeated in the *general* election for the House

5   He was defeated in the *primary* election for the Senate

6   He was defeated in the *general* election for the Senate

7   He did not return to this chamber, but the reason that he did not return is not given here

8   He died or resigned

9   He was in the most recent session of this chamber. Statuses during the next have not yet been determined

64   *This code is used in ALL columns catalogued* "status during the *next* session of the legislature"—the even-numbered ones from 26-64.

65   Legislator's experience in the other chamber of the legislature:

1   All the man's service was in this chamber

2   He served in the other chamber prior to his first session in this one

3   He served in the other chamber after his first session in this one but before his last session in this one

4   He served in the other chamber after his last session in this one

5   Both 2 and 3 are true

6   Both 2 and 4 are true

7   Both 3 and 4 are true

8   2, 3, and 4 are all true

66   His continuity of service in this chamber:

1   His service in this chamber was continuous; he had no layouts

2   His service in this chamber was interrupted by 1 layout

3   His service in this chamber was interrupted by 2 layouts

4   His service in this chamber was interrupted by 3 layouts

5   His service in this chamber was interrupted by 4 or more layouts

A layout is defined as an absence from the chamber for one or more sessions. Only absences occurring since 1925 have been counted.

Card
Column
Number   *Contents of Columns*

67   Cause of his final retirement from this chamber:
     2 He left to serve in the other chamber the next session
     3 He was defeated in the *primary* election for the House
     4 He was defeated in the *general* election for the House
     5 He was defeated in the *primary* election for the Senate
     6 He was defeated in the *general* election for the Senate
     7 He did not return to this chamber, but the reason that he
       did not return is not given here
     8 He died or resigned
     9 He was in the most recent session of this chamber. He has
       not retired.

68   Urban-rural category of his legislative district: specific to
     Indiana
     1 All districts which contain Indianapolis; always more than
       50% of the population was in Indianapolis.
     2 All districts which contain Fort Wayne; always more than
       50% of the population was in Fort Wayne.
     3 All districts which contain Lake County; always more than
       80% of the population was in the Chicago urbanized area
       and always more than 50% in the 3 cities of Gary, Ham-
       mond, and East Chicago.
     4 All districts which contain South Bend; always more than
       50% of the population was in South Bend.
     5 All districts which contain Evansville; always more than
       50% of the population was in Evansville.

     Code numbers 6 and 7 are applied to districts which con-
     tain all cities of the state (other than Fort Wayne, South
     Bend-Mishawaka, Evansville, and the cities in Lake Coun-
     ty) which were second or third class cities under all three
     censuses from 1930-1950 (i.e., they had 20,000 or more
     population). These cities:

Anderson	Lafayette	Muncie
Elkhart	Richmond	New Albany
Kokomo	Michigan City	Terre Haute
		Marion

     6 Code 6 applies to the districts which have more than 50%
       of their population living in one of these cities. In all dis-
       tricts except House Dist. 68, more than 50% of the popula-
       tion was in the city under all three censuses. (House Dist.

Card
Column
Number   *Contents of Columns*

68—Tippecanoe-Warren—had 50% of its population in La-
fayette for only two census periods.)

7 Code 7 applies to all remaining districts which contain any
of the cities in the above list. In all cases for all three censuses, less than 50% of the district's population was in the
city.

8 Districts having a city that was 10,000 or more at some
time during the period, but never as big as 20,000; and at
no time was 50% of the population in cities as big as 5,000.

9 Districts that at no time had a city as big as 10,000 population, and at no time was as much as 50% of the population in cities as big as 5,000.

0 Districts not falling into any of the above categories.

69 Number of counties in legislator's district

70 Number of members elected from that district
1 One member district
2 Two member district
3 Three member district
5 Five member district
9 Eleven member district

71-72 Year of birth: last two digits of the year of birth

73 Age category into which legislator falls at entry into legislature; use code below

74 Age category into which legislator falls at entry into this
chamber:
0 No information
1 21 to 29 years old
2 30 to 34 years old
3 35 to 39 years old
4 40 to 44 years old
5 45 to 49 years old
6 50 to 54 years old
7 55 to 59 years old
8 60 to 69 years old
9 70 years old or more

75 Age category into which legislator falls at last session in this
chamber:
0 No information
1 21 to 29 years old

Card
Column
Number   *Contents of Columns*

2 30 to 39 years old
3 40 to 44 years old
4 45 to 49 years old
5 50 to 54 years old
6 55 to 59 years old
7 60 to 64 years old
8 65 to 69 years old
9 70 years old or more

76 Occupation of legislator:
0 No information
1 Attorney
2 Farmer, livestock owner, bee-keeper, etc.
3 Insurance and real estate agent
4 Merchant, contractor, small businessman, advertising man, manufacturer, and industrialist
5 Laborer (includes union officials, machinists, tradesmen, etc.)
6 Salesman, clerk, and white collar worker
7 Newspaperman, editor, publisher, radio
8 Professional man other than lawyer and newspaperman: includes teachers and educational administrators, doctors, veterinarians, engineers, accountants, etc.
9 Not otherwise classified

77 Educational background:
0 No information
1 He did not attend high school
2 He attended high school but did not graduate
3 He graduated from high school but did not go further
4 He attended college but did not get a four year degree
5 He received a four year college degree or equivalent
6 He did not go to college but we do not know where he stopped before that
7 He attended high school and may have graduated
8 He at least graduated from high school and may have gone further
9 He at least attended college and may have a four year degree

78 Religious affiliation:
0 No information
1 Catholic: Roman Catholic, etc.
2 Methodist: M.E., Meth., 1st Methodist, etc.

Card
Column
Number   *Contents of Columns*

3 Christian: Christian Church, Congregational, Disciples of Christ, Church of Christ, etc.
4 Baptist: Primitive Baptist, Missionary Baptist, etc.
5 Presbyterian
6 Lutheran: Evangelical Lutheran, German Lutheran, etc.
7 German Anabaptist: United Brethren, Evangelical United Brethren, E.U.B., Church of the Brethren, Dunkers, etc.
8 Episcopalian
9 Not otherwise classified

79 Party affiliation:
1 Democrat
2 Republican

80 Flag column—irregularities in legislative service which require special attention:
0 No irregularities (all the information about this man can be recorded with use of appropriate digits in appropriate columns).
1 This man's length of service in the legislature exceeded nine sessions before he retired from the chamber. Thus, his "membership status in terms of legislative service" column (odd-numbered columns from 25 to 63) will repeat the digit "9" for those sessions in which he had more than 9 sessions' experience.
2 The man held more than nine chairmanships in this chamber since 1925 (this code is for use in conjunction with another deck of the Legislative Personnel Study).
3 The man did not always represent the same district in the legislature. Thus, the district code given for columns 11-12 might not be the correct code for a particular session. Columns 68-70 *may* also be affected by this, for they reflect the characteristics of the district given in columns 11-12. Thus, these columns (68-70) may not apply for the particular session when the man represents a district different from that which is given in columns 11-12. In general, the practice used in recording has been to give the district in which he *last served* as his district number in columns 11-12.
4 Both 1 and 2 are true in regard to this man.
5 This man changed party affiliation; his later party is recorded.

APPENDIX A-4 **ROLL CALL VOTING**

These cards contain the voting positions taken by each legislator on every "contested" roll call vote which occurred in the chamber of service. (A contested roll call vote is defined as any vote on which at least 10% of the membership of the chamber is recorded voting "yes" and at least 10% is recorded voting "no.")

Card
Column
Number   CATALOG OF CONTENTS

 1-2   State Identification Code: *12* (Indiana)

 3-4   Study Code: *11* (Roll Call Votes Recorded for *House* Members)
        12 (Roll Call Votes Recorded for *Senate* Members)

 5-6   Session of Legislature: last two digits of the year of session

   7   Set Identification Number: the particular group of roll call votes which have been recorded for the above session

 8-10 Identification of the particular legislator whose voting positions have been recorded on a given card

11-12 The legislative district the above man represented in legislature

  13   His party affiliation

  14   His occupation

  15   The urban-rural nature of the legislative district that he represented

  16   The voting positions assumed by the legislator on every "contested" roll call vote which occurred in the chamber of service. Each column from #16 to #80 contains the results of his vote on a *specific* roll call vote. The same column is used to record the vote of all Senators or Representatives for a par-

80　ticular measure voted on in the appropriate chamber. Columns 5-6 and column 7 aid in identifying which specific vote is recorded in which column. For example, in the 1949 House session all the cards of, say, set #1 may contain the vote on a highway bill in, say, column #37. Thus, for that particular year and set, column #37 will record the votes of all representatives with reference to that particular bill. *Which* specific roll call vote is recorded in *which* column can only be known with reference to a listing of the "contested" votes and their card locations.

Card Column Number	*Contents of Columns*

7　Set Identification Number: the particular group of roll call votes which have been recorded for a legislative session:

1 The *first* group of contested roll call votes occurring in a given session of the legislature. (As the legislature proceeds in its daily activities and as "contested" roll call votes develop, these votes are recorded in order of their occurrence —beginning with column #16 on Set #1. After 65 such votes have been recorded in columns #16-80, the end of the card is reached and it becomes necessary to begin a second set, Set #2, which is then used to record an additional 65 contested roll call votes before another set is needed.)

2 The *second* group of contested roll call votes . . . . (refer to the above explanation)

0 The *tenth* group . . . . (a total of 650 roll call votes can be recorded for a single session with the use of this code)

8-10　Identification of the particular legislator whose voting positions have been recorded on a given card: This identification code is the same as that used in Study 10, Appendix A-3. These numbers are different for House and Senate members.

11-12　The legislative district the above man represented in the legislature: This is a two digit code referring to House and Senate legislative districts.

13　His party affiliation:
1 Democrat
2 Republican

Card
Column
Number   *Contents of Columns*

14   His occupation:
     0 No information
     1 Attorney
     2 Farmer, livestock owner, bee-keeper, etc.
     3 Insurance and real estate agent
     4 Merchant, contractor, small businessman, advertising man, manufacturer, and industrialist
     5 Laborer (includes union officials, machinists, tradesmen, etc.)
     6 Salesman, clerk, and white collar worker
     7 Newspaperman, editor, publisher, radio
     8 Professional man other than lawyer and newspaperman: includes teachers and educational administrators, doctors, veterinarians, engineers, accountants, etc.
     9 Not otherwise classified

15   The urban-rural nature of the legislative district he represents: (see code for column 68 in Study 10, Appendix A-3)

16   The voting positions assumed by the legislator on every "contested" roll call vote which occurred in the chamber of service:

80   1 The legislator voted *yes* on this roll call vote.
     2 The legislator voted *no* on this roll call vote.
     3 The legislator was not recorded as voting on this particular roll call vote.
     Any number which is not a *1* or a *2* is to be interpreted as a *3*. It had been tried to record a *condition* for not voting, such as "excused," "present, but not voting," etc., but it was learned that the official Indiana Journals were not consistent in their reporting of these conditions. Therefore, it is safer to disregard these more subtle categories and treat all digits which are not a "1" or a "2" as a "3"—indicative of a simple "not voting" condition.

COMMITTEE ASSIGNMENTS

These cards contain, along with other relevant information concerning legislators, the committee assignments of each member of a given legislative session.

Card
Column
Number   CATALOG OF CONTENTS

1-2   State Identification Code: *12* (Indiana)

3-4   Study Code: *13* (Committee Assignments of Legislators)

5-6   Session of Legislature: last two digits of year of session

7   Legislative chamber to which the legislator belongs

8-10   Identification of the particular legislator whose committee assignments have been recorded for this session

11-12   Legislative district represented by the above man

13   His party affiliation

14   His occupation

15   The urban-rural nature of the legislative district that he represented

16   His education

17   His length of service in legislature, including this session

18   His status during *next* session of legislature

19   The positions of authority he held in the committee structure

20   Total number of committees of which he was a member

21   The committee assignments of the legislator in a legislative chamber with N committees. (N may range up to 6o.) For each chamber in each legislative session, a specific column has been used to record membership on a given committee. Beginning with column 21, the committees have been as-

N signed to the columns in sequential order in accordance with
their alphabetical listing in the back of the official Journal.
The numbers of these columns containing the membership of
a given committee are identical to the code numbers used to
identify the committees in the Legislative History Study,
#43—Appendix A-6. Thus, a bill referred to committee #33
on that Study will have been sent to the committee identified
by column #33 in this Study.

Card
Column
Number   *Contents of Columns*

7 The legislative chamber to which the legislator belongs:
1 House
2 Senate

8-10 Identification of the particular legislator whose committee
assignments have been recorded for this session: This identification code is the same as that used in Study 10, Appendix A-3.

11-12 The legislative district the above man represented in the
legislature: This is a two digit code referring to House and
Senate legislative districts.

13 His party affiliation:
1 Democrat
2 Republican

14 His occupation:
0 No information
1 Attorney
2 Farmer, livestock owner, bee-keeper, etc.
3 Insurance and real estate agent
4 Merchant, contractor, small businessman, advertising, manufacturer, and industrialist
5 Laborer (includes union officials, machinists, tradesmen,
etc.)
6 Salesman, clerk, and white collar worker
7 Newspaperman, editor, publisher, radio
8 Professional man other than lawyer and newspaperman:
includes teachers and educational administrators, doctors,
veterinarians, engineers, accountants, etc.
9 Not otherwise classified

Card Column Number	Contents of Columns

17   His length of service in the legislature including this session:
1 This is his *first* session in the legislature
2 This is his *second* session in the legislature

9 This is *at least* his 9th session in the legislature; he *may* have served more than 9 sessions.

18   His status during the *next* session of the legislature:
1 He returned to this chamber the next session
2 He served in the *other* chamber the next session
3 He was defeated in the primary election for the House
4 He was defeated in the general election for the House
5 He was defeated in the primary election for the Senate
6 He was defeated in the general election for the Senate
7 He did not return to the legislature, and the reason that he did not return is unknown
8 He died or resigned
9 He is serving in a current session and status for the next session cannot be determined

19   The positions of authority he held in the committee structure:
0 The man held no positions of authority on any committees
1 He had *one* ranking membership on a committee
2 He had *two* ranking memberships
3 He had *one* committee chairmanship
4 He had one committee chairmanship and *one* ranking membership
5 He had one committee chairmanship and *two* ranking memberships
6 He had *two* committee chairmanships
7 He had two committee chairmanships and *one* ranking membership
8 He had two committee chairmanships and *two* ranking memberships
9 Not otherwise classified

21   The committee assignments of a legislator in a legislative
↓   chamber with N committees. The session-by-session listing of
     legislative committees will disclose the column-codes used for
     recording committee membership according to this code:
N   0 The legislator was not a member of this column's
       committee
     1 He was a member with no position of authority
     2 He was the ranking member on this column's committee
     3 He was the chairman of this column's committee

LEGISLATIVE HISTORIES OF BILLS

These cards contain information pertaining to the legislative history of every measure introduced into the legislature during the sessions for which data have been recorded. Included in the legislative history are codes relating to the sponsorship of each measure, the committee of referral, action taken by that committee, action taken on the floor, the fate of the measure in the second chamber, the governor's action, etc. (These codes were constructed several years ago for "counter-sorter" data processing. Consequently, they do not conform to the coding suggestions in Chapter V.)

Card
Column
Number CATALOG OF CONTENTS

1-2	State Identification code: *12* (Indiana)
3-4	Study Code: *43* (Legislative History)
5-6	Session of legislature: last two digits of year of session
7	Type of legislation: House/Senate, Bill or Resolution
8-10	Identifying number of specific measure
11	Number of sponsors for measure in originating chamber
12-14	Identifying number of measure's first-named sponsor in originating chamber
15	His party affiliation
16	His occupation
17	Number of sessions of experience he has had in legislature
18-19	Legislative district the man represented
20	Urban-rural category into which his district falls
21-23	Identifying number of measure's second-named sponsor
24	His party affiliation

*Card
Column
Number*

25   His occupation

26   Number of sessions of experience he has had in legislature

27-28   Legislative district the man represented

29   Urban-rural category into which his district falls

30-37   Unassigned: contains zeros

38   Number of committees to which measure was referred in originating chamber

39-40   Identification of final committee to which bill was referred

41   Chamber action on committee's majority report

42   Chamber action on committee's minority report

43   Chamber's efforts to remove bill from committee's consideration

44   Summary of action at committee stage

45   Action taken on floor at passage stage

46   Amendments made after being reported out of committee

47   Floor stage in legislative process at which bill was amended

48   Result of final vote on passage

49   Result of preceding vote on passage—if such vote occurred

50   Result of still earlier vote on passage—if such vote occurred

51   Summary of action taken on bill by *originating* chamber

52   Number of committees to which bill was referred in *second* chamber

53-54   Identification number of final committee to which bill was referred

55   Chamber action on committee's majority report

56   Chamber action on committee's minority report

57   Chamber's efforts to remove bill from committee's consideration

58   Summary of committee action

59   Action taken on floor at passage stage

60   Amendments made after being reported out of committee

61   Floor stage in legislative process at which bill was amended

62   Result of final vote on passage

63   Result of preceding vote on passage—if such vote occurred

64   Result of still earlier vote on passage—if such vote occurred

65   Summary of action taken on bill by *second* chamber

66   Initiating chamber's reaction to second chamber's amendment

67   Reference to conference committee and result of its action

68   Both chambers' reaction to conference committee report

69   Reference to *second* conference committee and result of its action

70   Both chambers' reaction to second conference committee report

71   Reference to *third* conference committee and result of its action

72   Both chambers' reaction to third conference committee report

73   Amendments made by conference committee and adopted by legislature

74   Governor's action on measure

75   Appropriate course of action to be followed subsequent to governor's veto

76   Initiating chamber's reaction to governor's veto

77   Second chamber's reaction to governor's veto

78-79   Special flag code designed to handle legislative irregularities

80   Master summary of legislative history

Card Column Number	*Contents of Columns*
7	Type of legislation:
	1 Senate Bill
	2 Senate Joint Resolution
	3 Senate Concurrent Resolution

Card
Column
Number   *Contents of Columns*
       4 House Bill
       5 House Joint Resolution
       6 House Concurrent Resolution

12-14 Identifying number of measure's *first*-named and *second*-
&   named sponsor: These identifying numbers are the same as
21-23 those used in Study 10, Appendix A-3.

15 His party affiliation:
&   1 Democrat
24 2 Republican

16 His occupation:
&   0 No information
25 1 Attorney
    2 Farmer, livestock owner, bee-keeper, etc.
    3 Insurance and real estate agent
    4 Merchant, contractor, small businessman, advertising, man-
      ufacturer, and industrialist
    5 Laborer (includes union officials, machinists, tradesmen,
      etc.)
    6 Salesman, clerk, and white collar worker
    7 Newspaperman, editor, publisher, radio
    8 Professional man other than lawyer and newspaperman:
      includes teachers and educational administrators, doctors,
      veterinarians, engineers, accountants, etc.
    9 Not otherwise classified

17 Number of sessions of experience he has had in the legisla-
&   ture:
26 1 This was his 1st session in the legislature
    2 This was his 2nd sessiond in the legislature
    3 This was his 3rd session in the legislature
    4 This was his 4th session in the legislature
    5 This was his 5th session in the legislature
    6 This was his 6th session in the legislature
    7 This was his 7th session in the legislature
    8 This was his 8th session in the legislature
    9 This was *at least* his 9th session in the legislature. Between
      1925 and 1961, a few men served more than 9 sessions.

18-19 Legislative district the men represented:
&   This is a two digit code referring to House and Senate legis-
27-28 lative districts.

Card
Column
Number   Contents of Columns

20   Urban-rural category into which his district falls. (See codes
&   for column 68, Study 10, Appendix A-3.)
29

38   Number of committees to which bill was referred:
&   0 Not applicable; no committee handled bill
52   1 One committee handled bill
     2 Although there were intervening committees, the original
       committee finally handled bill
     3 The bill was handled finally by a committee other than
       original committee
     4 No committee involved in handling bill; it was acted upon
       on the floor of chamber
     5 The bill was assigned to committee, but there was no
       record of a committee report and the chamber handled the
       bill
     6 Special committee handled bill

39-40 Identification of final committee to which bill was referred:
&   These identification numbers, which differ for each chamber
53-54 during each session, are the same as those used for the cor-
       responding session and chamber in the Committee Assign-
       ment Study.

41   Chamber action on the committee's majority report:
&   0 Not applicable
55   1 The bill was not reported out (this includes situations in
       which committee requested and was granted more time for
       consideration, although it still did not provide a report on
       the bill)
     2 The chamber adopted the majority report: that the bill
       pass without amendment
     3 The chamber adopted the majority report: that the bill
       pass after amendment
     4 The chamber adopted the majority report which reported
       the bill without amendment and without recommendation
     5 The chamber adopted the majority report which reported
       the bill with amendment, but without recommendation
     6 The chamber adopted an unfavorable committee report
       (this includes being reported with amendment striking out
       enactment clause, reported for indefinite postponement, or
       reported with a motion to table the bill)
     7 The chamber adopted the majority report: that the bill be
       recommitted to another committee

Card Column Number	Contents of Columns

8 The bill was taken from the committee by action of the chamber

9 The chamber adopted the minority report of the committee. The nature of this report is described in the following column:

42 Chamber action on the committee's minority report:

& 0 Not applicable

43 2 The minority report was that the bill pass without amendment

3 The minority report was that the bill pass after amendment

4 The minority report proposed to report out the original bill without recommendation

5 The minority report proposed to report out an amended bill without recommendation

6 The minority report proposed an unfavorable report (this includes being reported with an amendment to strike out the enacting clause or a motion to table the bill)

7 The minority report was that the bill be indefinitely postponed

43 Chamber's efforts to remove bill from committee's consideration:

& ation:

57 0 The chamber did not attempt to remove the bill from the committee's consideration

1 A motion to have the bill reported out of committee failed and the bill was not reported out. It remained in committee

2 A motion to have the bill reported out of committee failed, but the bill was reported out later

3 A motion for bill to be reported out passed by the chamber

4 A motion to have the bill recommitted to a new committee failed (i.e., it was withdrawn, defeated, or there was no record of action; the bill stayed in this committee)

5 A motion to have the bill recommitted to a new committee failed, but the bill was recommitted to another committee

6 A motion to have the bill recommitted to a new committee was passed

44 Summary of action at the committee stage:

& 0 Not applicable; the bill was not referred to committee

58 1 The bill was not reported out of committee

2 The bill was reported out without amendment

3 The bill was reported out with amendment

4 The bill was withdrawn while still in committee

Card
Column
Number   *Contents of Columns*

5 The bill was ordered from the committee by the chamber, and the bill was handled by the chamber
6 The bill was reported out for recommitment to another committee
7 The bill was reported out for indefinite postponement, or for tabling
8 Chamber disregarded committee report

45   Action taken on the floor at the passage stage:
&   0 The bill terminated previous to passage stage
59   1 A vote on passage was taken
     2 The bill did not come to a vote on passage, and it was not withdrawn
     3 The bill was withdrawn after being reported out of committee

46   Amendments made after being reported out of committee:
&   0 Not applicable; the bill terminated earlier
60   1 The bill was not amended
     2 It was amended by its author with chamber vote
     3 It was amended by the chamber acting as a Committee of the Whole
     4 It was amended on a motion from the floor by a legislator other than its author
     5 It was amended by Committee on Phraseology
     6 It was amended by a committee of one
     7 It was amended by Committee of the Whole and by one or more of the other means given above
     8 It was amended by two or more of the above means, *not* including Committee of the Whole
     9 It was amended by a *specially-appointed* committee of two or more

47   Floor stage in legislative process at which bill was amended:
&   0 Not applicable; bill was amended in committee, was terminated earlier, or was not amended
61   1 It was amended prior to or at time of second reading
     2 It was amended prior to or at time of third reading
     3 It was amended after third reading, but prior to vote on passage
     4 Any combination of the above three
     5 It was amended after third reading and *after* vote on passage

48   Result of final vote on passage:
&   0 Not applicable; bill terminated previous to passage stage
49   1 The bill passed by a constitutional majority although it was
&   contested
50   2 The bill passed by a constitutional majority and was *not*
&   contested
62   3 It was defeated by a constitutional majority but was con-
&   tested
63   4 It was defeated by an uncontested constitutional majority
&   5 It failed enactment for lack of a constitutional majority,
64   but a majority voted for the bill in a contested vote. (This
       bill may be reconsidered for passage at a later time)
     6 It failed enactment for lack of a constitutional majority,
       although no one voted against the bill. (This bill may be
       reconsidered for passage at a later time)
     7 It failed for lack of a constitutional majority, and a major-
       ity voted against the bill in a contested vote. (This bill may
       be reconsidered at a later time)
     8 It failed for lack of a constitutional majority, and everyone
       voted against the bill. (This bill may be reconsidered at a
       later time)
     9 The bill was defeated on the floor for a reason not classified
       above. This includes situations of tie votes, and measures
       which did not receive a roll call vote on the third reading

51   Summary of action taken on the bill by the chamber:
&   0 Not applicable; the bill terminated earlier
65   1 The bill did not survive the vote on its passage
     2 The bill passed this chamber and was sent to the other
       chamber which acted on the bill
     3 The bill was withdrawn while in this chamber
     4 The bill did not arrive at the voting stage and no further
       action was recorded
     5 The bill passed but no further action was recorded
     6 The bill passed the initiating chamber and was sent to the
       other chamber but was then recalled from that chamber;
       no further action was recorded, or the bill was indefinitely
       postponed
     7 The bill was killed by a chamber vote which was taken
       before the passage stage. This includes a vote for indefinite
       postponement, tabling and striking out enactment clause

Card Column Number	Contents of Columns

8 The bill originally passed, but it was reconsidered and placed back on the third reading where it died—because of indefinite postponement or no further action taken

66 Initiating chamber's reaction to second chamber's amendment:
0 Not applicable; the bill terminated earlier
1 There was no amendment of bill by second chamber
2 It was amended by second chamber, and initiating chamber accepted the amendment
3 It was amended by second chamber, and initiating chamber voted *not* to concur in the amendment
4 It was amended by second chamber, and initiating chamber did not act on the amendment
5 It was amended by second chamber, and initiating chamber acted with reference to the amendment, but no vote was taken

67
&
69
&
71

Reference to Conference Committee and result of its action:
0 Not applicable; bill terminated earlier or no amendments were made by the second chamber
1 A conference committee was designated by both chambers and agreement was reached by that committee
2 A conference committee was designed by both chambers but there was no further entry in the Journal
3 A conference committee was appointed. However, it reported that it reached no agreement, and there was no further entry in the Journal
4 A conference committee was appointed. However, it reported that it reached no agreement and the House failed to designate members for a subsequent conference committee
5 A conference committee was appointed. However, it reported that it reached no agreement and the Senate failed to designate members for a subsequent conference committee
6 A conference committee was appointed. However, it reported that it reached no agreement and both chambers failed to designate members for a subsequent conference committee

*Card
Column
Number*   *Contents of Columns*

7 A conference committee was appointed. However, it reported that it reached no agreement and a new conference
committee was appointed
8 The bill was withdrawn at this stage
9 One chamber appointed members to the conference committee, but the other did not; therefore there was no meeting and no report

68   Both chambers' reaction to conference committee report:
&   0 Not applicable; the bill terminated earlier or there was no
70   conference committee report
&   1 Both chambers accepted committee report
72   2 Both chambers rejected committee report
3 Both chambers took no action on conference committee
report
4 The initiating chamber accepted the report, but the second
chamber rejected it
5 The initiating chamber accepted the report, but the second
chamber took no action on it
6 The initiating chamber rejected the report, but the second
chamber accepted it
7 The initiating chamber rejected the report, but the second
chamber took no action on it
8 The initiating chamber took no action on the report, and
the second chamber rejected it
9 The initiating chamber took no action on the report, and
the second chamber accepted it

73   Amendments made by the conference committee and adopted
by the legislature:
0 Not applicable
1 The conference committee made amendments although it
was appointed only to amend the title
2 The conference committee passed the bill in original form,
striking out amendments added earlier
3 The conference committee struck out *some* of the original
amendments and made further amendments
4 The conference committee struck out *all* of the original
amendments and made further amendments
5 The conference committee agreed on all original amendments and made further amendments
6 The conference committee struck out some of the original
amendments but agreed on the others

Card
Column
Number   *Contents of Columns*

      7 The conference committee accepted the amendments of the second chamber
      8 The conference committee completely re-wrote the bill

74 Governor's action on the measure:
      0 Not applicable; the bill was terminated earlier
      1 The Governor signed the bill during the first 59 days of the session
      2 The Governor signed the bill during the last two days of the session
      3 The bill became effective without the Governor's signature
      4 The Governor vetoed the bill, and returned it with his message of objection
      5 The Governor vetoed the bill, which was presented to him during the last two days of the session, by failing to act upon it
      6 The Governor refused to receive the bill, which was presented to him during the last two days of the session
      7 The bill was recalled from the governor by the originating chamber. No further action was recorded in the Journal

75 Appropriate course of action to be followed subsequent to the Governor's veto:
      0 Not applicable; the bill terminated earlier, or there was no veto
      1 Action on overriding the Governor's veto is proper only in this session of the legislature
      2 Action on overriding the Governor's veto is proper only in the following session of the legislature

76 Chamber's reaction to the Governor's veto:
&   0 Not applicable; the bill terminated earlier, or the Gover-
77 nor did not veto the bill
      1 A motion to override the Governor's veto carried by a constitutional majority this session
      2 A motion to override the Governor's veto failed; a majority voted against the motion
      3 A motion to override the Governor's veto failed; a majority voted for the motion, but it lacked the required constitutional majority
      4 It was proper to attempt to override the veto that session, but no action was taken
      5 A motion to override the Governor's veto carried by a constitutional majority in the subsequent session

*Card
Column
Number*   *Contents of Columns*

    6 A motion to override the veto failed in the subsequent session: a majority voted against the motion

    7 A motion to override the veto failed in the subsequent session: a majority voted for the motion, but it lacked the required constitutional majority

    8 It was proper to act in the subsequent session to override the veto, but no action was taken in that session

78-79 Special flag codes designed to handle legislative irregularities:

(*Codes 20-39 refer to action in initiating chamber*)

  20 The rules were suspended in handling the bill on the floor

  21 The second chamber amended the bill; the first chamber withdrew a motion to concur in the amendment, and indefinitely postponed the bill

  22 The bill was referred to a committee, but it advanced to the second reading without a committee report or any committee action

  23 The bill was not referred to a committee but the chamber adopted a motion to supply the committee report

(*Codes 40-59 refer to action in the second chamber*)

  40 The rules were suspended in handling the bill on floor

  41 No committee was involved; the bill was handled by chamber

  43 No committee was involved, and no action was recorded in Journal

  44 The conference committee appointed to work on title made amendments on bill

  45 Committee introduced new bill under "amendment"

(*Codes 60-79 refer to action in both chambers*)

  60 No committee handled the bill in the first chamber, and the rules were suspended in the second

  70 Bill followed a course contrary to legislative procedure

  80 Master summary of legislative history:

    0 The bill terminated without reference to a committee or without a formal vote in the initiating chamber. This includes bills which have been withdrawn immediately after introduction, those which lack references in the Journal, etc.

    1 The bill terminated at the committee stage of the initiating chamber

Card
Column
Number   *Contents of Columns*

  2 The bill died on the floor of the initiating chamber
  3 The bill passed the initiating chamber
  4 The bill died at the committee stage of the second
     chamber
  5 The bill died on the floor of the second chamber
  6 The bill passed the second chamber
  7 The bill died at the conference committee stage
  8 The Governor's veto was effective
  9 The bill became law

CODING CONVENTIONS

A. The basic scheme. (Taken from the Survey Research Center *Manual for Coders*)

Code Content

1. "*Yes*" ("good" or most positive)

5. "*No*" ("bad" or least positive)

7. "Other" (not specified in preceding code categories) The respondent mentions an item which, because of its infrequent occurrence as a response does not have a particular category designated for it. These responses are *valid* but miscellaneous. The "other" category is *not* low priority and should be treated by the coder like any other perfectly good code.

8. "*I don't know*" or any similar indication *by the respondent* that, because of ignorance or memory failure, he cannot give an opinion or has no attitude toward the subject in question.

9. "*Not ascertained*" This means that the *coder* cannot ascertain how to categorize a particular response in terms of the code for any of the following four reasons:

    a. The *respondent obviously misunderstood the question* or did not reply in terms of the question. For instance, in answer to an absolute question, the respondent gives only a comparative answer, with no other indication of his position. (Q. "Are times good or bad now?" Response: "Times are better than they were.") Or the reverse situation in which the respondent gives only an absolute answer to a question that calls for a comparative one. (Q. "Are times better or worse than they were a year ago?" Response: "Times are good now.")

    b. The *coder* simply *cannot understand what the respondent has said;* the answer just does not make sense, perhaps due to poor or incomplete transcription of the verbatim response by the interviewer.

      c. The question *should have been asked but was not,* and no conclusive inference can be made from other responses.

      d. The respondent's answer is so equivocal and broad (and less specific than the code categories) that it might be seen as *fitting several categories equally well.*

  0. *"Inapplicable"* (also "None")

      a. Any response to the question would be impossible under the circumstances, and therefore the question was deliberately not asked of that respondent. (The respondent owns his home; the question on "amount of rent paid yearly" would be inapplicable.)

      b. A sufficient number of columns is available to code two or more items in a particular code (reasons, etc.) but only one item is coded in the first column. The columns for other items are coded "0" when only one item is mentioned in the response.

      c. "0" is also used to categorize "None," indicating the absence of the particular item being classified. For instance, in a code classifying number of children in the respondent's household, "0" would be the symbol for "no children."

In a double column code the last four categories would be 77, 88, 99, and 00.

B. *Agreement*
    1. Agree strongly
    2. Agree, but not very strongly
    3. Not sure, it depends
    4. Disagree, but not very strongly
    5. Disagree strongly

C. *State*: this code is consistent with Bureau of the Census regional definitions, with the exception of Delaware, which the Bureau considers a Border State.

    New England (first digit indicates region)
      01. Connecticut
      02. Maine
      03. Massachusetts
      04. New Hampshire
      05. Rhode Island
      06. Vermont

Middle Atlantic
   11. Delaware
   12. New Jersey
   13. New York
   14. Pennsylvania

East North Central
   21. Illinois
   22. Indiana
   23. Michigan
   24. Ohio
   25. Wisconsin

West North Central
   31. Iowa
   32. Kansas
   33. Minnesota
   34. Missouri
   35. Nebraska
   36. North Dakota
   37. South Dakota

Solid South
   41. Alabama
   42. Arkansas
   43. Florida
   44. Georgia
   45. Louisiana
   46. Mississippi
   47. North Carolina
   48. South Carolina
   49. Texas
   40. Virginia

Border States
   51. Kentucky
   52. Maryland
   53. Oklahoma
   54. Tennessee
   55. Washington, D. C.
   56. West Virginia

Mountain States
   61. Arizona
   62. Colorado
   63. Idaho
   64. Montana

65.   Nevada
66.   New Mexico
67.   Utah
68.   Wyoming

Western States
71.   California
72.   Oregon
73.   Washington

D.   *County.* The three digit codes published in the 1952 or 1962 *County and City Data Book*, published by the Bureau of the Census, are standard. This code basically arranges the counties of a state in alphabetical order, and assigns 001 to the first county, 002 to the second, etc. There are exceptions, however, in that a few units which are not counties are also included.

E.   *Congressional District.* A two digit field containing the actual number of the district is recommended. Thus the first district of a state is coded 01. At-large districts are coded according to contest, with the first race coded 98, the second 97, the third 96, etc. The 99 code is reserved as a missing data category (a respondent doesn't know the number of the district in which he resides, for example).

F.   *Age.* Usual practice is to code present age in a two column field. However, an excellent alternative is to preserve the last two digits of year of birth in a two column field.

G.   *Income, net worth, savings, etc.* A seven column field will preserve detailed information about the few multi-millionaires that might appear in a sample.

H.   *Number of children, number of adults in household, etc.* A field wide enough to code highest number in sample should be defined.

I.   *Sex.*
1.   Male
2.   Female

J.   *Race*
1.   White
2.   Negro
7.   Other

PREPARATION OF CONTROL CARDS FOR NUCROS

NUCROS is a general program for preparing multivariate cross-classifications in accordance with instructions provided by the user for his data processing problems. In common with virtually all general programs, the NUCROS program deck must be followed by a set of control cards containing these specific instructions. NUCROS uses the information punched into the control cards to determine how to process the raw data cards that follow immediately afterwards.

Two control card layout sheets, presented in Figures C-1 and C-2, serve as guides for correct preparation of the control cards. The proper order of the input for execution on the IBM 709 IBSYS monitor system in operation *at Northwestern* is as follows:

1. *Two* FORTRAN IV Northwestern University Computing Center Identification Cards
2. "$EXECUTE" card ⎰ (control the processing of object decks
3. "$IBJOB" card ⎱ for FORTRAN IV runs)
4. The NUCROS binary language object deck
5. "7 DATA FOLLOWS" card (prepares the program to receive the control cards and data cards which follow)
6. Control Cards #1-#12
7. Recording Control Cards (optional)
8. Variable Identification Cards (optional)
9. Raw data cards

If the program is to be run through a second cycle or more, then the above must be followed with:

10. Control Cards #2-#12 for the second cycle
11. Recoding Control Cards (optional)
12. Variable Identification Cards (optional)
13. Second set of raw data cards (or rewind data tape, see below)

A number punched into columns 1-2 of control card #1 tells the main program how many times it will be executed—how many "cycles" are requested. A maximum of 40 variables and 72 tables can be processed for each cycle of the program with a maximum of 99 cycles per run. For normal runs demanding only one cycle of operation, the number 01 should be punched in these columns.

Columns #2-#73 of the 2nd and 3rd control cards can be used for punching any kind of alphabetical or numerical information (called "alphanumeric") that the user would like to have identifying the output produced by this execution of the program. The information punched in these cards will simply be printed out on the first page of the output. Although these cards may be left blank if desired, they *must* be included in the control card sequence.

The 4th control card tells the main program the major parameters of the data processing problem, and instructs it as to which of several options will be called, if any. This information is contained on control card #4 as follows:

Columns   *Control Information*

  1-4   The number of *cases* to be processed

  5-6   The number of *variables* to be processed

  7-8   The number of *tables* to be prepared

  9-10   *Variable identification option*: This feature permits the labeling of each table automatically with an alphanumeric description of each variable involved in the cross-classification. The computer obtains the descriptions from information punched into columns 1-72 of the variable identification cards, one for each variable, ordered according to the sequence of the variables on the raw data cards. If this variable identification feature is desired, then *one* variable identification card for *each* variable to be processed must be present to be read in immediately after all the control cards and before the data cards. Any number larger than zero punched into columns 9-10 will exercise the option. If these columns are left blank or are punched 00 this feature will be bypassed and *no* variable identification cards should be included.

  11-12   *Variable recoding option*: This feature enables variables to be recoded in the machine by addition, subtraction, or division by any number less than 100. It also permits one- to five-digit data to be regrouped into intervals of specified size. Any number larger than zero punched into columns 11-12 will exercise this option, and the appropriate number of recoding control cards (see below) must follow card #12. If these columns are left blank or are punched 00 this feature will be bypassed and *no* recoding cards should be included.

If the recoding option is exercised, the machine will call for at least two more cards to be read immediately after the last standard control card #12. The first of these recoding control cards can be imagined as containing a two column field for each possible variable, or 40 fields in all. The first such field in columns 1-2 would correspond to variable #1 and so on in ascending order to columns 79-80 for variable #40. Any or all of the variables can be recorded according to these options:

Code   Option

01   Recode by *adding* some constant to the value
02   Recode by *subtracting* some constant to the value
03   Recode by *dividing* some constant to the value
04   Recode by *regrouping* the data into specified intervals
05   Recode by *regrouping* the data into specified intervals *and addition*
06   Recode by *regrouping* the data into specified intervals *and subtraction*
07   Recode by *regrouping* the data into specified intervals *and division*

Fields on the first recoding card that correspond to variables that are not to be recoded should be left blank.

The *constants* to be used for the addition, subtraction, or division recoding operations should be given in the corresponding fields of the *second* recoding control card. If, for example, it is desired to recode variable #7 by subtracting a value of *one* from each category, the code number 02 should be punched in the seventh field of the *first* recoding control card and the constant 01 in the seventh field of the *second* recoding control card. As many variables as desired can be recoded at any time, and any variable recoded by subtraction will never be assigned a negative value by the machine but will be set to zero if the subtraction code exceeds the value of the variable for a given case.

If coding by *regrouping* (punch 04) is specified for one or more of the variables, then the computer will read one or more cards, depending on the number of variables to be recoded in this manner. Each card can be imagined as being arranged in 16 five-column fields (from columns 1-80) providing a maximum of 16 categories into which each variable might be regrouped. Reading from left to right, the first five-column field should contain the *upper limit* of the first interval into which the data are to be regrouped, the second five-column field should contain the upper limit of the second interval, and so on. Assume, for example, it is desired to recode raw age figures from a sample survey into these categories: under 21, 21 to 30, 31 to 40, 41 to 50, and 51 to age 100. The first card in the pair of regrouping cards should contain the value 00020 in columns 1-5, 00030 in columns 6-10, 00040 in columns 11-15, 00050 in columns 16-20, and 00100 in columns 21-25. The fields on recoding control card #2 should be left blank if the recoding is done by regrouping without adding, subtracting, or dividing. But this second card must be present, even if regrouping alone is being done and the card is blank. If the other options are requested along with regrouping, the regrouping will be done *before* addition, subtraction, or division.

13-14   *Data tape option*: This feature permits the raw data to be contained on a separate data tape instead of being read in from punchcards after the control cards. It is an especially useful feature if the number of cases is large or if many executions are requested using the same data (see the following option). If used, the separate data tape should be hung on tape unit 1. Any number larger than zero in columns 13-14 will cause the data to be read in from tape unit 1. If these columns are left blank or punched oo the option will be bypassed and the data read in from the regular monitor tape 5, where the input data from different jobs in the monitor run are usually loaded.

15-16   *Data tape rewind option*: This feature can only be used in conjunction with the data tape option (col. 13-14). Any number larger than zero in columns 15-16 will cause the separate data tape on unit 1 to rewind *after* each execution of the program. This permits the researchers to handle more than 40 variables or prepare more than 72 tables for one computer run with the same data, if stored on tape. If these columns are left blank or punched oo, the data tape will not rewind.

17-18   *Chi-square option*: Any number greater than zero in these columns will cause chi-square values and the contingency coefficient (C) to be computed for each bivariate distribution in every table. The zero row and zero column frequencies are *omitted* from these calculations. If the zero category for any variable is desired in the calculations, the variable can be recoded by adding 1 to every category (see instructions regarding the preparation of recoding control cards). If these columns are left blank or punched oo chi-square and C will not be calculated.

19-20   *Column and row percentages option:* Any number greater than zero in these columns will cause two additional tables to be printed for each contingency table. The first will contain the percentages by columns and the second by rows. The zero column and zero row frequencies will be eliminated from the calculation of percentages. If the zero category for any variable is desired in the calculation, the variable can be recoded by adding 1 to every category (see instructions regarding the preparation of recoding control cards). If these columns are left blank or punched oo no percentages will be computed.

21-22   *Correlation coefficient option:* Any number greater than zero in these columns will cause the computation of several correlation coefficients. The coefficients computed for each table depend on its numbers of *rows* and *columns* (excluding the zero categories):

Size of Table	*Correlation coefficients*
n × n	Kendall tau-b, Goodman-Kruskal gamma, Somers D_{yx} and D_{xy}
n × m	Kendall tau-c, Goodman-Kruskal gamma, Somers D_{yx} and D_{xy}

The Size of Table column refers to the number of rows and columns *after* subtracting the zero categories, for the zero row and zero column frequencies will be excluded from the computation of these coefficients. If the zero category for any variable is desired in the calculation, the variable can be recoded by adding 1 to every category (see instructions regarding the preparation of recoding control cards). (The subroutine that computes these coefficients was written by Malcolm Spector, while a senior in Political Science at Northwestern. See the abstract of his program in *Behavioral Science,* 10 (1965), forthcoming).

Control cards #5, #6, and #7 enable the user of the program to tell the computer which variables he wants to be read in for cross-classification purposes and where these are located on his data cards. A series of symbols is entered on these cards to state the *format* of the variables. By means of these symbols, the computer can be told, for example, to ignore or skip the first 10 columns of a card, pick up a variable in column 11, skip the next three columns, pick up two variables in columns 15 and 16, skip to the next data card for this case, etc. The computer will then regard the very *first* variable it reads as variable #1, the next one as variable #2, and so on, in consecutive order, reading the card from left to right.

The format statement must always begin with the punched-hole code for a left parenthesis and end with a right parenthesis (see page 17). The letter "X" punched in a format statement means that one column on the card should be ignored or skipped; "3X" means that 3 columns should be skipped. In general, "nX" specifies that n columns of the data card should be skipped, but "X" may be used alone without the number 1 to skip one column.

The letter "I" punched into the format statement is used in this program to signify that a variable is to be read in from the specified card location. Thus, the expression (4X,I1) instructs the machine to skip the first four columns on a card and read in a single column variable from column 5. A two-column variable can be read in by writing "I2"; a three-column variable by writing "I3"; and so on. If seven different one-column variables are to be picked up in columns 11-17, the expression for the purpose can be written (10X, 7I1), where "nIm" tells the computer to read in n variables each of which are m columns wide.

If there is more than one data card per case, a slash "/" instructs the computer to go to the next card and begin reading in column #1. Thus the expression (12X,3I2/I1) will cause the machine to skip the first 12 columns of the first card; read in three variables each two-columns wide from columns 13-14, 15-16, and 17-18; skip to the second card for that case; and read in one variable from the first column of the card.

If the entire format statement exceeds 72 columns in length, the symbols must be continued on control card #6, which is also limited to 72 columns. Expecially lengthy format statements may need to be continued on card #7. Even if the entire format statement can be recorded on card #5, cards #6 and #7 *must* be included, for the computer will always try to read three format cards.

Blank columns may be used in the format statement to clarify the printing for humans, but they are ignored by the machine. Commas may be used to separate a skip expression from a following instruction to pick up a variable, but they need not be included. Thus (12X3I2) is a valid expression. Commas are required, however, after an instruction to pick up a variable, and the following expression (3I212X) would *not* be valid. The correct expression is (3I2,12X).

As already mentioned, the computer will assign identifying numbers to the variables according to the *order* in which they are read. The first variable read—regardless of the number of its column location—will be considered variable #1 and the next variable picked up from the card will be considered variable #2. An understanding of this procedure is important, for the user of the program must refer to the variables by the same numbers in instructing the machine which variables are to be cross-classified in which tables. If the machine, therefore, reads in party identification as the first variable and voting preference as the second variable, the user can construct a contingency table from these variables simply by punching 01 and 02 in the appropriate fields of control cards #9 and #10 (see below for more information).

The machine must be told the size of the tables it should construct. This is done by control card #8, which states the highest *value* of a variable that has not been recoded by regrouping or division. The number of categories in the rows or columns of a table using that variable will be determined by the value entered in the appropriate field of control card #8, which has 40 two-digit fields corresponding to the variables read into the computer: the first field (columns 1-2) corresponds to variable #1, etc.

The values entered in these fields need not conform to the actual codes for any variable. Assume that religion has been coded for the respondents in a survey as follows:

Code	Information	% in Sample
0	No response	9
1	Protestant	50
2	Catholic	35
3	Jewish	5
4	Other	1
		———
		100%

The researcher may decide to exclude catgories "3" and "4" from tables involving religion because of the small proportion of cases they contain. If this is desired, he could punch 02 in the third field of control card #8 to prevent the cases for categories 3 and 4 from appearing in the table. (As mentioned earlier in the discussion of control card #4, the zeros in the data would be excluded in calculating chi-square, correlation coefficients, and the percentages by rows and columns, if these options are requested.) If a variable has been recoded by regrouping or division, then the resulting number of categories *minus one* should be entered as the highest "value" for the variable on card #8.

Cards #9, #10, #11, and #12 are used to instruct the machine which variables to use in constructing each table. The user identifies these variables by the order in which they were read by the machine. Each two-column field in card #9 names the variable that will appear along the *columns* of a given table, while the corresponding field in card #10 specifies the variable that will appear along the *rows* of every table. The corresponding field in card #11 specifies any *third* variable to be used in constructing a given table, and the field in card #12 names any *fourth* desired in the table.

The first field (columns 1-2) for each of these cards corresponds to the first *table* the computer will construct. If the user wishes to cross-tabulate variable #26 by variable #13 in table #1, he punches 26 in columns 1-2 of card #9 and 13 in columns 1-2 of card #10. Variable #26 will then appear along the columns of the first contingency table and variable #13 in the rows. If only a bivariate distribution is desired, the corresponding fields in cards #11 and #12 should be left blank. If, however, the user wants to cross-classify the same pair of variables while holding a third variable constant, he should punch the number of the third variable—whatever it might be—into columns 1-2 of card #11. A fourth variable can be introduced in the table the same way with the use of card #12.

When a third variable is used in a table, a separate sub-table is prepared for each category of the third variable. If a two category party affiliation code (Democrat and Republican) is used for the third variable, the first two variables would be cross-classified separately for Democrats and then for Republicans. The zero category for third variables is not used in preparing sub-tables, but the variable can be recoded by adding one to each category if a sub-table is desired for that category. Understand that *one* sub-table will be generated for *each* category of a third variable. It is possible to generate up to 99 such sub-tables for each table.

In the interests of parsimony, the introduction of third variables into the analysis should be done with attention to the number of sub-tables to be generated in the process. If consistent with the theoretical concerns of the research, try to use as third variables those with few categories, using those with more categories as first and second variables. Even more attention should be given to the number of sub-tables to be generated when a *fourth* variable is introduced, for the number of sub-tables to be prepared in this instance will be equal to the number of categories for the third variable *multiplied* by the number of categories for the fourth.

It should be pointed out that Figure C-1 indicates an "a" and "b" card for each of the four table specification cards, #9, #10, #11, and #12. A maximum of 40 tables can be specified and requested with the use of the 40 two-column fields of the "a" cards in this group. If more than 40 tables are desired, the specifications must be continued on the "b" cards, up to a maximum of 72 tables. *Important*: Although the "a" and "b" cards are grouped together on the layout page for ease in constructing tables, they *must* be rearranged in the following fashion before being fed into the computer: card #9a and #9b, #10a and #10b, #11a and #11b, and #12a and #12b. These cards *are* arranged in the proper order for the computer in Figure C-3, which shows a print-out of the actual NUCROS control cards used for processing 338 cases from the sample survey discussed in Chapter VI. It would be helpful to match each of these cards with their counter-

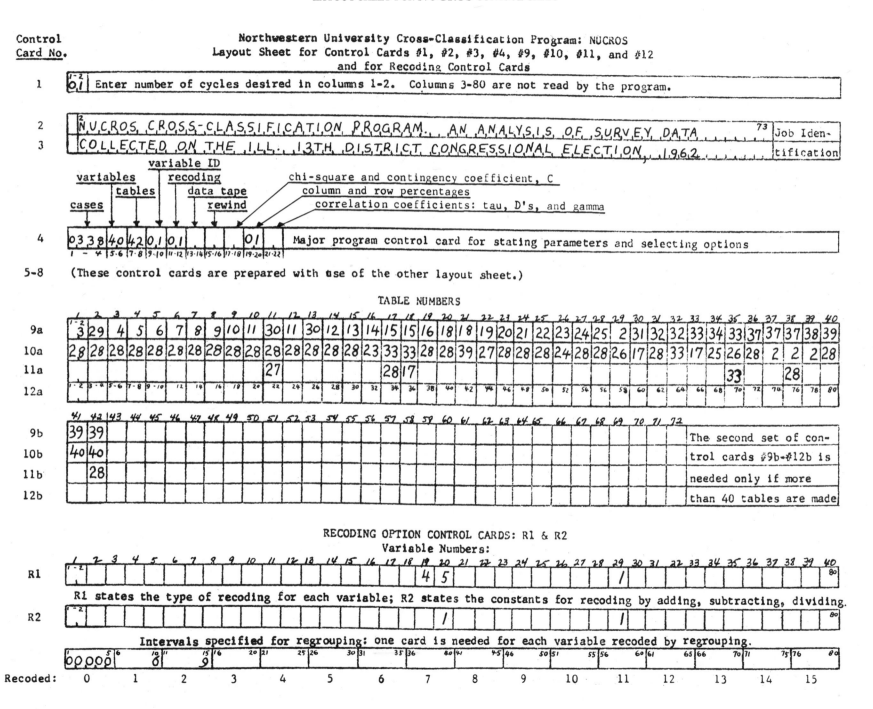

FIGURE C-1
LAYOUT SHEET FOR NUCROS CONTROL CARDS

Figure C-2
LAYOUT SHEET FOR NUCROS VARIABLE IDENTIFICATION CARDS

Northwestern University Cross-Classification Program: NUCROS
Layout Sheet for Control Cards #5, #6, #7, and #8
and for Variable Identification Cards

Location of Variables: Card	Columns	Control Cards #5-#7: Format Statement	Variable Number	Variable Identification Cards: Alphanumeric punches in Columns 1-72	Control Card #8: Highest Value of Variable	Punched in Columns
1	6	(5X, I1,	1	NUMBER OF TIMES INTERVIEWED	3	1-2
	10-11	3X, I2,	2	TOWNSHIP OR WARD	11	3-4
	21	9X, I1,	3	INTEREST IN THE ELECTION-ASKED BEFORE THE ELECTION	6	5-6
	29	7X,	4	DO YOU KNOW THE CONGRESSIONAL DISTRICT NUMBER	4	7-8
	30		5	WHICH PARTY USUALLY WINS IN THIS DISTRICT	6	9-10
	31		6	HOW DID THE REAPPORTIONMENT AFFECT THE 13TH DISTRICT	9	11-12
	32		7	WILL THE REAPPORTIONMENT HELP THE DEMOCRATS OR REPUBLICANS	6	13-14
	33	5I1,	8	DO YOU EXPECT THE DEMOCRATS OR REPUBLICANS TO WIN HERE IN NOVEMBER	6	15-16
	35	X,	9	DID YOU VOTE IN THE PRIMARY ELECTION	4	17-18
	36	2I1,	10	FOR WHOM DID YOU VOTE IN THE PRIMARY	9	19-20
	38	X, I1,	11	DO YOU KNOW THE NAMES OF THE CANDIDATES FOR CONGRESS -ASKED BEFORE	9	21-22
	40	X,	12	HAVE YOU READ OR HEARD ABOUT RUMSFELD	3	23-24
	41	2I1/	13	HAVE YOU READ OR HEARD ABOUT KENNEDY	3	25-26
2	29	28X, I1,	14	DO YOU THINK YOU WILL VOTE IN NOVEMBER	6	27-28
	32	2X,	15	HOW WILL YOU VOTE FOR CONGRESS	6	29-30
	33		16	WHEN DID YOU DECIDE HOW TO VOTE	8	31-32
	34	3I1,	17	PARTY IDENTIFICATION	9	33-34
	36	X, I1,	18	HAVE YOU ALWAYS VOTED FOR THE SAME PARTY	8	35-36
	38	X, I1,	19	FORMAL EDUCATION (RECODED 0-6-9)	2	37-38
	39-40	I2,	20	AGE (RECODED 20-30-40-50-99)	5	39-40
	43	2X, I1,	21	OCCUPATION	9	41-42
	45	X, I1,	22	RELIGION	3	43-44
	49	3X,	23	HOW LONG HAVE YOU LIVED IN THIS HOUSE	9	45-46
	50	2I1,	24	WHERE DID YOU LIVE BEFORE YOU MOVED HERE	5	47-48
	54	3X,	25	INCOME	9	49-50
	55	2I1,	26	SEX	2	51-52
	70	14X,	27	COLLEGE OR NON-COLLEGE EDUCATION	2	53-54
	71	2I1/	28	DEMOCRAT 1-2, INDEPENDENT 3-5, AND REPUBLICAN 6-7	3	55-56
3	21	20X,	29	INTEREST IN THE ELECTION - ASKED AFTERWARDS	6	57-58
	22	2I1,	30	DO YOU KNOW THE NAMES OF THE CANDIDATES - ASKED AFTERWARDS	9	59-60
	24	X,	31	DID YOU VOTE IN THE ELECTION	3	61-62
	25	2I1,	32	HOW WOULD YOU HAVE VOTED IF YOU HAD VOTED	4	63-64
	35	9X, I1,	33	WHO DID YOU VOTE FOR	5	65-66
	36-37		34	WHY DID YOU VOTE FOR HIM - FIRST-NAMED REASON	17	67-68
	38-39	2I2,	35	WHY DID YOU NOTE FOR HIM - SECOND-NAMED REASON	17	69-70
	41	X, I1,	36	DID YOU VOTE A STRAIGHT TICKET	8	71-72
	53	11X, I1,	37	WERE YOU CONTACTED BY A POLITICAL PARTY DURING THE CAMPAIGN	9	73-74
	58	4X, I1/	38	WHICH PARTY DID THE BETTER JOB OF ADVERTISING ITS CANDIDATES	4	75-76
4	42	41X, I1,	39	HAVE YOU EVER CHANGED PARTY IDENTIFICATION	7	77-78
	44	X, I1)	40	WHY DID YOU CHANGE PARTIES	8	79-80

parts on the control card layout sheets, Figure C-1 and C-2, to insure that their functions are clearly understood.

After reading these control cards, the computer reads in the data and begins the processing operations. Before printing out the cross-classification tables (as shown in Chapter VI, Figures VI-1 and VI-2), the computer will rearrange the information contained on the control cards and print a summary of their instructions as displayed in Figures C-4 and C-5.

FIGURE C-3
TABULATOR PRINTOUT OF NUCROS CONTROL CARDS

```
CONTROL
CARDS
#1  01
  2   NUCROS CROSS-CLASSIFICATION PROGRAM.  AN ANALYSIS OF SURVEY DATA
  3   COLLECTED ON THE ILL. 13TH DISTRICT CONGRESSIONAL ELECTION, 1962
  4   033840420101      01
  5   (5X,I1,3X,I2,9X,I1,7X,511,X,2I1,X,I1,X,2I1/28X,I1,2X,3I1,X,I1,X,I1,I2,
  6   2X,I1,X,I1,3X,2I1,3X,2I1,14X,2I1/20X,2I1,X,2I1,9X,I1,2I2,X,I1,1IX,I1,
  7   4X,I1/4IX,I1,X,I1)
  8   311 6 4 6 9 6 6 4 9 9 3 3 6 6 8 9 8 2 5 9 3 9 5 9 2 2 3 6 9 3 4 51717 8 9 4 7 8
 9a  329  4  5  6  7  8  910111301130121314151516181819202122232425  231323233343333737373839
 9b 3939
10a 282828202828202626262830282862333332828392728282624282826176833172526628 2 2 228
10b 4040
11a                                  27             2617                                33    28
11b  28
12a
12b
R1                                                        4  5                          1
R2                                                           1                          1
     00000      6    9
     00000     30   40    50   99 ←—— RECODING VALUES
     NUMBER OF TIMES INTERVIEWED
     TOWNSHIP OR WARD
     INTEREST IN THE ELECTION--ASKED BEFORE THE ELECTION
     DO YOU KNOW THE CONGRESSIONAL DISTRICT NUMBER
     WHICH PARTY USUALLY WINS IN THIS DISTRICT
     HOW DID THE REAPPORTIONMENT AFFECT THE 13TH DISTRICT
     WILL THE REAPPORTIONMENT HELP THE DEMOCRATS OR REPUBLICANS
     DO YOU EXPECT THE DEMOCRATS OR REPUBLICANS TO WIN HERE IN NOVEMBER
     DID YOU VOTE IN THE PRIMARY ELECTION
     FOR WHOM DID YOU VOTE IN THE PRIMARY
     DO YOU KNOW THE NAMES OF THE CANDIDATES FOR CONGRESS--ASKED BEFORE
     HAVE YOU READ OR HEARD ABOUT RUMSFELD
     HAVE YOU READ OR HEARD ABOUT KENNEDY
     DO YOU THINK YOU WILL VOTE IN NOVEMBER
     HOW WILL YOU VOTE FOR CONGRESS
     WHEN DID YOU DECIDE HOW TO VOTE
     PARTY IDENTIFICATION
     HAVE YOU ALWAYS VOTED FOR THE SAME PARTY
     FORMAL EDUCATION (RECODED 0-6-9)
     AGE (RECODED  0-30-40-50-99)
     OCCUPATION
     RELIGION
     HOW LONG HAVE YOU LIVED IN THIS HOUSE
     WHERE DID YOU LIVE BEFORE YOU MOVED HERE
     INCOME
     SEX
     COLLEGE OR NON-COLLEGE EDUCATION
     DEMOCRAT 1-2, INDEPENDENT 3-5, AND REPUBLICAN 6-7
     INTEREST IN THE ELECTION--ASKED AFTERWARDS
     DO YOU KNOW THE NAMES OF THE CANDIDATES--ASKED AFTERWARDS
     DID YOU VOTE IN THE ELECTION
     WHO WOULD YOU HAVE VOTED FOR IF YOU HAD VOTED
     WHO DID YOU VOTE FOR
     WHY DID YOU VOTE FOR HIM--FIRST NAMED REASON
     WHY DID YOU VOTE FOR HIM--SECOND NAMED REASON
     DID YOU VOTE A STRAIGHT TICKET
     WERE YOU CONTACTED BY A POLITICAL PARTY DURING THE CAMPAIGN
     WHICH PARTY DID THE BETTER JOB OF ADVERTISING ITS CANDIDATES
     HAVE YOU EVER CHANGED PARTY IDENTIFICATIONS
     WHY DID YOU CHANGE PARTIES
```

CONTROL CARDS

VARIABLE IDENTIFICATION CARDS

FIGURE C-4
COMPUTER PRINTOUT OF NUCROS CONTROL CARDS AFTER PROCESSING

```
NUCRUS CROSS-CLASSIFICATION PROGRAM.  AN ANALYSIS OF SURVEY DATA
COLLECTED ON THE ILL. 13TH DISTRICT CONGRESSIONAL ELECTION, 1962

TOTAL CASES USED =  338      CYCLE NO.    1 OF   1

VARIABLE   1  2  3  4  5  6  7  8  9 10 11 12 13 14 15 16 17 18 19 20 21 22 23 24 25 26 27 28 29 30 31 32 33 34 35 36 37 38 39 40
MAX.VALUE  3 11  6  4  6  9  6  4  9  9  3  6  6  3  6  8  8  2  5  9  5  9  5  2  2  9  3  6  9  3  4  5 17 17  8  9  4  7  8
```

TABLE NO.	VARIABLES			MAXIMUM VALUES		
1	3	28		6	3	
2	29	28		6	3	
3	4	28		4	3	
4	5	28		6	3	
5	6	28		9	3	
6	7	28		6	3	
7	8	28		4	3	
8	9	28		9	3	
9	10	28		9	3	
10	11	28		9	3	
11	30	28		9	3	
12	11	30		9	9	
13	30	28	27	9	3	2
14	12	28		3	3	
15	13	28		3	3	
16	14	23		6	9	
17	15	33	28	6	5	3
18	15	33	17	6	5	9
19	16	28		8	3	
20	18	28		8	3	
21	18	39		8	7	
22	19	27		2	2	
23	20	28		5	3	
24	21	28		9	3	
25	22	28		3	3	
26	23	24		9	5	
27	24	28		9	3	
28	25	28		9	3	
29	2	26		11	2	
30	31	17		3	9	
31	32	28		9	3	
32	32	33		4	5	
33	33	17		5	9	
34	34	25		17	9	
35	33	26	33	5	2	5
36	37	28		9	3	

TABLE NO.	VARIABLES			MAXIMUM VALUES		
37	37	2	28	9	11	3
38	38	2		9	11	
39	39	28		4	11	
40	39	40		7	3	
41	39	40	28	7	8	3
42	39	40		7	8	

RECODING OPTION CALLED FOR

VAR.NO.	CODE	CONSTANT	RECODED CATEGORIES (UPPER LIMITS)				
19	4	NONE	0	6	9		
20	5	1	0	30	40	50	99
29	1	1	NONE				

VAR.NO.

1 NUMBER OF TIMES INTERVIEWED
2 TOWNSHIP OR WARD
3 INTEREST IN THE ELECTION--ASKED BEFORE THE ELECTION
4 DO YOU KNOW THE CONGRESSIONAL DISTRICT NUMBER
5 WHICH PARTY USUALLY WINS IN THIS DISTRICT
6 HOW DID THE REAPPORTIONMENT AFFECT THE 13TH DISTRICT
7 WILL THE REAPPORTIONMENT HELP THE DEMOCRATS OR REPUBLICANS
8 DO YOU EXPECT THE DEMOCRATS OR REPUBLICANS TO WIN HERE IN NOVEMBER
9 DID YOU VOTE IN THE PRIMARY ELECTION
10 FOR WHOM DID YOU VOTE IN THE PRIMARY
11 DO YOU KNOW THE NAMES OF THE CANDIDATES FOR CONGRESS--ASKED BEFORE
12 HAVE YOU READ OR HEARD ABOUT RUMSFELD
13 HAVE YOU READ OR HEARD ABOUT KENNEDY
14 DO YOU THINK YOU WILL VOTE IN NOVEMBER
15 HOW WILL YOU VOTE FOR CONGRESS
16 WHEN DID YOU DECIDE HOW TO VOTE
17 PARTY IDENTIFICATION
18 HAVE YOU ALWAYS VOTED FOR THE SAME PARTY
19 FORMAL EDUCATION (RECODED 0-6-9)
20 AGE (RECODED 0-30-40-50-99)
21 OCCUPATION
22 RELIGION
23 HOW LONG HAVE YOU LIVED IN THIS HOUSE
24 WHERE DID YOU LIVE BEFORE YOU MOVED HERE
25 INCOME
26 SEX
27 COLLEGE OR NON-COLLEGE EDUCATION
28 DEMOCRAT 1-2, INDEPENDENT 3-5, AND REPUBLICAN 6-7
29 INTEREST IN THE ELECTION--ASKED AFTERWARDS
30 DO YOU KNOW THE NAMES OF THE CANDIDATES--ASKED AFTERWARDS
31 DID YOU VOTE IN THE ELECTION
32 WHO WOULD YOU HAVE VOTED FOR IF YOU HAD VOTED
33 WHO DID YOU VOTE FOR
34 WHY DID YOU VOTE FOR HIM--FIRST NAMED REASON
35 WHY DID YOU VOTE FOR HIM--SECOND NAMED REASON
36 DID YOU VOTE A STRAIGHT TICKET
37 WERE YOU CONTACTED BY A POLITICAL PARTY DURING THE CAMPAIGN
38 WHICH PARTY DID THE BETTER JOB OF ADVERTISING ITS CANDIDATES
39 HAVE YOU EVER CHANGED PARTY IDENTIFICATIONS
40 WHY DID YOU CHANGE PARTIES

FIGURE C-5
COMPUTER PRINTOUT OF NUCROS RECODING AND
VARIABLE IDENTIFICATION CARDS

APPENDIX C-2

FORTRAN IV NUCROS COMPUTER PROGRAM

```
C    GENERAL PROGRAM FOR CROSS CLASSIFICATION WITH AUTOMATIC CODING
     DIMENSION LAD(350,40),MAX(40),KIND(40),KONST(40),MBRAK(16),FMT(36)
     DIMENSION NTAB(101,21),NRTOT(101),NCLT(21)
     DIMENSION TAB(101,21),RTOT(101),CLT(21),PCENT(21)
     DIMENSION NDEEP(72),NDIM(4,72),MXTEMP(4)
     DIMENSION STORE(40,12)
     DIMENSION CKK(24)
     EQUIVALENCE(NTAB,TAB)
     NADA=0
C
C
     NDONE = 0
     READ  (5,7)NPROB
   7 FORMAT (4012)
C
C    READ AND PRINT TITLES
 500 NDONE = NDONE +1
     REWIND 2
     REWIND 3
     REWIND 4
     WRITE (6,800)
 800 FORMAT (1H1)
     READ(5,10)(CKK(I),I=1,24)
     WRITE(6,5)(CKK(I),I=1,24)
   5 FORMAT(1X,12A6)
C
C    READ CONTROL CARDS 4-8
     READ (5,6) NOBS,NVAR,NTABLE,IDVAR,NCODE, INPUT,NSAME,NCHI,NPCT,NTAU
     READ (5,10)(FMT(J),J= 1,36)
  10 FORMAT (12A6)
     LCHI = MINO (NCHI/NCHI + NTAU/NTAU, 1)
     LPCT = MINO(NPCT,1)
     WRITE (6,185) NOBS,NDONE,NPROB
     READ (5,7) (MAX(J),J=1,NVAR)
     WRITE (6,9) (J,J=1,NVAR)
     WRITE (6,423)(MAX(J),J=1,NVAR)
   6 FORMAT (I4,9I2)
 185 FORMAT(/20H TOTAL CASES USED = I4,5X,10HCYCLE NO. I3,4H OF I3      )
 780 FORMAT (1H0)
   9 FORMAT (//11H VARIABLE  ,40I3)
 423 FORMAT (11H MAX.VALUE  ,40I3)
C
C    READ AND PRINT CONTROL CDS 9,10,11,12... DETERMINE ALL TABLE DEPTHS
     DO 1000 I=1,4
1000 READ (5,7) (NDIM(I,K),K=1,NTABLE)
     DO 472 K=1,NTABLE
     NDEEP(K)=2
     DO 472 I=3,4
     IF (NDIM(I,K)) 472,472,470
 470 NDEEP(K) = I
 472 CONTINUE
     WRITE (6,424)
     IF(NTABLE-36)9001,9001,9002
9001 WRITE(6,781)
     GO TO 9003
9002 WRITE(6,426)
9003 CONTINUE
```

```
      LTABLE = MINO(NTABLE,36)
      DO 4 L=1,LTABLE
      K=L
      NDEPTH = NDEEP(K)
      WRITE (6,8) K,(NDIM(I,K),I=1,NDEPTH)
      DO 550 I=1,NDEPTH
      J = NDIM(I,K)
  550 MXTEMP(I) = MAX(J)
      WRITE (6,425) (MXTEMP(I),I=1,NDEPTH)
      K=L+36
      IF (K .GT. NTABLE) GO TO 427
      NDEPTH = NDEEP(K)
      WRITE (6,428) K,(NDIM(I,K),I=1,NDEPTH)
      DO 429 I=1,NDEPTH
      J = NDIM(I,K)
  429 MXTEMP(I) = MAX(J)
      WRITE (6,430) (MXTEMP(I),I=1,NDEPTH)
      GO TO 4
  427 WRITE (6,781)
    4 CONTINUE
    8 FORMAT (1H+,9X16,7X,4I4)
  424 FORMAT (//1H+,9X9HTABLE NO.,6X9HVARIABLES,7X14HMAXIMUM VALUES)
  425 FORMAT (1H+,38X,4I4)
  42C FORMAT (75X9HTABLE NO.,6X9HVARIABLES,7X14HMAXIMUM VALUES)
  428 FORMAT (1H+,74X,16,7X,4I4)
  43C FORMAT (104X,4I4)
  781 FORMAT (X)
C
C   READ AND PRINT RECODE-CONTROL-CARDS, IF RECODING OPTED
      IF (NCODE) 20,20,19
   19 WRITE (6,186)
      READ (5,7) (KIND(J),J=1,NVAR)
      READ (5,7) (KONST(J),J=1,NVAR)
      DO 400 J=1,NVAR
      NOPER = KIND(J)
      IF (NOPER) 400,400,401
  401 IF (NOPER-3) 402,402,403
  402 WRITE (6,188) J,NOPER,KONST(J)
      GO TO 400
  403 READ(5,422) MBRAK
      WRITE (3) MBRAK
      IF (NOPER .EQ. 4) WRITE (6,187) J,NOPER,MBRAK
      IF (NOPER .GT. 4) WRITE (6,9004) J,NOPER,KONST(J),MBRAK
  400 CONTINUE
  422 FORMAT (16I5)
  186 FORMAT (27H1RECODING OPTION CALLED FOR // 4X,67H VAR.NO.  CODE
     X CONSTANT    RECODED CATEGORIES (UPPER LIMITS)     )
  188 FORMAT (8X12,6X11,9X13,10X4HNONE)
  187 FORMAT ( 8X12,6X11,9X4HNONE,6X,16I6)
 9004 FORMAT(8X12,6X11,9X13,7X,16I6)
      REWIND 3
C
C   READ AND PRINT VAR NAMES IF OPTED
   20 IF (IDVAR) 480,480,495
  495 WRITE (6,83)
      DO 490 I=1,NVAR
      READ(5,82)(STORE(I,J),J=1,12)
  490 WRITE(6,57)I,(STORE(I,J),J=1,12)
   83 FORMAT (8H1VAR.NO.//)
   82 FORMAT(12A6)
   57 FORMAT(I5,2X,12A6)
C
C   INITIALIZE FOR FIRST BATCH
  480 NBATCH = MINO (NOBS,350)
      NOBS = NOBS-NBATCH
      IBATCH=1
      IOSW=24
      LINE = 60
C
C
C   READ A BATCH OF DATA CARDS
  299 IF (INPUT) 300,300,301
  300 READ (5,FMT) ((LAD(N,J),J=1,NVAR),N=1,NBATCH)
      GO TO 302
  301 READ (1,FMT) ((LAD(N,J),J=1,NVAR),N=1,NBATCH)
C
C   RECODE VARIABLES IF OPTED
```

```
302 IF (NCODE) 485,485,483
483 DO 32 J=1,NVAR
    NOPER = KIND(J)
    IF (NOPER) 32, 32, 176
176 GO TO (23,24,25,52,52,52,52),NOPER
C
C   DO TYPE 1,2,OR 3 RECODING
 23 DO 1001 I=1,NBATCH
1001 LAD(I,J) = LAD(I,J) + KONST(J)
    GO TO 32
 24 DO 1003 I=1,NBATCH
1003 LAD(I,J) = MAXO(LAD(I,J) - KONST(J), 0)
    GO TO 32
 25 DO 1002 I=1,NBATCH
1002 LAD(I,J) = LAD(I,J) / KONST(J)
    GO TO 32
C
C   DO TYPE 4 RECODING
 52 READ(3) MBRAK
    DO 29 I=1,NBATCH
    DO 28 K=1,16
    IF (LAD(I,J)-MBRAK(K)) 27,27,28
 28 CONTINUE
    LAD(I,J) = 20
    GO TO 29
 27 LAD(I,J) = K-1
 29 CONTINUE
    IF(NOPER-4)32,32,7638
7638 NOPER=NOPER-4
    GO TO 176
 32 CONTINUE
    REWIND 3
C
C   DEFINE TABLE DEPTH, MAX.VALUES, VARS TO BE USED...FOR EACH TABLE
485 DO 115 KT=1,NTABLE
    NDEPTH = NDEEP(KT)
    J1 = NDIM(1,KT)
    J2 = NDIM(2,KT)
    MAXA = MAX(J1) +1
    MAXB = MAX(J2) +1
    MAXC = 1
    MAXD = 1
    LREQ = 10 + MAXB + 2*LCHI
    LREQPC = LPCT * (MAXB-1+6)
    GO TO (36,36,33,34),NDEPTH
 34 J4 = NDIM(4,KT)
    MAXD = MAX(J4)
 33 J3 = NDIM(3,KT)
    MAXC = MAX(J3)
    LREQ = LREQ +2
C
 36 DO 115 L3 = 1,MAXC
    DO 115 L4 = 1,MAXD
    IF (IBATCH-1) 41,41,42
C   ZERO OUT TABLE AREA IF FIRST BATCH
 41 DO 43 I=1,MAXB
    DO 43 J=1,MAXA
 43 NTAB(I,J) = 0
    GO TO 44
C   OTHERWISE READ INTO TABLE-AREA STORED-RESULTS FROM PREVIOUS BATCH(ES)
 42 IF (IOSW-24) 46,46,47
 46 READ (2) ((NTAB(I,J),J=1,MAXA),I=1,MAXB)
    GO TO 44
 47 READ (4) ((NTAB(I,J),J=1,MAXA),I=1,MAXB)
C
C   DO A TABLE.  TEST 3RD AND 4TH-DIMENSION VARIABLES FOR APPROP VALUE
C   BEFORE COUNTING THE OBSERVATION (WHERE 3RD OR 4TH DIM IS USED)
 44 DO 45 N=1,NBATCH
    IF (NDEPTH-3) 40,35,39
 39 IF (LAD(N,J4) - L4) 45,35,45
 35 IF (LAD(N,J3) - L3) 45,40,45
 40 L1 = LAD(N,J1) +1
    L2 = LAD(N,J2) +1
    IF (L1.GT.MAXA .OR. L2.GT.MAXB) GO TO 45
    NTAB(L2,L1) = NTAB(L2,L1) +1
 45 CONTINUE
C
```

```
C   IF MORE OBSERVATIONS REMAIN, STORE THIS TABLE (RESULTS TO DATE)
    IF (NOBS) 75,75,48
 48 IF (IOSW-24) 50,50,60
 50 WRITE (4) ((NTAB(I,J),J=1,MAXA),I=1,MAXB)
    GO TO 115
 60 WRITE (2) ((NTAB(I,J),J=1,MAXA),I=1,MAXB)
    GO TO 115
C
C
C   IF NO MORE OBSERVATIONS WRITE OUT THIS TABLE
 75 LINE = LINE + LREQ
    IF(LINE+2*LREQPC-58)431,431,811
431 WRITE(6,780)
    GO TO 76
811 WRITE (6,800)
    LINE=LREQ-1
 76 GO TO (822,822,823,824),NDEPTH
C   TWO-DIMENSION TITLE
822 IF(IDVAR)522,522,523
523 WRITE(6,524)KT,J1,(STORE(J1,J),J=1,12),J2,(STORE(J2,J),J=1,12)
   1 ,MAXA,MAXB
524 FORMAT(7X,11H TABLE NO. ,I3,10X,13HVARIABLE NO. ,I2,2X, 12A6,   /
   1 25X,6HVRS.  ,13HVARIABLE NO. ,I2,2X, 12A6,   / 7X,13HTABLE SIZE =
   2 ,I3,5H  BY  ,I3)
    GO TO 86
522 WRITE (6,80) KT,J1,J2,MAXA,MAXB
 80 FORMAT (    10X,11H TABLE NO. I3,5X,13HVARIABLE NO. I2,3X,9HVRS. N
   10. I2//13X,13HTABLE SIZE = I3,5H  BY I3  )
    GO TO 86
C   THREE-DIMENSION TITLE
823 IF(IDVAR)525,525,526
526 WRITE(6,527)KT,J1,(STORE(J1,J),J=1,12),J2,(STORE(J2,J),J=1,12),J3,
   1 (STORE(J3,J),J=1,12),MAXA,MAXB,L3
527 FORMAT(7X,11H TABLE NO. I3,10X,13HVARIABLE NO. I2,2X, 12A6,
   .1 2(/25X,6HVRS.  ,13HVARIABLE NO. I2,2X, 12A6)        // 7X,13HTABLE
   2SIZE =  I3,5H  BY  I3,10X,16H3RD DIMENSION = I3)
    GO TO 86
525 WRITE (6,77) KT,J1,J2,J3,MAXA,MAXB,L3
 77 FORMAT (    10X,11H TABLE NO. I3,5X,13HVARIABLE NO. I2,3X,9HVRS. N
   10. I2,3X,9HVRS. NO. I2//13X,13HTABLE SIZE = I3,5H  BY I3//13X,16H3
   2RD DIMENSION = I3 )
    GO TO 86
C   FOUR-DIMENSION TITLE
824 IF(IDVAR)528,528,529
529 WRITE(6,530)KT,J1,(STORE(J1,J),J=1,12),J2,(STORE(J2,J),J=1,12),J3,
   1 (STORE(J3,J),J=1,12),J4,(STORE(J4,J),J=1,12),MAXA,MAXB,L3,L4
530 FORMAT(7X,11H TABLE NO. I3,10X,13HVARIABLE NO. I2,2X, 12A6,
   1 3(/25X,6HVRS.  ,13HVARIABLE NO. I2,2X, 12A6)        // 7X,13HTABLE
   2SIZE =  I3,5H  BY  I3,10X,16H3RD DIMENSION = I3,5X,16H4TH DIMENSIO
   3N =   I3)
    GO TO 86
528 WRITE (6,72) KT,J1,J2,J3,J4,MAXA,MAXB,L3,L4
 72 FORMAT (    10X,11H TABLE NO. I3,5X,13HVARIABLE NO. I2,3X,9HVRS. N
   10. I2,3X,9HVRS. NO. I2,3X,9HVRS. NO. I2//13X,13HTABLE SIZE = I3,5H
   2 BY I3//13X,16H3RD DIMENSION = I3,5X,16H4TH DIMENSION = I3  )
 86 CONTINUE
C
C
C   PRINT BODY OF MAP, COMPUTE AND PRINT COLUMN AND ROW TOTALS
 84 MSUB = MAXA-1
    WRITE (6,91) (IH,IH=NADA,MSUB)
    WRITE (6,781)
    NGRTO =0
    DO 85 J=1,MAXA
 85 NCLT(J)=0
    DO 100 I=1,MAXB
    ISUB = I-1
    NRTOT(I)=0
    DO 90 J=1,MAXA
    NRTOT(I)= NRTOT(I) + NTAB(I,J)
 90 NCLT(J) = NCLT(J) + NTAB(I,J)
    WRITE (6,105) ISUB,NRTOT(I),(NTAB(I,J),J=1,MAXA)
100 NGRTO = NGRTO + NRTOT(I)
    WRITE (6,106) NGRTO,(NCLT(J),J=1,MAXA)
 91 FORMAT (/17X,3HTOT,3X,2I15)
105 FORMAT (9X13,I8,3X,2I15)
106 FORMAT ( /9X5HTOTAL,I6,3X,2I15)
```

```
C
C
C   DO CHISQUARE AND/OR PERCENTS AND/OR COEFFICIENTS, IF OPTED
C   GET FLOATING-PT EQUIVALENTS...DEDUCT ZERO ROW,COLUMN FROM TOTALS
        IF (NCHI + NPCT + NTAU) 115,115,404
  404 NGRTO = NGRTO - NCLT(1) - NRTOT(1) + NTAB(1,1)
        GRTO = NGRTO
        DO 405 I=2,MAXB
        NRTOT(I) = NRTOT(I) - NTAB(I,1)
  405 RTOT(I) = NRTOT(I)
        DO 406 J=2,MAXA
        NCLT(J) = NCLT(J) - NTAB(1,J)
  406 CLT(J) = NCLT(J)
        DO 407 I=2,MAXB
        DO 407 J=2,MAXA
  407 TAB(I,J) = NTAB(I,J)
C
        IF (NCHI + NTAU) 410,410,605
  605 IF(NCHI) 606,606,408
  606 WRITE (6,781)
        GO TO 304
  408 CHISQ = 0.0
        DO 409 I=2,MAXB
        DO 409 J=2,MAXA
        A = (CLT(J)*RTOT(I)) / GRTO
        B = (TAB(I,J)-A)  **2
  409 CHISQ = CHISQ + B/A
        CRXC=(CHISQ/(CHISQ+GRTO))**.5
        WRITE(6,608)CHISQ,CRXC
  608 FORMAT(/1H+,6X,12HCHI SQUARE = ,F8.3,3X,4HC = ,F5.3)
        IF(NTAU)604,604,304
  604 WRITE (6,781)
        GO TO 410
C
C   DO ALL CORRELATION COEFFICIENTS
C   NTAU IS NOT USED BY THE SUBROUTINE, BUT MAY BE USED TO
C   EXERCISE OPTIONS IN ALTERNATE SUBROUTINES
  304 CALL COEFT(TAB,MAXB,MAXA,NTAU)
C
C
C   DO COLUMN PERCENTS
  410 IF (NPCT) 115,115,411
  411 LINE = LINE + LREQPC
        IF (LINE-58) 412,412,413
  412 WRITE (6,108)
        GO TO 414
  413 WRITE (6,800)
        WRITE (6,108)
        WRITE (6,113) (IH,IH=1,MSUB)
        WRITE (6,781)
        LINE = LREQPC + 3
  108 FORMAT(//7X,40HPERCENTS BY COLUMN FROM THE ABOVE MATRIX//)
  113 FORMAT (17X,3HTOT,8X,20I5)
C
  414 DO 416 I=2,MAXB
        ISUB = I-1
        DO 415 J=2,MAXA
  415 PCENT(J) = TAB(I,J) / CLT(J)
  416 WRITE (6,109) ISUB,NRTOT(I),(PCENT(J),J=2,MAXA)
        WRITE (6,111) NGRTO,(NCLT(J),J=2,MAXA)
  109 FORMAT (9X13,I8,9X,2P20F5.1)
  111 FORMAT ( /9X5HTOTAL,I6,8X,20I5)
C
C   DO ROW PERCENTS
        LINE = LINE + LREQPC
        IF (LINE-58) 417,417,418
  417 WRITE (6,114)
        GO TO 419
  418 WRITE (6,800)
        WRITE (6,114)
        WRITE (6,113) (IH,IH=1,MSUB)
        WRITE (6,781)
        LINE = LREQPC +3
  114 FORMAT(//7X,38HPERCENTS BY ROW FROM THE ABOVE MATRIX //)
C
  419 DO 421 I=2,MAXB
        ISUB = I-1
```

```
      DO 420 J=2,MAXA
420 PCENT(J) = TAB(I,J) / RTOT(I)
421 WRITE (6,109) ISUB,NRTOT(I),(PCENT(J),J=2,MAXA)
      WRITE (6,111) NGRTO,(NCLT(J),J=2,MAXA)
C
115 CONTINUE
C
C  PREPARE PROCESS NEXT BATCH IF ANY
      IF (NOBS) 150,150,130
130 NBATCH = MINO (NOBS,350)
      NOBS = NOBS - NBATCH
      IBATCH  = IBATCH +1
      IF (IOSW-24) 12,12,13
 12 IOSW =42
      GO TO 15
 13 IOSW = 24
 15 REWIND 2
      REWIND 4
      GO TO 299
C
C  PREPARE PROCESS NEXT PROBLEM IF ANY
150 IF (NPROB-NDONE) 160, 160, 155
155 IF (NSAME) 500, 500, 157
157 REWIND 1
      GO TO 500
160 WRITE (6,189) NPROB
189 FORMAT (1H1, I3, 33H CYCLES COMPLETED - THIS JOB DONE      )
      STOP
      END
$IBFTC COEFT    DECK
      SUBROUTINE COEFT(A,II,JJ,NTAU)
      DIMENSION A(101,21),TI(101),TJ(21)
 82 IF(II-JJ)86,85,86
 85 IPT=2
      GO TO 84
 86 IPT=3
 84 CONTINUE
      SUM=0.
      DO 2 I=2,II
      DO 2 J=2,JJ
  2 SUM=SUM+A(I,J)
      P=0.
      IX=II-1
      JX=JJ-1
      DO 10 I=2,IX
      DO 10 J=2,JX
      IY=I+1
      JY=J+1
  2 SUM=SUM+A(I,J)
      P=0.
      IX=II-1
      JX=JJ-1
      DO 10 I=2,IX
      DO 10 J=2,JX
      IY=I+1
      JY=J+1
      DO 10 K=IY,II
      DO 10 L=JY,JJ
 10 P=P+A(I,J)*A(K,L)
      Q=0.
      DO 11 I=2,IX
      DO 11 J=3,JJ
      IN=I+1
      JY=J-1
      DO 11 K=IN,II
      DO 11 L=2,JY
 11 Q=Q+A(I,J)*A(K,L)
      S=P-Q
      GAMMA=(P-Q)/(P+Q)
100 DO 21 I=2,II
      TI(I)=0.
      DO 21 J=2,JJ
 21 TI(I)=TI(I)+A(I,J)
      DO 22 J=2,JJ
      TJ(J)=0.
      DO 22 I=2,II
 22 TJ(J)=TJ(J)+A(I,J)
```

```
      XU=0.
      DO 55 J=2,JJ
   55 XU=XU+ TJ(J)**2
      XU= .5*(SUM**2-XU)
      YU=0.
      DO 56 I=2,II
   56 YU=YU+TI(I)**2
      YU=.5*(SUM**2-YU)
      DYX=S/XU
      DXY= S/YU
      IF(IPT-2)57,57,102
   57 CONTINUE
      T=0.
      DO 23 I=2,II
   23 T=T+.5*TI(I)*(TI(I)-1.)
      U=0.
      DO 24 J=2,JJ
   24 U=U+.5*TJ(J)*(TJ(J)-1.)
      BI=(SUM*(SUM-1.)*.5-T)**(.5)
      BJ=(SUM*(SUM-1.)*.5-U)**(.5)
      TAUB=S/(BI*BJ)
  104 WRITE(6,301) TAUB,GAMMA,DXY,DYX
      RETURN
  102 IF(II-JJ)5,5,6
    5 AM=II-1
      GO TO 12
    6 AM=JJ-1
   12 TAUC=S/((.5*SUM**2*(AM-1.)/AM))
      WRITE(6,302)TAUC,GAMMA ,DXY,DYX
      RETURN
  301 FORMAT(1H+,41X,8HTAU-B = ,F6.3,3X,8HGAMMA = ,F6.3,3X,6HDXY = ,F6.3
     1,3X,6HDYX = ,F6.3)
  302 FORMAT(1H+,41X,8HTAU-C = ,F6.3,3X,8HGAMMA = ,F6.3,3X,6HDXY = ,F6.3
     1,3X,6HDYX = ,F6.3)
      END
```

INDEX

The index to this book was prepared on an IBM 709 computer using the keyword indexing techniques described in Chapter VIII, pages 188-200. To use the index, scan the vertical column of alphabetized keywords. Page number references are usually given to the right of the keywords. But parts of longer entries will be "wrapped around" so that page numbers are printed to the left of the keywords.

To my knowledge, Lester W. Milbrath was the first political scientist (and possibly the first author) to use a computer for indexing his books. Both *The Washington Lobbyists* and *Political Participation* (Chicago: Rand McNally, 1963 and 1965) were indexed in this manner. In each case, however, the published index was set in type from the computer output and has a "conventional" appearance. The index below was reproduced directly from the computer output.

The main advantage of indexing books with a computer is efficiency. Working directly from page proofs, I keypunched 541 lines of index entries (one-card-per-line) in less than five hours. The computer took 10.87 minutes to generate and alphabetize 1070 separate keywords from the 541 lines. Another three minutes or so were required to print the index on the IBM 1401.

KEYWORDS

```
               J. AAGAARD, 209N
02                ABSTRACTING INPUT FOR TRIAL PROGRAM, 200-2
        SEARCHING ABSTRACTS WITH TRIAL PROGRAM, 202-206
                  ACCESS TIME TO MEMORY, 100
   IBM 403 AND 407 ACCOUNTING MACHINES ( TABULATORS ), 70-76
                  ACCOUNTING MACHINE (SEE TABULATOR)
           MEMORY ADDRESS, 100
      PUNCHCARDS-- ADVANTAGES, 7-11
194               AFRICAN AND MIDDLE EAST KWOC BIBLIOGRAPHY,
                  AGGREGATE DATA, 174
                  AGGREGATE DATA, 19
               C. ALGER, 40-42
               C. ALGER, 45N
               H. ALKER, 44N
                  ALPHABETIC AND NUMERIC DATA, 16
```